NTOA 44

Anne Dawson

Freedom as Liberating Power

NOVUM TESTAMENTUM ET ORBIS ANTIQUUS (NTOA)

Im Auftrag des Biblischen Instituts
der Universität Freiburg Schweiz
herausgegeben von Max Küchler
in Zusammenarbeit mit Gerd Theissen

The Author

Anne Dawson, born 1942 in Canberra, Australia. Academic background: BEd (CCAE Canberra), MLittStudies (University of Queensland), PhD (University of Queensland).

Anne Dawson has taught in primary, secondary and tertiary education institutions. From 1977–1989 she taught at McAuley College in the teacher education programme. Since 1990 she has been teaching at the Brisbane College of Theology in Queensland. She is currently lecturing in Studies in Christian Spirituality and is coordinator of the programme.

Novum Testamentum et Orbis Antiquus   44

Anne Dawson

Freedom as Liberating Power

A socio-political reading of the ἐξουσία texts
in the Gospel of Mark

Universitätsverlag Freiburg Schweiz
Vandenhoeck & Ruprecht Göttingen
2000

Die Deutsche Bibliothek – CIP-Einheitsaufnahme

Dawson, Anne:
Freedom as liberating power: a socio-political reading of the ἐξουσία texts in the Gospel of
Mark / Anne Dawson. – Freiburg [Schweiz]: Univ.-Verl.; Göttingen: Vandenhoeck und
Ruprecht, 2000
  (Novum testamentum et orbis antiquus; 44)
  Zugl.: Queensland, Univ., Diss., 1996
  ISBN 3-525-53944-4
  ISBN 3-7278-1285-0

Veröffentlicht mit Unterstützung des Hochschulrates Freiburg Schweiz, des
Rektorates der Universität Freiburg Schweiz, der Ursulinen der Provinz Australien
und der University of Queensland (Dept. Studies in Religion).

Die Druckvorlagen der Textseiten wurden von der Autorin
reprofertig zur Verfügung gestellt.

© 2000 by Universitätsverlag Freiburg Schweiz
Paulusdruckerei Freiburg Schweiz
ISBN 3-7278-1285-0 (Universitätsverlag)
ISBN 3-525-53944-4 (Vandenhoeck & Ruprecht)
ISSN 1420-4592 (Novum Testam. orb. antiq.)

To Anne and Frank
my parents

Acknowledgments

The completion of this work, would not have been possible without the help of a number of people. In particular, I would like to acknowledge Michael Lattke, Professor of New Testament and Early Christianity Studies in the Department of Studies in Religion at the University of Queensland, who shares my interest in the topic of Christian freedom. Professor Lattke's scholarly expertise, his alertness to available publications and resources, as well as his critique of this project, have been invaluable.

I would like to thank Adela Yarbro Collins from the Divinity School at the University of Chicago, Detlev Dormeyer from the University of Münster, and Robert Crotty from the University of South Australia, who read an earlier version of this work and who have provided helpful comments. I owe a special debt of gratitude to Max Küchler and Gerd Theissen, editors of the NTOA series and well regarded for their scholarship in the area of Early Christianity, who also offered helpful suggestions and encouraged the publication of this work. While I thank all of these scholars, I acknowledge that the responsibility for this work is entirely mine.

I would like to pay special tribute to the following people for their assistance in various ways: the Department of Studies in Religion at the University of Queensland, where my interest in biblical studies was supported, and for a financial contribution provided by the Department which has made the publication of this work possible; my colleagues at Pius XII Seminary Banyo, member school of the Brisbane College of Theology, and in particular Elaine Wainwright, with whom I have had a number of informal discussions which have generated ideas for the project; Carolyn Willadsen, for her ready assistance regarding access to library resources; Janice Howard, for proof reading the Latin texts incorporated into this work; the Ursuline Sisters in the Australian Province who have provided encouragement and financial support from the beginning of this project through to its completion for publication.

Last, but certainly not least, I want to express my deep gratitude to my family who have always shown a keen interest in any of the projects I have undertaken.

25 November, 1999   Anne Dawson
Brisbane

Table of Contents

Chapter Four   **The Gospel of Mark**   **95-120**

Chapter Five   **The ἐξουσία of Jesus and the Disciples**   **121-170**

Technical Preface

The Latin and Greek references from the *Res Gestae Divi Augusti* are taken from Ekkehard WEBER (ed). 1970. **Augustus: meine Taten:** *Res Gestae Divi Augusti,* nach dem Monumentum Ancyranum, Apolloniense und Antiochenum. Lateinisch–Griechisch–Deutsch. München: Heimeran.

References to the English translation from the Latin are taken from Edwin JUDGE (ed). 1985a [1983]. "Augustus in the *Res Gestae.*" In **Augustus and Roman History: Documents and Papers for Student Use**. North Ryde, Australia: Macquarie University, 131-171.

Direct quotations from the Bible in Greek and English are taken from the **Synopsis of the Four Gospels. Greek-English Edition of the Synoptis Quattuor Evangeliorum.** Completely revised on the basis of the Greek text of Nestle-Aland 26th Edition and Greek New Testament 3rd Edition. The English text is the Second Edition of the Revised Standard Version. [Stuttgart:] United Bible Societies, 1975.

CHAPTER ONE

Introduction to the Study

Preamble

Freedom is "the central topic of the New Testament proclamation (κήρυγμα)" (Lattke 1993, 37). In the New Testament literature, the Greek word group for "freedom" (ἐλεύθερος, ἐλευθερόω, ἐλευθερία, ἀπελεύθερος) appears most frequently in the Gospel of John and in the Pauline literature particularly in the *Hauptbriefe* (Romans, 1-2 Corinthians, Galatians), in which the concept of Christian freedom is considered thematically (Niederwimmer 1990, 432).[1] While the word group occurs a number of times in these Christian texts, it appears only once in the synoptic tradition, namely in Mt 17:26. In this context reference is to the "sons" or citizens of earthly kings who do not have to pay tax because of their status as free people. By inference those who are citizens of God's reign are also free. Although the word group ἐλευθερία (et al.) is not found in the synoptic texts, an important point to which Niederwimmer (1990, 432) draws attention is that "only part of the history of liberation is seen in NT texts which have these words; that history begins already in the work of the earthly Jesus." It was also Käsemann's view (1968, 55-58) that the notion of Christian freedom is grounded in the teachings and actions of Jesus of Nazareth and that the author of the Markan text developed his Gospel with the concept of freedom as its underlying theme. On that basis, according to Käsemann, Mark's Gospel may in fact be termed the "Gospel of freedom." Given that the concept of freedom is central to the *kerygma* of early Christianity, and given that the word ἐλευθερία does not appear in the Gospel of Mark, the question then arises as to how or in what way the Gospel of Mark witnesses to the concept of freedom.

Christian Freedom

The notion of Christian freedom that is contained in the Pauline writings is couched in theological, doctrinal and philosophical terms which describe the nature of Christian

---

[1] For more extensive discussion of the term ἐλευθερία in the New Testament texts see Niederwimmer (1966); Nestle (1967); Panimolle (1988); Vollenweider (1989).

freedom, the status of the free Christian person and the free Christian community, and the "world" in which the free Christian person and free Christian community lives (Böckle 1980, 114-123). Within the context of early Christianity the Pauline emphasis of Christian freedom tended to focus more specifically on the notion of freedom in terms of its christological dimension rather than on the *praxis* of freedom within the social context. As Christianity expanded into the Greco-Roman world of the first century CE, two major issues began to emerge regarding the proclamation of Christian freedom. Firstly, Christian communities had to contend with the politics of the dominant ethos of the Roman empire as they struggled to remain faithful to their commitment as followers of the "good news" that Jesus had proclaimed. In their interaction with non-Christian groups and public officials, the Christian communities had to encounter the hostility metered out to them by asserting their right and freedom to choose a way of life which had been effectively outlawed by officialdom. This meant that the interpretation of the concept of Christian freedom which was central to the Christian way of life was in danger of being used as a political catchcry to boost morale and hope, in much the same way that ἐλευθερία and *libertas* had become rallying political catchcries in the Greek and Roman worlds.[2] Secondly, as Christianity became enculturated into the Greco-Roman world, the situation arose in some Christian communities, where Christian freedom was regarded as a licence to do and act as one pleased, irrespective of the social and moral consequences.[3] The author of the Markan Gospel, therefore, has provided a corrective to the esoteric and distorted interpretation of the notion of Christian freedom that was beginning to develop in first century Christian communities.[4] By returning to the actual source of the concept of freedom grounded in the teachings and actions of Jesus, the author of Mark's Gospel sought to recapture the essence of the concept of freedom that Jesus proclaimed, in order to locate its meaning with reference to the lived reality of the first century world and its consequent universal significance (Käsemann 1968, 55-58).

Freedom and the Human Condition

It would be fair to say that no other concept has evoked as much passion in the human spirit as the concept of freedom. Throughout history the nature of freedom has been the subject of much political discourse and the reason for political action wherever people have come together or have been forced together in socially defined units. The struggle

---

[2] The letters to the Corinthians address the issue of a distorted notion of Christian freedom.

[3] See particularly Käsemann's discussion (1968) 59-84.

[4] See also Collins (1988) 148 who states that Mark was written to provide a controlling text for the Jesus tradition.

for freedom has been undertaken by individuals, communities and nations. The paradox, of course is that the human quest for freedom has often been interpreted as a justification for wars, social upheaval and atrocities perpetrated on other people. The promise of freedom has been the catchcry of the proponents of monarchism, republicanism, communism, capitalism, totalitarianism, and democracy, each acting as the "voice" of freedom for the people under its rule. Yet for all the propaganda surrounding the promise of freedom by the dominant political powers, the fact remains that individuals, groups and nations have continued to experience non-freedom to a greater or lesser extent. Freedom has been bestowed on some and denied to others. It has been jealously guarded and zealously defended. Its absence has caused some to protest and others to remain silent. Its presence and its absence have always impacted on the very fabric of human living.

There have been individuals who by their actions, have been held up to future generations as people who demonstrated that freedom is not just a philosophical and unattainable idea, but that it is an inalienable right of every human being and fundamental to human living. In the Christian tradition there have been people who have chosen the possibility of martyrdom rather than succumb to the exploitation and dominating control by the political powers of the day, be they church powers or state powers. These people exercised their power of choice with regard to what they held as their belief. Others may have not been confronted with martyrdom but nevertheless chose a way of living that challenged social and political situations of oppression. In more recent times, there have been people who have spoken and acted on behalf of freedom in spite of the threat of suffering and even death. The witness to freedom by some people has altered the course of history. For example, Martin Luther King demanded for his black sisters and brothers the freedom from the oppression of white dominant culture in the United States of America, and demanded that they be treated with the dignity that rightfully belongs to any human being. Steve Biko and Nelson Mandela to name but two, spoke out on behalf of the people in their struggle for freedom and equality in South Africa. Mahatma Gandhi called on the people to take a stance with him, of passive resistance against the exploitation and violent domination of the people by the political powers in India. Archbishop Romero chose to stand with the poor in their opposition against the oppressive government regime of El Salvador. The men and women involved in liberation movements of South America, Africa, and Asia, as well as the indigenous people of many countries such as Australia, New Zealand and nations of the South Pacific region, have called for freedom from political oppression and the right to be in control of their destiny. The voices in the women's movement have also called for freedom from oppressive patriarchal structures. In all these cases freedom has been sought against the prevailing structures, customs or laws which have or would have kept them enslaved to dominant powers. These women and men have witnessed to the fact that the reality and *praxis* of freedom is an attainable goal.

Just what has contributed to situations of non-freedom, is of course, generally complex and is determined by the cultural context and ideological values that are espoused within that cultural context. However, a glance across the history of the western tradition shows that particularly where there has been a major shift in terms of so-called economic and political advancement of a nation, a corresponding shift in the curtailment of freedom of its people or of other people has also resulted. This is not to deny the positive outcomes in such "revolutions." But all too often these revolutions have occurred without due regard and care for the well-being of all people. By way of example, the industrial revolution in the late 18th and early 19th centuries in England spawned the social dislocation, resultant misery and enslavement to overlords that subsequently occurred in the latter part of the 18th century and throughout the 19th century. The search for new lands and trade that was encouraged by European political powers in the 14th, 15th and 16th centuries resulted in colonial domination, slavery and in many cases the annihilation of indigenous peoples in many parts of the so-called New World of North America and South America. The "christianising" of the Roman empire in the reign of Constantine assured the church's position and the influence of its leaders in the running of political and economic affairs for many centuries, and at the same time it continued the *status quo* of powerlessness and subservience that the general populace experienced as a result of power being the prerogative of a few.

Western tradition, of course, has been very much influenced by Greek and Roman culture of ancient times. At the height of their political ascendancy as "world leaders," both Greece and Rome exerted enormous power and domination over other cultures in the bid for expansion and the control of territories. The fortunes that Rome and Greece acquired through the conquest of other nations resulted in a major shift in political and cultural norms and expectations throughout the ancient Mediterranean world. When Rome, as a result of Augustus' military exploits, became the dominant world power in the first century BCE, freedom was promised to those nations conquered by Rome. However as Augustus himself was to state, freedom was given only to those nations "which could with safety be pardoned" (*RG* 3). The implication of course was that the so-called "freedom" of those nations conquered by Rome, depended entirely on Augustus' disposition towards them and their acquiescence to Augustus' rule. In all of these examples mentioned here, what was regarded as freedom by the dominant group was certainly experienced as non-freedom by other groups.

The Political Context of Judaea in the First Century

The Judaic world of the first century CE was one of those foreign nations that Augustus deemed worthy of pardon. Consequently, Rome believed that in granting this pardon, the freedom of the people in the region of Palestine could be assured. However, as Borg's study indicates (1984, 29), the people of Palestine took a different view because Roman control which was maintained by military occupation clearly had a significant detrimental impact on the religious, social, political and economic life of the Jews (Borg 1984, 29). While generally on the part of the Jews there was hostility towards Rome, at the same time there were individuals and groups among them who pledged loyalty to Rome because of the rewards that such loyalty was able to secure. Those who pledged this loyalty were mostly those who held the power within the Judaic political system. In this way these people secured their so-called freedom even if it meant being subservient to Rome. Nevertheless, in the context of being subject to Rome, the granting of certain freedoms to the Jews meant that they were able to maintain a degree of control over their internal affairs. Broadly speaking it was the appeal to their adherence to the conventional wisdom of their tradition which provided them with the means of political bargaining regarding their status and so-called "autonomy" under foreign domination.

Goal of the Study

This study will demonstrate that the Gospel of Mark proclaims a concept of freedom which is radically different from the concept of freedom that was espoused by the dominant culture of the Mediterranean world. It will be argued that the ideology of the dominant culture is given expression in the text of the *Res Gestae* inscription. This inscription or text provides an interpretation of the achievements of Augustus on behalf of the citizens of Rome with the claim that these achievements had secured not only their freedom but indeed the freedom of the whole world. It represented the "voice" at the centre of the world under Roman rule. In other words it became the "dominant political consciousness" of the Mediterranean world. In the Gospel of Mark, the author interprets for his readers the message of Jesus of Nazareth who preached in the regions of Palestine proclaiming the freedom of the "reign of God," and who intentionally challenged the principles and practices on which the freedom proclaimed by Rome was based. Jesus' proclamation represented the "voice" at the margins of society. The ways in which the concept of freedom in the Gospel of Mark differed substantially from the notion of freedom that was promulgated by the ruling powers of Rome and Judaea, is the particular focus of this study.

Approach to the Study

Because the freedom of people is essentially a socio-political issue, this study will entail a socio-political reading of the Gospel of Mark. The term "political" in this case refers to what Borg (1994, 98) describes as the "broader definition of politics" in that it "builds on the semantic associations of its Greek root *polis* ... politics concerns the shape and shaping of the city, and by extension the shape and shaping of a society's life." The framework or methodology for the study is socio-rhetorical and draws on the insights of those scholars whose focus in recent years has been the development and refining of a socio-rhetorical framework for interpreting biblical texts.[5] These scholars in turn have been particularly influenced by the ground breaking scholarship of George Kennedy whose study of the rhetoric of ancient literary texts led him to explore the rhetoric and rhetorical function of Christian scriptures as texts which were influenced by the rhetorical conventions of classical Greek and Roman literature.

A focus on the rhetorical aspect of literary texts as George Kennedy (1984, 4) explains, considers the text in its final form and "looks at it from the point of view of the author's or editor's intent, the unified results, and how it would be perceived by an audience or near contemporaries." A number of scholars have applied the critical method which Kennedy adapted from the classical rhetorical model, with a view to identifying the purpose of the selected New Testament text and the intention of its author. Wuellner (1987, 458-460) for example, applies this rhetorical critical model to 1 Corinthian 9 and concludes that "the much cited and much misunderstood diatribe has emerged at last as essentially epideictic in purpose." A first century reader would have been aware of the "signs" within the text which would have indicated its epideictic purpose. However, a modern reader might miss it if he or she was unaware of the rhetorical forms inherent in the text. A reader in the first century CE would have been accustomed to these forms. Obviously with the purpose of the text defined, the meaning of the text becomes clearer to the modern reader. Schüssler Fiorenza (1987, 386-403) also draws on a variation of Kennedy's model to "explore the questions, methods, and strategies involved in the interpretation" of 1 Corinthians, and in an earlier study Schüssler Fiorenza (1985, 144-165) also applied a rhetorical critical approach to the study of Revelation 14:1-5. Through these studies, she demonstrated that in the case of 1 Corinthians, Paul's rhetoric is to be understood as an active response to the situation of the Corinthian church (1987, 388), and with reference to Revelation 14:1-5 she states: "Revelation must be understood as a poetic-rhetorical

---

[5] There are a number of scholars whose work reflects a socio-rhetorical approach to the interpretations of early Christian texts. See in particular that of Tannehill (1981; 1984); Schüssler Fiorenza (1985; 1989); Mack (1988; 1990); Myers (1988); Tolbert (1989); Thibeaux (1992); Malbon (1993); Matera (1993); Oakman (1994); Powell (1993); Robbins (1987; 1992; 1993; 1994).

construction of an alternative symbolic universe that "fits" its historical-rhetorical situation" (1985, 146). In each of these examples the meaning of the text is drawn from the rhetoric that is contained within the text. The significance of rhetorical criticism for interpreting New Testament texts is that it provides ways of understanding "the social and ideological dynamics of the first-century movements and help us determine what exactly the new persuasion was" (Mack 1990, 94).

A socio-rhetorical framework adds another dimension into the interpretative process of rhetorical criticism with its focus on the consideration of the social environment in the cultural context as it is reflected in the rhetoric of a "text." The text, of course, may be a literary text or a non-literary text. Robbins (1992, xxiv) explains that a socio-rhetorical approach to a text "presupposes that language is a social possession and that one of the social functions of language is to tell a story." A phenomenon of modern interpretation of New Testament texts is the multiplicity of methods and approaches, which indicates the growing awareness of the complexity of the task of interpretation.[6] For this reason, as Robbins (1992, xxiv) explains, there is a need to develop "an interdisciplinary method grounded in a multi-disciplinary approach that uses both transdisciplinary and disciplinary practices in its interpretative strategies." The nature of socio-rhetorical criticism is that it draws on a multi-disciplinary approach (Robbins 1992, xxiv). One of the features of socio-rhetorical criticism to which Robbins (1992, xxiv) draws attention, is its relationship to the science of Semiotics. Basically, Semiotics may be defined as a field of enquiry into the nature and function of signs as a form of communication within a society (Stibbe 1990, 618). Applied to the area of literary criticism it too, can be seen as a multi-disciplinary approach whereby interpreters study literary texts as signifiers with the aim of discovering "the operations and conventions by which the reader understands what is signified" (Stibbe 1990, 619). Its focus is that of identifying distinction rather than opposition, and its "bias is dialogical rather than dualistic as it seeks similarities and differences that both interrelate and differentiate different phenomena" (Robbins 1990, xxiv).

My approach to the study of the concept of freedom in the Gospel of Mark draws on the insights of those scholars whose focus in recent years has been the development and refining of a socio-rhetorical framework for interpreting biblical texts. I use the word "approaches" deliberately as the nature of socio-rhetorical criticism is eclectic and as such there are various ways of approaching the text within the socio-rhetorical paradigm.[7] In the approach that I have adopted in my exploration of the topic of freedom in the Gospel of Mark, the explanations of interpretative processes adopted by

---

[6] For an excellent discussion of methodological approaches to the interpretation of New Testament texts, see Sandra Schneider (1991) 97-128.

[7] For example, see the rhetorical approach that Thibeaux (1992) adopts in her analysis of Luke 7:36-50.

Robbins (1992; 1994), Schneiders (1991) and Malbon (1993), have been particularly influential.

One of the presuppositions that underlies my enquiry is that texts have contexts which are both intrinsic and extrinsic to the text in question. These contexts can be both on a micro-scale and a macro-scale. The meaning to be gained from a text is largely dependent on the reader's understanding of both the contexts in which the text is embodied, and the contexts which are embodied within the text itself. As Malbon (1993, 82) explains, all texts have both "internal" and "external" contexts. A focus on the "internal" aspects of the texts is to look at the text as "mirror" which reflects what is contained in the text, and that the interpretive process consists of identifying such elements as the language, style, genre and rhetoric contained within the text with the purpose of identifying "the text's meaning and significance" (Malbon 1993, 82). A focus on the "external" aspects is to look at the text as a "window" through which one can view and consider the political, cultural, religious or literary world of the text (Malbon 1993, 82). A consideration of the text as both window and mirror, as Malbon explains, is "necessary to the interpretative task in its fullest sense." Both the literary context and the historical context, as well as the internal and external contexts of both the literary and historical contexts, have to be considered as a set of interrelating elements within the interpretative process. The difficulty, Malbon (1993, 82) suggests, is the problem "of relating the two views in a way that does justice to both."

Schneiders identifies three possible interpretive outcomes of text analysis. Like Malbon, Schneiders (1991, 113) also suggests that the interpretive process entails viewing the text as a "window" through which the interpreter is able to identify, to a degree, "the historical, theological and ideological agenda and the ancient world in which that community lived," and as a "mirror" by which she means that "the reader is revealed to her-or himself in the process of engaging in the text." However, Schneiders adds a third outcome, that of identifying "the significance of the text for the present: the implications of the biblical material for contemporary theological reflection, the text's challenge for the contemporary believer, its transformative potential" (Schneiders 1991, 113). According to Schneiders (1991, 113) each of these three areas can be termed as "the world *behind* the text (i.e., text as window), the world *of* the text (i.e., the text as linguistic system and as mirror), and the world *before* the text (i.e., the text as transformative)." In the interpretative process, it is possible to use a combination of the three interests, but as Schneiders (1991, 113) explains there will be differences in the weight of interest. It depends on the particular interest or interests of the interpreter as to which area or areas would be more strongly emphasised (Schneiders (1991, 113).

Robbins also claims that the interpretative process involves working at two "texts" at the same time. By that he means both reading the text and opening the world of the text. He also identifies four main contexts which he calls "textures" of the text. The first he identifies is that of the "inner texture." The goal of inner textual analysis is to identify the elements within the text "from the simple repetition of signs to the most subtle argumentative strategies" (Robbins 1994, 171). According to Robbins (1994, 171-179), every text has subtexts which in turn contain codes or signs such as structural elements for example, repetition and progression. It also considers such elements as dialogue within the text and the form of the dialogue, narration and plot. The second area with which rhetorical criticism is concerned is the intertextual element. The focus here is on a comparative analysis of the text with other texts. The comparison may be drawn from textual units within the total text or it may be drawn from two totally "different" texts. The third element in the socio-rhetorical paradigm is the "social and cultural" texture. The text reflects its socio-cultural milieu and the analysis of this dimension provides an insight into the conditions giving rise to the composition of the text (Robbins 1994, 185). The fourth element is the ideological texture which, as its name suggests, inquires into the area "of whose self-interests are being negotiated" within the text (Robbins 1994, 194). Again in the interpretive process as Robbins envisions it, the weight of interests is not equal. He cites the works of four scholars which illustrate the specific "interest" or "interests" that each is pursuing, even though the term "texture" is not identified explicitly by these scholars themselves (1992, xxx-xxxiv). Robbins explains that Elliott's emphasis is on the social and cultural texture, Myers' focus is on the ideological texture, Mack's interest is on the intertextuality of the texts, while Scott's emphasis is on the inner texture of the text. Robbins' interest in his work *Jesus the Teacher*, is on the inner texture and the intertexture of the texts in the Gospel of Mark (1992, xxx).

The Rhetorical Situation

A second presupposition that underlies my enquiry is that all texts are rhetorical in that they come into being in response to a situation (Bitzer 1968, 9). All texts are a product of a writer's desire to persuade his/her reader of a point of view regarding a "situation." Schüssler Fiorenza has demonstrated this point in her analysis of both 1 Corinthians and Revelation 14:1-5.

The Gospel of Mark is a product of the socio-cultural and literary context of the Mediterranean world in the first century CE. Its author was obviously someone whose assessment of a "situation" in the first century CE was such that it called for a response or in Bitzer's words, the situation "invited utterance" (1968, 4). My assumption is that the societal context of first century Mediterranean world was influenced and in many ways shaped by the dominant ideological political power of the time which was a legacy of the reign of Augustus. The testimony of that influence, as has already been mentioned is found in the *Res Gestae* inscription which projected the "dominant consciousness" in the Mediterranean world. It is for this reason that a study of the *Res Gestae* inscription is an important consideration in my approach to the concept of freedom in the Gospel of Mark.

It must be stated that unlike other socio-rhetorical studies which tend to find parallels between New Testament texts and other literary texts from the Greco-Roman world, the study of Mark's Gospel and of the *Res Gestae* inscription in this work, is not undertaken with the purpose of identifying parallels between these texts. Rather, the study of the *Res Gestae* from a socio-rhetorical perspective provides an insight into the meaning and purpose that the *Res Gestae* conveyed throughout the Mediterranean world of the first century CE. It may be argued, of course, that many people in the first century and particularly those living in the Syrian and Palestinian regions of the Mediterranean world, may never have heard of the *Res Gestae* inscription, let alone have read it. While this may be so, it will be argued that its influence would have extended into the many areas of the Mediterranean world. An inscription, by its very nature, is a public document, and as such, is accessible to all (Danker 1982, 28-29). Whether or not the *Res Gestae* was read by the passers-by, it nevertheless would have stood as a monument or "text" and as such would have "signified" its content. Even if the *Res Gestae* inscription was unknown to some people, the very "behaviour" of the general populace would have reflected the presence of its ethos. Reactions to the ethos may have been positive, negative or ambivalent. Nevertheless, the observed "behaviour" of the people to which another text or other texts bear witness provides evidence of its pervasiveness and its acceptance or rejection within that society. These other texts may have been of a literary nature, such as the writings of Josephus and the writings of Philo, or they may be non-literary such as architectural designs of buildings, other monuments, inscriptions and coinage.

It is in the context of the ethos of political domination at whatever level, but particularly at the structural levels of government and societal institutions that the Gospel of Mark interprets the message that Jesus proclaimed in his teachings and through his actions. Its message is political in the sense that it initiates a conceptual change of the meaning of freedom.[8] The text of the *Res Gestae* and the text of Mark's Gospel contain the "language" through which the specific perspectives of the concept of freedom can be discerned. The study, therefore, will focus on each of these texts in order to identify the specific sense and reference regarding freedom as a political concept.

Skinner (1989, 8) explains that "[t]he surest sign that a group or society has entered into the self-conscious possession of a new concept is that a corresponding vocabulary

---

[8] See Farr's discussion of the politics of conceptual change (1989) 25-31.

will be developed, a vocabulary which can then be used to pick out and discuss the concept with consistency." The discussion, therefore, will identify the "vocabulary" that reflects the consistent theme of freedom contained in each of the texts.

In the case of the *Res Gestae*, it will be demonstrated that although the word *libertas* (liberty) occurs at the beginning of the text, it is the language or "vocabulary" of the office of *triumvir potestas*, rendered in the Greek as δημαρχικὴ ἐξουσία in the context of the text, that conveys the sense of the meaning of freedom that the *Res Gestae* is promoting. This term which was used in connection with the higher officials of Roman administration, occurs at significant points in the text.

In the Gospel of Mark, the term ἐλευθερία (*libertas*) does not occur at all. However, it is the term ἐξουσία with its meaning of "freedom to act" that conveys the concept of freedom that the Gospel author is wishing to emphasise. There is no proof, of course, that the Gospel author selected the term ἐξουσία as a corrective to the notion of freedom that the *Res Gestae* was promoting. But in selecting this "vocabulary," the intention was to show that freedom was not the acceptance of societal structures that oppressed and impoverished people, nor was it a passive acceptance of another person's beneficence which left the recipient unable to choose, act or decide for himself or herself. Mark's Gospel portrays a picture of Jesus who acted with ἐξουσία and who called on his followers to act likewise. In doing so, Jesus in fact subverted the notion of freedom that Rome proclaimed.[9]

In discussing the concept of freedom contained in these two documents, the approach will be attentive to the contexts *within* the texts and the contexts *of* the texts. Accordingly attention will be given to the literary and historical dimensions, both internal and external to the texts. It will analyse the "textures" within the texts, namely the inner texture, intertexture, social and cultural texture and the ideology. It will discuss these "textures" in the light of the documents as both revealing the world of the text and the world behind the text.

The socio-political context of the Greco-Roman world of the eastern part of the Roman empire in the first century CE is the subject of chapters two and three of this work. Chapter two presents a detailed rhetorical analysis of the text of the *Res Gestae*, and a discussion of its influence in the Mediterranean world of the first century CE.[10] This is followed in chapter three by a study of the theme of freedom in the Greco-

---

[9] The theme of ἐξουσία in the Gospel of Mark is the subject of a study by Scholtissek (1992). His work differs from this thesis in that his focus is on the christological aspect of the ἐξουσία (*Vollmacht*) of Jesus. See also Scholtissek (1993) for a discussion of the theme of ἐξουσία in the Old Testament and Jewish literature.

[10] I have identified a chiastic structure in the *Res Gestae* and will argue that this structure is fundamental to the message that the *Res Gestae* is promoting. From the research I have undertaken and to my knowledge, this chiastic structure has not been previously identified by any other scholar.

Mediterranean world of the first century CE, and its implications for the people both in the region of Asia Minor and for the Jews living in the region of Palestine. Chapter four considers the more recent scholarship concerning the provenance of the Markan text as well as scholarly views regarding its genre, structure and function as a literary document. Chapters five and six consider the theme of ἐξουσία in the Gospel of Mark against the background of the socio-political context of the first century CE. Chapter five identifies the nature of ἐξουσία that Jesus proclaimed in his teaching and in his actions, and the response of his disciples to that ἐξουσία in and around the region of Galilee. Chapter six discusses Jesus' critique of the Jerusalem establishment and the ultimate test there of both the ἐξουσία of Jesus and that of the disciples.

Finally, it is the concern for "the world *before* the text" that has prompted this enquiry in the first place. My reason for undertaking this study is socio-political in the sense that my understanding of the true nature of politics is a sharing of power within society. Although there are expressions in today's world, of the kind of freedom that Jesus proclaimed, the general human experience is of a world in which there is a distorted understanding of the meaning of freedom. It is a world in which dominant powers continue to exploit, oppress or block the life-growth of those deprived of power. This was the same kind of world that the community of Mark experienced:

> Nimmt man all dies zusammen, so läßt der Evangelist keinen Zweifel daran, daß er seine Gemeinde in einem Unrechts-Staat leben sieht, der durch Machtmißbrauch, Unterdrückung und Gewalt geprägt wird. (Söding 1995, 193).

It is by returning to the source of Christian freedom which the Gospel of Mark interprets, and by reinterpreting its message of freedom against the background of its socio-political context, that the message of Christian freedom can be seen in a new light, and may thus be retrieved and reconceptualised as meaningful *praxis* in the modern world.

CHAPTER TWO

Res Gestae Divi Augusti

The *Res Gestae* in the Mediterranean World

(a) Ancient Historical Evidence

The *Res Gestae* was intended to be an inscribed public document. Evidence for this is found in the writings of Suetonius (*Aug.* 101.2) and also that of Cassius Dio (56.33). In the final chapter of his account of the life of *Divus Augustus*, Suetonius relates that Augustus had drawn up a will fourteen months before his death in 14 CE. According to Suetonius the will was written partly by Augustus, and partly by his freedmen Polybius and Hilarion. It was written in two books and deposited with the vestal virgins (Suet. *Aug.* 101.1). As Edward Champlin (1989, 155) points out "temples were the standard repositories for the original copies of wills and other valuable documents." After the death of Augustus, the will and three other sealed documents were opened and read aloud in the Senate (Suet. *Aug.* 101.2). The first of the three scrolls contained directions for Augustus' funeral, the second was an account of all that he had accomplished. Modern scholarship refers to this account as the "Index" (Judge 1985, 5), or more commonly as the "Res Gestae."[1] Suetonius says that it was the wish of Augustus that this account was to be inscribed on bronze tablets and set up at the entrance of his Mausoleum.[2] The third scroll was a summary of the condition of the empire (Suet. *Aug.* 101.4). All of these scrolls seem to have been lost to posterity, as was the original inscription, the *Res Gestae,* at the entrance of the Mausoleum.

Ancient Roman historians apparently have made little direct reference to the *Res Gestae*. This seems rather strange in that source material related to the document would have been readily accessible.[3] In his overview of recent scholarship on this particular matter, Edwin Ramage states that some scholars claim that there are significant

---

[1] *Res Gestae Divi Augusti* is the title that Theodor Mommsen (1883) 1-39 assigned to the Monumentum Ancyranum and Monumentum Apollonium which are discussed in this chapter.

[2] Having such a document inscribed in bronze and placed in front of his Mausoleum would not have been all that unusual, as there were instances where the achievements of other dignitaries had been inscribed on monuments. See Gagé (1977) 29-30.

[3] Whether Suetonius, in writing his biography of Augustus in 120 CE, would have had direct access to these documents and to the inscription is debatable. It is generally held that Suetonius would have had access to a substantial amount of material from histories and memoirs which are now lost. For a more extensive discussion, see Rolfe (1970) xviii; Gagé (1977) 40; Ramage (1987) 150.

influences from the *Res Gestae* in the writings of Suetonius, Velleius and Dio, and that others have argued that there is also evidence of influences of the *Res Gestae* in Valerius Maximus, Seneca and Tacitus (1987, 147).[4] While Ramage is of the opinion that the arguments for such references are not really convincing, he does support the view that there is evidence of the influence of the *Res Gestae* in the writings of Suetonius (1987, 147). As well as mentioning the existence of such a document (Suet. *Aug.* 101.4), Suetonius also quotes from it:

> *Fecisse se ludos ait suo nomine quater, pro aliis magistratibus, qui aut abessent aut non sufficerent, ter et vicies (Aug. 43.1)*

> He says that he gave games four times in his own name and twenty-three times for other magistrates, who were either away from Rome or lacked means.[5]

Jean Gagé likewise refers to this example and also claims that Suetonius' choice of words, and sometimes rare words, show a striking resemblance to sections of the *Res Gestae* (1977, 39). He cites the example of the term *Curulis triumphos (Res Gestae* 4.1, cf. Suet. *Aug.* 22) which, he says, is seldom found elsewhere in writings of the Augustan and post-Augustan periods. He also points out that chapter 22 of Suetonius' biography of Augustus has obviously been drawn substantially from chapter 13 and also, but to a lesser extent, from chapter 4 of the *Res Gestae* (1977, 38). Gagé claims that Suetonius, like other historians of the time would have cited from memory, the texts that were generally well known. This would seem to explain the use of more indirect references rather than direct references to the *Res Gestae* which, Gagé argues, can be detected in both the writings of Suetonius as well as in other writings of the Augustan and post-Augustan periods (1977, 39-40; 210). Ramage takes a somewhat different view. He argues that the *Res Gestae* does not seem to have been used either directly or indirectly to any great extent by Roman historians, and he claims that the reason for this lack of interest in the *Res Gestae* as source material is that "the eulogistic nature of the *Res Gestae* would not have suited the designs of a Tacitus or a Suetonius or even a Velleius" (1987, 150).

---

[4] Alfred Heuss (1975) 91, claims that Velleius' encomiastic portrayal of Octavian's return from Alexandria and the period of the crossing of the Rubicon was influenced by the *Res Gestae*.

[5] The text from the *Res Gestae* reads: *Ludos feci meo nomine quater, aliorem autem magistratuum vicem ter at viciens* (22.2). I put on games four times in my own name and twenty three times I took over the responsibility for them from other magistrates.

(b) Modern Historical Evidence

In spite of the seemingly apparent lack of interest in the *Res Gestae* by ancient Roman historians, the fact that the existence of such a document and its inscription is attested in the writings of Suetonius is vitally important, as it substantiates the authenticity of the copies of the *Res Gestae* which have been subsequently discovered in more recent times, in what was the eastern part of the Roman world. The first of these copies was found on the walls of a mosque at Ancyra in 1555. Epigraphical evidence confirms that this was the site of what once had been the temple of Roma and Augustus (Gagé 1977, 4, n. 2). The inscription which was placed on the walls of the temple is now referred to as the "Monumentum Ancyranum".[6] The inscription was written in both Latin and Greek, with the Latin text inscribed on six columns on the interior walls of the vestibule of the temple, while the Greek text was spread out in nineteen columns over the exterior left wall (Gagé 1977, 5).[7] The Greek text is not always a direct translation of the Latin text, but is a very close paraphrase (Brunt & Moore 1967, 2). Bilingual inscriptions were not uncommon in the Greco-Roman world. An inscription now located in the Burdur museum in southern Turkey and which at considerable length details the requisitioning of transport in the Roman empire, is written in both Latin and Greek. According to Stephen Mitchell (1976, 109) this inscription "dates to the beginning of the reign of Tiberius." Mitchell compares the language used in this inscription with that of the *Res Gestae*, and makes the following observation:

> The language of both the Latin and the Greek texts, and the forms of the words used, correspond closely with the practice of the time as we know it from other inscriptions, and in particular with the *Res Gestae Divi Augusti* which must have been inscribed at about the same date.[8]

A second discovery of the inscription of the Res *Gestae* was found in the ruins of the town of Apollonia in Pisidia. The text that has been unearthed here is the Greek version. Although fragments of the text had been found in a number of places in Apollonia for over a century, little attention was given to them until 1930 when substantially more portions of the text were found. The fragments were of considerable

---

[6] It was not until 1861 that the first serious publication of the *Monumentum Ancyranum* was produced. The 1865 edition of the text was completed under the direction of the German scholar, Theodor Mommsen. The critical edition which was published in 1883 forms the basis on which all subsequent scholarly work has been based. See Ramage (1987) 122. Further critical editions, Ernst Diehl (1910).

[7] Gagé relies on the photographs taken by M. Schede for the information regarding the physical arrangement of the texts on the walls of what was the original temple of Roma and Augustus.

[8] Mitchell points out that bilingual inscriptions of any length are unusual in the Roman Empire, but not unique. See examples cited by Mitchell (1976), 110. Research by Jorma Kaimo (1979) 60, indicates that official inscriptions in antiquity constituted above all a medium of information and were written or transcribed in the language of the people for whom the inscription was intended.

importance for they were able to supply some of what was missing or what was indecipherable of the Greek text of the Monumentum Ancyranum (Gagé 1977, 6). Whether or not there was a Latin version of the inscription along with the Greek text is not known, as no Latin fragments have been found. Unlike the inscription of the *Res Gestae* at Ancyra, the inscription found at Apollonia was not located in a temple. It is thought to have been inscribed on the pedestals supporting the statues of the *divus* Augustus, Tiberius, Livia and the princes Germanicus and Drusus. These statues were grouped together and honoured in the same way that they were found to have been grouped at Laonia and honoured by the Gytheates (Gagé 1977, 6).[9]

In 1914 William Ramsay discovered a third copy of the inscription in the town of Antioch, which is also situated in Pisidia. The fragments that were found are the Latin version of the inscription. In a further expedition to the site in 1924, a far greater number of the fragments was unearthed. The discovery of these fragments was also of special significance in that they supplemented some of the missing Latin elements of the Monumentum Ancyranum (Gagé 1977, 7). The actual site for this inscription at Antioch is uncertain. Gagé suggests that it may have been inscribed either on the pedestals of statues of honour or on a triumphant gate. He says that what is certain is that the text was written on ten columns. These columns formed a passage between two public thoroughfares. Above one of the thoroughfares is the title *platea Augusta* and over the other is the title *platea Tiberiana* 1977, 7 n.1).[10]

The discovery of the inscriptions of the *Res Gestae* in various places in Asia Minor, as well as the testimony of Suetonius that such an inscription existed in Rome, point to the fact that the *Res Gestae Divi Augusti* reached a geographically widespread audience. Suetonius reports that Augustus wanted the *Index* to be inscribed on bronze tablets and set up at the entrance of the Mausoleum (*Aug.* 101.4). This structure which Augustus had erected during his sixth consulship in 28 BCE, was situated between the Via Flaminia and the bank of the Tiber and was surrounded by a large park which was open to the public (Strabo 5.3.9; Suet. *Aug.* 101.4). Zanker (1988, 73) explains that the Mausoleum was a huge edifice and "far overshadowed all earlier such structures in Rome and could only be likened to the tomb of the Carian dynast Mausolus, one of the Seven Wonders of the world." Presumably then, the inscription would have been very visible both to the citizens of Rome and visitors to Rome when they visited this park area and shrine. At Ancyra, visitors to the temple of Roma and Augustus would have been well acquainted with this visible testimony to Augustus and the influence of

---

[9] There seems to have been quite a strong imperial cult at Gytheum, a town near Sparta in the Peloponnese. The arrangements for this cult were inscribed to ensure the permanency of the cult. See Price (1984) 60-1; 210-11.

[10] Gagé (1977) draws on the work of W. Ramsay and A. v. Premerstein for this information. For a detailed analysis and discussion of the arrangement of the text see also A. v. Premerstein (1964) 198-225; H. Volkmann (1942) 41-44; Barini (1937) v-xii.

Rome. At Apollonia the rituals associated with the imperial cults would have been enacted in the public space where the statues stood. Hence the inscription would have been on view to the people as they engaged in their cultic rituals. The inscription at Antioch which was written on the walls of two presumably important public thoroughfares, would not have gone unnoticed by people passing through these thoroughfares.

On the Monumentum Ancyranum there is an explicit statement written in both Latin and Greek, that the inscription is a copy of the Roman inscription:

> *Rerum gestarum divi Augusti, quibus orbem terra[rum] imperio populi*
> *Rom[a]ni subiecit, et impensarum quas in rem publicam populumque*
> *Romanum fecit, incisarum in duabus aheneis pilis, quae su[n]t Romae*
> *positae, exemplar sub[i]ectum.*

> Below is a copy of the acts of the Deified Augustus by which he placed
> the whole world under the sovereignty of the Roman people, as engraved
> upon two bronze columns which have been set up in Rome.

> Μεθηρμηνευμέναι ὑπεγράφησαν πράξεις τε καὶ δωρεαὶ
> Σεβαστοῦ Θεοῦ, ἃς ἀπέλιπεν ἐπὶ Ῥώμης ἐνκεχαγμένας
> χαλχαῖς στήλαις δυσίν.

> Below is a translation of the acts and donations of the Deified Augustus
> as left by him inscribed on two bronze columns at Rome.

This statement, as well as the evidence from the three different locations of the *Res Gestae* in the eastern part of the Roman world, suggests that after the death of Augustus a number of copies of the *Res Gestae* must have existed. They may have been either copies of the original manuscript of the *Res Gestae* or manuscript copies of the inscription taken from the walls of the mausoleum in Rome. Since the inscriptions that have been discovered have come from areas that are geographically quite distant from one another, and because they have also been found at different sites, it can be presumed that copies of the *Res Gestae* probably found their way into many different communities. According to research undertaken by Charlesworth (1924) and Lionel Casson (1974), the mobility of peoples in the ancient Roman world was quite extensive. As well as the deployment of armies to various places in the Roman world, other activities such as those associated with trade, official business, mail services, pilgrimages and recreational pursuits were all reasons for people travelling from one place to another throughout the Mediterranean areas. Joseph Fitzmyer's study of the languages in Palestine also bears witness to the diffusion of languages, particularly Greek and Latin, in the ancient Mediterranean world (1991, 127-162). This is another indication of the mobility of people as well as the mobilisation of commercial interests and services throughout this part of the world. It can be presumed, then, that an inscription such as the *Res Gestae* would have been known, if not throughout the whole of the Mediterranean world, then certainly by people living in or travelling through large cities and towns throughout the eastern part of the Roman world, particularly where imperial cults had been established or where large cities and towns had been dedicated to the Roman ruler.[11]

The Purpose and Intended Audience of the *Res Gestae*

(a) Overview of Scholarship

Since Mommsen's extensive work on the text of the *Res Gestae* in the latter half of the nineteenth century up until the present time, scholarship related to the inscription has ranged from "matters of text criticism and questions of type and purposes to issues involving the content and real nature of the document" (Ramage 1987, 119). A survey of the scholarship cited by Volkmann (1942, 1-94), Danker (1982, 258), and also by Ramage (1987, 117-157), demonstrates that scholarship on the inscription has been quite extensive. The earliest survey of the literature on the *Res Gestae* was provided by Gardthausen (1904, 874-880) who covered the years from 1881 to 1903. Ramage (1987, 117) also refers to the work of Besnier, who covered the years 1883 to 1912. During this period scholarly investigation centred on the form of the text, translations and new editions, the influences of the text in the writings of Suetonius, as well as the debate on Kornemann's theory regarding the stages of composition of the text (Ramage 1987, 117-8). Volkmann's survey (1942, 1-94) covers the years 1914-1941. These years saw the discoveries of more fragments of the Apollonian text and also the Antiochian text, and as a consequence much scholarly investigation was devoted to revised editions and translations.[12] Attention was also given to the authorship of the copies of the text, authorship of the superscription and the appendix, as well as to elements of style, language and the literary character of the text.

Ramage provides a synopsis of these earlier investigations, but concentrates on the scholarship of the *Res Gestae* undertaken since 1941. Ramage claims that nothing of significance has been added to the scholarship undertaken before 1941 regarding the

---

[11] In ancient times inscriptions to or about popular figures or gods could be found over a wide geographical area. For example a number of inscriptions with reference to the cult of Isis which spread from Egypt to many places in the Greek world, have been found in Asia Minor. In 1969 such an inscription was discovered at Maroneia which was part of the Roman province of Macedonia. The content of the inscription of 1 *Kyme* 41, in praise of Isis, is regarded as evidence of the universal importance of this cult for Hellenistic Greeks and Romans. See Horsley (1981) 12-21. Also Danker (1982) 176-86. For evidence of the extent of Roman imperial cult in Asia Minor, see Price 1984.

[12] Shipley (1979); Gagé, (1977); Volkmann (1942) 1-37.

discovery, physical remains or reconstruction of the text (1987, 118-9). Instead scholars seem to have turned their attention to commentaries and translations of the text, the style and language of both the Latin and Greek texts with reference to form, purpose and literary character, and also studies that involve investigations on specific content within the text and aspects of the text which relate to wider issues, but where the text "is not the primary focus of the writer" (1987, 119-44). Ramage claims that the work on the text which was completed in the earlier part of this century has been the most successful accomplishment relating to the inscription (1987, 119). His assessment is that, apart from the work on textual reconstruction, most of the scholarship that has been carried out in relation to the *Res Gestae* inscription has been rather disappointing, and that with a few exceptions, "the document has been the victim of speculation and theorizing" (1987, 119).

According to Ramage, the study that has created and continues to create the most interest and the most debate is that relating to the form and purpose of the document (1987, 136). This debate began as early as 1884, when a German scholar by the name of Bormann, identified characteristics which suggested to him that the *Res Gestae* was a *"Grabinschrift* or *elogium sepulcrale"* (Ramage 1987, 136). While there were some who agreed with Bormann at that time, there were a number of scholars who proposed other possibilities, for example, that it was a political testament, an account book of what Augustus had achieved for the people and what the people had given to him, a document "in anticipation of and preparation for his deification" (1987, 136). Theodor Mommsen, who can arguably be said to have carried out the most extensive work on the text of the *Res Gestae,* was initially reluctant to categorise the document under a specific class of composition (Shipley 1979, 337). Eventually, as Ramage points out, he "allowed himself to be drawn into the controversy" (1987, 136). According to Ramage, Mommsen's conclusion was that the document was not "a eulogistic epitaph or a justification for apotheosis" but rather, he claims, it was "a statement of accounts (*Rechenschaftsbericht)* in a political sense; it was the summary of the emperor's long rule and was to be connected with similar documents produced by earlier rulers like Darius in the East" (1987, 136). Other theories that have since been proposed relating to the nature of the document are that it is a political testament directed to the *plebs urbana,* a statement of debit and credit, an account of Augustus' stewardship, a testimony of his life or an epitaph (Shipley 1979, 337; Gagé 1977, 25-31; Ramage 1987, 136-9).

In exploring the question regarding the purpose of the *Res Gestae,* scholars have tended to focus specifically on the content and arrangement of the content of the text. In the earlier part of this century W. L. Westermann, for example, concentrated on the internal evidence of the text. He noticed that there was little mention of other people's names in the text, and concluded that Augustus would have omitted proper names in the

Res Gestae, "consciously and with a purpose" (1911, 4). He pointed out that the names that Augustus does mention are those which refer to the male members of Augustus' family, and he argued that this evidence demonstrates that Augustus "was preparing the way for the succession in his family" (1911, 5-6). He claimed that Augustus was able to "make use of the account of his deeds to justify the inheritance of power in his family and influence the senate's opinion in favour of Tiberius" (1911, 10). According to Westermann, Augustus believed that in setting the document in front of the Mausoleum, the people of Rome would become used to "the idea of the inherited monarchy" (1911, 10).

Writing some seventy years after Westermann, Yavetz also took up the question of the purpose of the *Res Gestae.* He argued against the theory which some scholars had held, that the *Res Gestae* was addressed "to the *plebs urbana* of Rome" (1984, 8). He claimed that it was the educated *iuventus* that Augustus specifically had in mind when composing the *Res Gestae.* Drawing on selected references in the *Res Gestae* as well as "external" evidence from writings emanating from the Augustan era, Yavetz argued that Augustus was conscious that his rule had ushered in a new era, and since "the older generation would not be amenable to change, he took a strong personal interest in the education of the *iuventus,* caring not only for their physical fitness, but also for what he saw as their moral and spiritual well-being" (1984, 18). According to Yavetz, Augustus "wanted to set an example for future generations, and was not satisfied with being *imperio maximus.* His goal was to become *exemplo maior*" (1984, 20).

Apart from the significant work carried out on the reconstruction of the text of the *Res Gestae* which Ramage praises, he is critical of many approaches to the study of the *Res Gestae* because, in his view, scholars have tended to rely on information external to the text, rather than look to the text itself in the first instance. In his exploration of the question regarding both the form and purpose of the *Res Gestae,* Ramage breaks new ground in that he adopts a methodology which, he says, is intended "to draw information from the *RG* and not to impress ideas from outside it" (1987, 12). He describes his approach as "a close reading of the text which takes into account both individual passages and the document as a whole" (1987, 12). He begins his study by focusing on the rhetoric in the document. Under the heading of rhetoric he lists four elements, namely, aspects of organisation, use of the first person, emphasis and precedent, and matters of reliability. From his discussion of these rhetorical elements in conjunction with the arrangement of the content of the text, Ramage draws the conclusion that the main purpose Augustus had in mind was explication, by which he means that Augustus "was out to describe in a clear, succinct manner the new form of government, the principate, that he had established in Rome" (1987, 11). Ramage argues that the *Res Gestae* was "part of a program of instruction addressed by Augustus to his successor," and that this explanation would have been helpful to

"Tiberius and his successors, and the Roman people generally, to better understand the principate and the philosophy behind it" (1987, 115-6).

For the past century, the arrangement of the content of the *Res Gestae* is an area that has attracted the interest of scholars. In order to ascertain the major elements or issues that are emphasised in the document scholars have tended to organise the content of the text under specific categories. The following five examples illustrate the various conclusions that have been drawn. Mommsen's identification of the organisation of the content of the text has generally formed the basis from which subsequent scholars have identified other categories or more specific sub-categories.

According to Hardy (1923, 14) Mommsen identifies three distinct components, namely:

> (a) a statement of various honours, titles and offices received by
>   Augustus, 1-4
> (b) a statement of moneys spent on public objects, 15-24
> (c) an account of wars, conquests, and expeditions, 25-34

Hardy (1923, 14-17) on the other hand, identifies a fourfold classification, namely:

> (a) a summary of the *Res Gestae*, domestic and military, 1-3
> (b) a list of honours, titles and offices (cf. Mommsen) but which
>   are further subdivided into:
>   - the identification of domestic administration and government
>   - statements, positive or negative as to his constitutional position
>   - public acts, the noting of which serves to highlight his success
>   - honours of a more personal nature
> (c) the summary of the *impensae*
> (d) statements relating to "wars, expeditions by land and sea, extensions
>   - of the frontier, as well as annexations and diplomatic relations to
>   - foreign kings"

Gagé (1977, 13-14) identifies two major divisions, that of the *dites* (πράξεις) und *impensae* (δωρεαί). He then divides the text into three areas:

> (a) enumeration of civil and religious honours, both those received
>   and those declined throughout his career, 1-15
> (b) a list of expenses of all kinds in favour of the state and
>   the people, 15-24
> (c) a reminder of the history of both peaceful and conquering
>   exploits, 25-33

Judge (1985a, 132) identifies four sections:

> (a) *Honores*: sections 1-7 and special tributes 9-14
> (b) *Impensae*: 15-24
> (c) *Res Gestae*: 25-33
> (d) *Exemplum Virtutis*: 34-35

Ramage (1987, 17-19) follows Gagé, but makes further subdivisions:

> (a) introduction, summary of rise to power, 1-2
> -general summary of Augustus' military honours, 3.0-4.3
> -activities as civil leader, 4.4-5
> -civil positions held and refused, 5.1-7.2
> -list of his religious positions, 7.3
> -civil activities, 8
> -religious honours bestowed on Augustus, 9-13
> -extension of military, civil and religious honours, 14
> (b) Augustus' expenditures (*liberalitas*) civic, military and religious, 15-24
> (c) military campaigns leading to world domination, 25-33
> climax, (*pater patriae*) 34-5

Ramage claims that the arrangement of the content of the text into these categories supports his argument that Augustus had a "fairly clear plan in mind when he wrote the *RG*" (1987, 19). He draws attention to "the careful balance that exists between the introduction (1-2) and the conclusion (35-35)" (1987, 19). Ramage believes that this contrast, along with the other contrasts that he identifies in the text, substantiates his theory that the rhetoric which Augustus employs is intended to emphasise that "Octavian has come a long way, and the *RG* is designed to underline that fact" (1987, 20). He further explains that the qualities that were becoming obvious at the beginning of Augustus' career were "recognised many times over and have been institutionalised and idealised," and that "the *RG* is the story of this evolution" (1987, 20).

The other aspects of the rhetoric of the document to which Ramage draws attention are the use of the first person and the emphasis that is placed on precedent and numbers. Ramage claims that the combination of these two factors serve to focus the attention of both author and reader solely on Augustus. It is intended that Augustus be seen as "the constant focus of the action, whether it involves him as the doer or as the receiver" (1987, 28). His conclusion is that the *Res Gestae*, in emphasising the many precedents covering a wide spectrum of public activity, was meant to be a constant reminder to all, that the Romans had entered a new era with its own ideology firmly based in the best Roman traditions (1987, 32).

It is because the *Res Gestae* is written in the first person, that scholars generally hold that Augustus wrote the *Res Gestae* himself.[13] However, there has been some debate as to whether or not this is the case.[14] Nowhere does Suetonius explicitly state that Augustus wrote the *Index*. What he does say is that Augustus wrote part of his will and that the two freedmen, Polybius and Hilarion wrote the other part. As already mentioned, the will, written in two notebooks and the three scrolls, one of which was

---

[13] Suet. *Aug*, 101.4 and *Res Gestae* 35.2 are cited as evidence that the *Res Gestae* was written by Augustus.

[14] In this regard see the comment by Gagé (1977) 51-2.

the *Index*, were deposited with the Vestal Virgins, and after the death of Augustus all four documents were read in the Senate. The text does not say that Augustus himself wrote what was contained in the scrolls, and the fact that it was written in the first person does not necessarily indicate that Augustus wrote it or even composed it. There is evidence to show that there were epitaphs of ancient Egyptian dignitaries which were written in the first person (Aune 1989, 32).[15] Ramage claims that the last line of the *Res Gestae* is evidence that the *Res Gestae* was written by Augustus himself in the last year of his life (1987, 133). Whether or not Augustus wrote the *Index*, at least in its final form, is probably not verifiable. However if one can rely on the testimony of Suetonius which states that Augustus decreed that the *Index* was to be set up in front of his Mausoleum, it seems obvious that he would have at least known and would have approved the content of the document. What is certain, is that the document is written in the first person, and all the events, accomplishments, successes and honours that are enumerated are in relation to Augustus.

Scholarship on the text of the *Res Gestae* has, of course, revealed important and significant insights into elements of the document. However, there has been little progress towards an understanding of the rhetorical function of the document and the effect that this document was intended to have on the audience. An approach to a text from the perspective of rhetorical analysis, while taking into consideration questions relating to source, form and content of the text, takes the discussion beyond what Robbins (1992) describes as the "inner texture" of the text and towards an understanding of its rhetorical function and its intended effect. This calls for an identification of the genre of the text, and its stylistic arrangement as well as what is included as the content of the text. As the writing of the document was intentional, it can be assumed that the genre and the stylistic arrangement of the text as well as the selection of content was intentionally chosen and designed for maximum effect on its audience.

(b) The Genre of the *Res Gestae*

In the ancient Greek and Roman worlds, rhetorical discourse was divided into three major categories or "species," known as judicial, deliberative and epideictic (Arist., *Rhet.* I.ii.3). Judicial speech was used in trials before juries or judges, deliberative

---

[15] While not common, inscriptions dedicated to prominent persons or gods have been found to have been written in the first person, for example, the inscription on the mausoleum of Antiochos I of Kommagene dated approximately the middle of the first century BCE. See Danker (1982) 237-46. The aretology of Isis at Kyme is written in an autobiographical style. See Danker (1982) 197-9; Horsley (1981), 18-20. Also Lattke (1990) 495, for the many references to the use of the 'I-style' [Ich-Stil-Prädikationen] in ancient hymnology.

speech was employed in political debate within a council or assembly, while epideictic speech was considered appropriate for occasions of public memorial (Mack 1990, 34). Funeral orations and speeches delivered at festivals were occasions for epideictic speech (Kennedy 1983, 23). According to Aristotle, epideictic "has for its subject praise or blame" (Arist. *Rhet.* I.ii.3). In Hellenistic, Imperial and Byzantine periods it came to be used on occasions of public gatherings and more often than not had a political function, particularly when it was an "expression of loyalty to the state by an individual" (Kennedy 1983, 24). Epideictic speeches were a way of conveying to the general public "the values or ideals of the rulers themselves through the mouths of those who praised them" (Kennedy 1983, 24). Mack explains that wherever the aim of epideictic speech "was to marshal examples from the life of an individual (or the history of an institution) that could demonstrate the person's virtues and establish the basis for honor or memorial," it was termed an *encomium* (1990, 47-8). An explanation of the distinction between epideictic and encomium is given by Aristotle (Arist. *Rhet.* I.ix.33):

> praise [ἔπαινος] is language that sets forth greatness in virtue; hence it is necessary to show that a man's actions are virtuous. But encomium [ἐγκώμιον] deals with achievements—all attendant circumstances, such as noble birth and education, merely to conduce to persuasion; for it is probable that virtuous parents will have virtuous offspring and that a man will turn out as he had been brought up. Hence we pronounce an encomium on those who have achieved something. Achievements, in fact, are signs of moral habit.

Hermogenes, who set out elementary exercises detailing rules for the composition of encomia, describes encomium as the "setting forth of the good qualities that belong to someone in general or in particular." He explains that it "differs from praise (in general) in that the latter may be brief, as "Socrates was wise," whereas encomium is developed at some length" (Baldwin 1928, 30).[16]

Examples of encomia can be found in many contexts of the ancient Mediterranean world. Classical works such as Isocrates' *Evagoras* and Xenophon's *Agesilaus* are prose encomia (Aune 1989, 29). Isocrates' encomium *Evagoras* begins with an introduction to the subject (*l.* 1-11). The deeds and achievements of *Evagoras* are then enumerated (*l.* 12-64), and his virtues recounted (*l.*65-81). The pattern in the *Agesilaus* text, is firstly, a chronological account of deeds (*l.*1-2), which is then followed by an account of his virtues (*l.* 3-11). Aune explains that the pattern of encomium can be found in reverse order, in epitaphs of ancient Egyptian dignitaries. The first section of the encomium describes the life of the deceased as fulfilling idealistic rules of conduct, while the second part outlines the person's career (1989, 31-2). The inscription of the

---

[16] The elementary exercises that Hermogenes outlines are translated by Baldwin (1928) 23-38.

aretalogy of Isis found at Maroneia, explicitly states that it is an encomium (*l.* 6a; 12). The component parts of this encomium are quite obvious. The author begins with a statement indicating why Isis is deserving of praise (*l.* 3-12). He then refers to her origins and draws attention to the fact that she was the first daughter of Ge, "the mother of all" (*l.* 13-15). She is praised for her virtue (*l.* 16-21). This is followed by an enumeration of her achievements for humankind (*l.* 22-40...).[17] Encomia, however were not just reserved for dignitaries, gods, or goddesses. A Latin encomium entitled 'In Praise of Turia' was inscribed on two stone tablets in Rome. It is a tribute by a man to his wife who had remained faithful to him through forty-one years of marriage. For much of that time he had been forced to live in exile, and it was his wife who had constantly petitioned the authorities for his release, in spite of the harassment she received from Roman officials (Judge 1985a, 64-65). The general population of the ancient Mediterranean world, therefore, would have come across the literary form, encomium, in many and various life situations. Whether people had been formally taught rhetoric or not, they nevertheless would have been conscious of the hortatory function and persuasive nature of encomium.[18]

While the pattern of encomium in ancient classical literature did not follow a definitive prescribed formula, it generally contained the following characteristics:

1. Prologue	προοίμιον
2. Race and origins	γένος, γένεσις
3. Education	ἀνατροφή
4. Achievements	πράξεις
5. Comparison	σύγκρισις
6. Epilogue	ἐπίλογος

Hester (1991, 296), describes the essential features of these topics as follows:

προοίμιον: a statement which indicates the importance of the person or thing being praised, often with reference to the fact that the speaker feels inadequate to the task.

γένος and γένεσις: a reference to the ancestry and origins of the one being praised, and a reference to the circumstances of the person's birth, especially to any noteworthy fact or event associated with it.

ἀνατροφή: a review of the circumstances of the person's youth, particularly those that give an early indication of character. An important sub-category of this division was ἐπιτηδεύματα: deeds that illustrate choice guided by character.

---

[17] The author of the inscription explains that it is a copy of the one inscribed on the stele in the temple of Hephaistos in Memphis. See Danker (1982) 197. As the cult of Isis was quite widespread, perhaps other copies of this particular inscription also existed.

[18] Klaus Berger (1984) 1173-1184, provides a number of examples of encomia from ancient inscriptions encompassing both Christian and non-Christian texts.

πρᾶξεις: activities or achievements which illustrate the person's virtues.

σύγκρισις: comparison with others to highlight character. This was also one of the elementary exercises.

ἐπίλογος: a recapitulation and appeal to others to imitate virtues of the one being praised. The contents of the epilogue are dependent on the subject and circumstances just as in the προοίμιον.

According to Mack, the pattern of encomium "was not arranged as an exercise in logical argumentation, following instead a model that was broadly narrative in overall frame but essentially topical in outline" (1990, 48). Mack also draws attention to the fact that the occasion for an encomium required a degree of subtlety on the part of the rhetor so that he would not be seen to be arguing for a person's honour (1990, 48). Since the culture of the classical world was "oriented to honour and shame, the attribution of praise was a forceful means of persuasion" (1990, 48).

The *Res Gestae*, as its name implies, recounts the deeds or achievements of Augustus, and also elaborates his virtues. A close reading of the text reveals that the elements of encomium are evident in the *Res Gestae*, as the following components indicate:

Prologue:	1.1-1.9	Augustus refers to the fact that he was but a youth when his remarkable achievements began, and that it was on his own initiative that the Republic was liberated thereby bringing stability to the Republic.
Race/origins:	2.1	Reference here is made to his father, Julius Caesar who had adopted Octavian as his son.
Education	2.1-2.2	Choice of a military career; sought to avenge his father's death by sending those responsible into exile.
Achievements	3.1-29.2.39	Enumeration of Augustus' military honours: activities as a civil leader, as well as the positions he held and refused in this regard; list of religious positions and religious honours bestowed on him; expenditures lavishly bestowed for civic, military and religious developments; military campaigns leading to world domination.
Comparison	30.1-33.1	Comparison with others relating to military and diplomatic relations with rulers of countries beyond the Roman Empire.

| Epilogue | 34-35 | Emphasis on being given the title of "Augustus." A shield was presented by the people which bore an inscription naming the virtues for which he would be remembered: A man of "virtue, clemency, justice and piety." The senate and equestrian order bestowed on him the title of *pater patriae*. |

It would seem, then, that not only has the subject matter for the *Res Gestae* been chosen deliberately, but also the rhetorical "species," encomium, has been deliberately employed in order to convey its purpose. In identifying the text of the *Res Gestae* under the components that constitute encomium, the modern reader is thus in a better position to assess why Augustus chose to leave to posterity an account of his achievements. As an encomium written in an autobiographical style, it was not just meant to be a listing of Augustus' past achievements, or a tribute to Augustus for these deeds. Rather it is meant for posterity, to perpetuate both praise for Augustus and an affirmation of the power of Rome for which he was instrumental in establishing. The intention was to draw from the readers not just an intellectual assent to what had been achieved, but perhaps more significantly to draw forth from the readers an affective identification to what had been achieved for them through the power of Rome, and consequently draw from them their allegiance to the dictates and wishes emanating from Rome. There is no evidence to suggest that Augustus decreed that copies of the inscription be set up in other parts of the world. Whether or not the people of Ancyra, Apollonia or Antioch would have been interested in the detailed enumeration of events and achievements for which Augustus claimed to have been responsible, is open to speculation. However those who were responsible for setting up copies of the inscription of the *Res Gestae* in public places must have been aware of its effect as a medium of propaganda to the masses, with its message that not only the "iuventus" or the "plebs urbana," but all peoples allied with Rome could enjoy the benefits of the *Pax Romana* that Augustus had achieved on their behalf.

(c) Style

The style adopted throughout the *Res Gestae* is not the ornate Asiatic style, which Brunt & Moore (1967, 6-7) claim, would have been a feature of some funerary monuments. Apparently a plain style was consistent with Augustus' way of writing and speaking. Suetonius states that Augustus avoided "the vanity of attempts at epigram and an artificial order ... making it his chief aim to express his thoughts clearly as possible" (Suet. *Aug.* 86. 1). While this may be true, the plain style used for an inscription would have been chosen with deliberation. Bardon demonstrates that there is a conscious effort on the part of the author of the text of the *Res Gestae* to imitate an epigraphical style (1968, 46-62). He bases this claim on the fact that the author's use of syntax, choice of vocabulary and emphasis on traditional themes are likewise to be found in other epigraphs in the ancient Roman world. If the text was intended to be read by the population at large, then clarity of style would have been essential if it was to reach an audience with presumably a wide range of reading ability. The importance of clarity is emphasised by Demetrius in his rhetorical handbook *On Style* (221-222):

> The power of convincing depends on two things, lucidity and naturalness ... what is not lucid nor natural is not convincing. Accordingly exuberant and inflated language must not be sought after in a style meant to carry conviction ... These then are the main essentials of persuasiveness to which may be added ... that all possible points should not be punctiliously and tediously elaborated, but some should be left to the comprehension and inference of the hearer, who when he perceives what you have omitted becomes not only your hearer but your witness, and a very friendly witness too. For he thinks himself intelligent because you have afforded him the means of showing his intelligence. It seems like a slur on your hearer to tell him everything as though he were a simpleton.

Clarity of style no doubt would have added to the persuasive effect of the propaganda of the *Res Gestae*.

(d) Arrangement of the *Res Gestae*

Another important aspect of classical rhetoric is the arrangement of the elements of a text "into a unified structure" (Kennedy 1984, 23). Kennedy cites the advice that Plato gives in the *Phaedrus* (264c) that "every discourse should be like a living body in which the parts cohere like limbs" (1984, 23). In *Rhetorica ad Herennium* (IV. xlii. 54) the advice is quite clear:

> Refining consists in dwelling on the same topic and yet seeming to say something ever new. It is accomplished in two ways: by merely repeating the same idea, or by descanting upon it. We shall not repeat the same thing precisely—for that, to be sure, would weary the hearer and not refine the idea—but with changes ... Our changes will be verbal when, having expressed the idea once, we repeat it once again or oftener in other, equivalent terms, as follows: "No peril is so great that a wise man would think it ought to be avoided when the safety of the fatherland is at stake. When the lasting security of the state is in question, the man endowed with good principles will undoubtedly believe that in defence of the fortunes of the republic he ought to shun no crisis of life, and he will ever persist in the determination eagerly to enter, for the fatherland, any combat, however great the peril to life."

Ramage is correct when he says that Augustus had a clear plan in the writing of the *Res Gestae* (1987, 19). A significant aspect of the force of rhetoric in the *Res Gestae* is the careful balance of ideas. In order to prevent the reader from becoming bored with a long list of deeds and achievements, the author of the *Res Gestae* again followed the advice of eminent rhetoricians in using strategies of patterns of repetition, contrasts and progression of ideas. Ramage draws attention to the "careful balance" between the introduction (1-2) and the conclusion (34-35), and notes the contrasts that are evident in these chapters (1987, 19). According to Ramage these contrasts are intended to draw the reader's attention to the "fine qualities" apparent in Augustus as a youth (1-2) and which, reiterated throughout the text, are shown in the final chapters to have become "institutionalised and idealised" (1987, 20). With reference to the structure of the text, scholars seem to limit their observations of balance and contrast to these sections of the document, and then generally follow the sequential arrangements of the text. Ramage does propose some refinement of the pattern of organisation, which he claims addresses the problems relating to the lack of logical order in the text. He concedes that the enumeration of Augustus' religious positions (7.3) which follows the reference to civil positions (5.1-7.2) and precedes the account of civil activities, "seems a little disruptive," and he agrees with Gagé that the inclusion of the section dealing with the honours conferred on Gaius and Lucius (14) "seem a little out of place" (1987, 18). However, he argues that its position here can be justified because it "may be taken as an extending in a general way what has just been said about his military, civil and religious honours" (1987, 18). Ramage claims that chapters 15-24, which he categorises as an enumeration of expenditures by Augustus, is "tightly organised" (1987, 18). He notes Gagé's concern with chapter 24 dealing with the restoration of the temples in Asia Minor and which appears to Gagé as being out of place in the context of the preceding chapters. Ramage's response is that this chapter, like chapter 14 on the honours given to Gaius and Lucius, is intentionally placed in order to draw attention to the honours bestowed on Augustus (1987, 18).

The *Res Gestae* proper, according to Gagé (1977, 14) and Judge (1985a, 158), are contained in sections 25-33. Judge maintains that actual warfare is not emphasised here, but that the political themes of peace, security and prestige are the major concerns (1985a, 158). Ramage, however, takes a different view, arguing that this section "in a sense elaborates the *bella* referred to earlier in the military summary" in Chapter 3, and in a sense follows "quite logically from chapter 2. Augustus had left off at the point with mention at Philippi, and this section begins with the defeat of Sextus Pompey some six years later (25.1) with Actium following immediately" (1987, 18). His explanation attempts to address the problem that Gagé has with the civil wars appearing in both chapter 3.1 and also later in the document in chapter 25 (1987, 19). Gagé had claimed that the section 25-33 could be divided into two sections, namely the various military activities of Augustus (25-29) and an account of even more important military successes, "les exploits qui surpassent tous les précédents," and by which Augustus extended his influence beyond the boundaries of the Roman world (Gagé 1977,15). Ramage proposes an alternative division, claiming that there is an obvious and intentional contrast:

> Paragraphs 25-30 all involve military action of one kind or another ... By contrast chapters 31-33 comprise no military action ... but show Augustus as master of the world dealing with various peoples on a diplomatic level" (1987, 19).

Most scholars claim that the climax of the *Res Gestae* appears in the last two chapters 34-35, and that the connection with the first chapters is apparent and significant in terms of the achievements of Augustus (Brunt & Moore 1967, 5; Weber 1970, 92; Gagé 1977, 15; Judge 1985a, 169; Ramage 1987, 19). Ramage (1987, 20) explains the significance:

> The fine qualities, then, that were at best hinted at and just starting to make themselves felt at the beginning of his career and the beginning of the *RG* have by the end been recognised many times over and over and have even become institutionalised and idealised. The *RG* is the story of this evolution.

It seems that attempts at justifying the logic of a sequential order of events from a chronological perspective have not led to any further clarification as to what this inscription of the *Res Gestae* was meant to convey or what response it was intended to evoke from the reader.

A reading of the text with specific attention to its rhetorical arrangement, reveals that the pattern of balance and contrasts is a stylistic device that the author has adopted, not only with respect to the first and last chapters, but indeed throughout the whole of the *Res Gestae,* and which appears to have been used deliberately and for effect. The pattern of balance and contrast, known as chiasmus, was widely used in ancient texts and speeches by many different cultures and for different situations.[19] According to Welch "chiasmus was widely employed with equal fluency in both prose and poetry" (1981, 11).

In both classical Greek and Latin literature, chiasmus as a compositional technique appears as early as Homer and in the writings of Plato, and appears also in Latin poetry. Importantly, it is found particularly in the Latin poets of the Augustan period as Welch (1981, 250-68), Kennedy (1984, 28-9), along with other scholars, have clearly

---

[19] For evidence of the use of chiasmus in the ancient world, see Welch (1981).

demonstrated.[20] The many instances of its occurrence in the Christian Scriptures testify to its popular usage in the first century.[21]

As Welch explains, the function of chiasmus gives "order to thought and sounds, and thus it may give structure to the thought pattern and development of entire literary units, as well as structure to shorter sections whose composition is more dependent on immediate tones and rhythms" (1981, 11). He suggests that "this implies that the scope of chiasmus is limited only by the size of the unit within which the chiasm occurs" and that chiasmus as a compositional technique is "a significant ordering principle within, not only verses and sentences, but also within and throughout whole books and extensive poetical units, whose dimensions are virtually unlimited" (1981, 11).

Welch claims that while the inventiveness of grammatical chiastic patterns can be noted in the shorter verses and single sentences within literary works, it is in the "complex structural applications of the form" which present more interest and challenge (1981, 11). He explains the reason for this interest is that

> the form becomes more than a mere literary device, and more than a skeleton upon which thoughts and words are attached. When chiasmus achieves the level of ordering the flow of thoughts throughout an entire pericope, or of a sustained unfolding of an artistic verbal expression, the character of the form itself merges with the message and meaning of the passage. Indeed what is said is often no more than how it is said ... the task of understanding the meaning of a writing is never complete until its formular aspects as well as its thought contents have been grasped (1981, 11-2).

According to Welch, chiastic structure in ancient texts is increasingly drawing the attention of scholars because "the form appears frequently and is often executed with noteworthy precision" (1981, 12). He further adds that "the form can be aesthetically very pleasing due in part to its vast potential to coordinate rigorous and abrupt juxtapositions within a single unified literary system, all while focussing on a point of central concern" (1981, 12). Another aspect that Welch emphasises is its significance from an exegetical perspective, in that it can often provide "the basis of cogent

---

[20] For example, see Whitman's discussion of the geometric structure of the *Iliad* (1958) 249-84; the study by Duckworth (1962), on the structural patterns and proportions in the *Aeneid* particularly Chapters 1 & 2; Moskalew's discussion on repetition, genre and style in the *Aeneid* (1982) 21-72; Cairns' discussion of Propertius 4.6, (1984) 131-7; Elsner's reference to chiasmus in Horace's *Odes* 1.4 (1991) 59.

[21] For example Jeremias' article "Chiasmus in den Paulusbriefen" (1958) 145-56; architectonic designs in Luke-Acts in Talbert (1974); discussion of the structure of the Gospel of Mark in Myers (1988) 109-16; chiasmus in the discourse on freedom in John 8:30-6 in Panimolle (1988) 46-7; the chiastic pattern in Mark's Gospel 1:1-13 in Tolbert (1989) 11-2; the chiastic pattern in Galatians 2:16 in Hester (1991) 303; the discussion by Luter and Lee (1995) 89-101. Also Segert (1984) 1433-1462, for Semitic poetic structures in the literature of the New Testament.

alternatives to other text critical interpretations which have called for a drastic fragmentation of certain basic texts" (1981, 12).[22]

The identification of chiastic structures in ancient texts involves both subjective and objective judgements. Welch argues that defining what constitutes a literary unit and determining its beginning and ending is a subjective matter, "especially where multiple structures operate simultaneously or where a single system is composed of separated bicola" (1981, 13). However, he explains that the primary concern in identifying chiasmus is that of objectivity, which means that there must be verifiable evidence of chiasmus within the text. He provides an explanation of what this entails:

> In striving for objectivity, it is reasonable to require significant repetitions to be readily apparent, and the overall system to be well balanced. The second half of the system should tend to repeat the first half of the system in a recognizably inverted order, and the juxtaposition of the two central sections should be marked and highly accentuated. Longer passages are more defensibly chiastic where the same text also contains a fair amount of short chiasmus and other forms of parallelism as well. Key words, echoes, and balancing should be distinct and should serve defined purposes within the structure.

Talbert refers to the formal patterns of balances, contrasts and proportions in the arrangement of texts as "architectural designs" and the study of these patterns as "architectural analysis" which, he explains, "is a variety of the species style criticism within the genus literary criticism" (1974, 5).[23] In striving for objectivity in architecture analysis, Talbert proposes the employment of two criteria, or what he terms "safeguards" that act as controls on subjectivity, namely, "internal" controls and "external" controls. With reference to "internal" controls, Talbert explains that there should be "indications within the text of the writing itself that point to the existence of a given pattern" (1974, 8). This means firstly, that "a pattern controlling the arrangement of large units throughout an author's work, and in units of all sizes" should be discernible (1974, 8). Secondly it means that "one should be able to show that the pattern is located in the redactional activity of an author rather than in the tradition" (1974, 9). The other safeguard is that consisting of "external" controls, which, Talbert explains, are "indications outside the text that may render a proposed pattern probable or improbable" (1974, 9). He identifies three major "external" controls. Firstly he argues that since the approach of architecture analysis "assumes that writings in antiquity used certain conventional patterns for the organisation of their materials," then these conventional patterns "should be evident in more than one document and should

---

[22] See discussion of Near-eastern and Semitic texts as well as Greek and Latin literature in Welch, (1981).
[23] Although Talbert's main concern is with New Testament texts, he discusses, by way of example and comparison, classical texts of antiquity.

be found in a wide cross-section of writings in a document's milieu" (1974, 9). Secondly he draws attention to the fact that classical examples indicate that the architectonic designs governing a document's arrangements are also generally found in the visual art of the period, and he claims that wherever this is the case, "such parallels should be demonstrated" (1974, 9). A third external control that Talbert emphasises is "that behind various artistic tendencies there are certain cultural or aesthetic roots for these stylistic traits," by which he means that in arguing a case for the architecture of a piece of literature one should be able to demonstrate "that a given technique is indigenous to the cultural mentality" (1974, 9).

(e) Chiasmus in the *Res Gestae*

It can be demonstrated that the pattern of chiasmus is a feature of the text of the *Res Gestae,* and that it is intentionally employed to give structure to the thought pattern throughout the text. It is somewhat surprising that while scholarly investigations concerning the text of the *Res Gestae* have been numerous, it seems that the chiastic structure of the text has not been noticed. There have been some indications that scholars have explored some alternative possibilities of the arrangement of the text rather than that of a linear model. Gardthausen (1964, 1292), for example, notes the structural element that Kornemann had identified in that the honours mentioned in the text occur both at the midpoint of the text (9-14) and at the end (34-35) and which, he argues, suggests that the placement was a strategic intention to draw attention to the person of Augustus himself. Ramage (1987, 19) has also noted the connection between the beginning and the end of the text. Lauton (1946, 74-75) has identified what she regards as rare instances of chiasmus in the text. These instances occur in some grammatical constructions of sentences where the placement of the verb within the sentence forms the mid-point of the chiasmic pattern between the main clause and the subordinate clauses of the sentence.[24] However it would appear that no study has focussed on the chiastic structure of the text as a whole.

A close reading of the text reveals that the text contains two symmetrical segments. Each segment contains nine sections, with each of the sections in the first half of the text balanced by the nine sections in the second half in an inverted order. It will be argued that the two juxtaposed central sections are key to the meaning and purpose of the text. The chiastic pattern of the *Res Gestae* is illustrated on the following pages as follows:

---

[24] See also Lauton (1949) 107-123.

1.1   **A.** Age 19: *annos undeviginti natus*

1.2-2.1a   **B.** Assumes filial duty: *exercitum privato consilio et privata impensa comparavi ...*
                Honours received: *Eo nomine senatus decretis honorificis in ordinem suum me adlegit ... consularem locum sententiae dicendae tribuens et imperium mihi dedit ...*
                Takes responsibility as son to avenge death of his parent: *Qui parentem meum trucidaverunt ...*

2.1b   **C.** Wrested the res publica from those who were vying for control: *... et postea bellum inferentis rei publicae vici bis acie.*

3.1-4   **D.** Military campaigns: *Bella terra et mari civilia externaque toto in orbe terrarum saepe gessi ...*
                Emphasises his mercy and beneficence: *... victorque omnibus veniam petentibus civibus peperci. Externes gentes, quibus tuto ignosci potuit, conservare quam excidere malui.*
                Establishes his ability as a leader: *Millia civium Romanorum sub sacramento meo fuerunt circiter quingenta ...*

4.1-4   **E.** Given military honours for securing the safety of Rome: *Bis ovans triumphavi et tris egi curulis triumphos et appellatus sum viciens et semel imperator ... Ob res a me aut per legatos meos auspiciis meis terra marique prospere gestas quinquagiens et quinquiens decrevit senatus supplicandum esse dis immortalibus ...*

5.1-3   **F.** At own expense averted a national calamity of food shortage: *... Non sum deprecatus in summa frumenti penuria curationem annonae quam ita administravi ut intra dies paucos metu et periclo praesenti civitatem universam liberarem impensa et cura mea ...*

6.1-8.5   **G.** Organisation of political affairs and administration of government: *... senatu populoque Romano consentientibus ut curator legum et morum summa potestate solus crearer ... Patriciorum numerum auxi ... Senatum ter legi, et in consulatu sexto censum populi conlega M.Agrippa egi.*

9.1-12.2   **H.** Vows undertaken by the citizens because of concern for his welfare: *Vota pro valetudine mea suscipi per consules et sacerdotes quinto quoque anno senatus decrevit.*
                Recognised by the people to be included amongst the deity: *Nomen meum senatus consulto inclusum est in Saliare carmen, et sacrosanctus in perpetum ut essem et, quoad viverem, tribunicia potestas mihi esset, per legem sanctum est.*
                Altar built in his honour: *... aram Pacis Augustae senatus pro reditu meo consacrandam censuit ad campum Martium, in qua magistratus et secerdotes virginesque vestales anniversarium sacrificium facere iussit.*

13.1   **I.** Reference to his birth as the beginning of a new era of universal: peace: *Ianum Quirinum quem claussem esse maiores nostri voluerunt cum per totum imperium populi Romani terra marique esset parta victoriis pax, cum priusquam nascerer a condita urbe bis omnino clausum fuisse prodatur memoriae ter me principe senatus claudendum esse censuit.*
                The leading citizen: *me principe*

14.1-2   **I '.** Reference to his descendants; ensuring the continuation of the 'Pax Romana': *Filios meos, ... Gaium et Lucium Caesares honoris mei caussa senatus populusque Romanus ... consules designavit.* Each named as leader of the younger generation: *... principem iuventutis ... appellaverunt.*

15.1-19.2   **H '.** Gifts of money given to various sectors of the population: *Plebei Romanae viritim HS trecenos numeravi ex testamento patris mei, et nomine meo ... dedi.* His concern for the welfare of the people: *Quae mea congiaria pervenerunt ad hominum millia nunquam minus quinquaginta et ducenta ... Quater pecunia mea iuvi aerarium.* Restores and builds sacred shrines: *Curiam et continens ei Chalcidicum templumque Apollinis in Palatio cum porticibus ... aedes in Capitolio Iovis Feretri ... aedem Matris Magnae in Palatio feci.*

20.1-23.1   **G '.** Organisation and expenditure for public works and public events: *Capitolium et Pompeium theatrum utrumque opus impensa grandi refeci ... In privato solo Martis Ultoris templum forumque Augustum ex manibiis feci ...Ter munus gladiatorium dedi meo nomine ... Navalis proeli spectaclum populo dedi ...*

24.1-2   **F '.** At own expense restored the fortunes to the people of Rome: *... Statuae meae ... argenteae steterunt in urbe XXC circiter quas ipse sustuli exque ea pecunia dona aurea in aede Apollinis ... posui.*

25.1-29.2   **E '.** Military campaigns establish Rome as the leading nation: *Mare pacavi a praedonibus ... Omnium provinciarum populi Romani quibus finitimae fuerunt genres quae non parerent imperio nostro fines auxi. Aegyptum imperio populi Romani adieci ... Colonias in Africa, Sicilia, ... Syria ... Pisidia militum deduxi.*

30.1-33:1   **D '.** Former enemies become allies. Establishes the supremacy of Rome over all nations: *Pannoniorum gentes ... devictas per Ti. Neronem, qui tum erat privignus et legatus meus, imperio populi Romani subieci prototulique fines Illyrici ad ripam fluminis Danui.* Other nations become dependent on Rome and appreciate his beneficence: *Ad me ex India regum legationes saepe missae sunt ... Ad me supplices confugerunt reges...*

34.1   **C '.** Restores res publica to the control of the people of Rome: *... rem publicam ex mea potestate in senatus populique Romani arbitrium transtuli.*

34.2-35.1   **B '.** Honours received: *... Quo pro merito meo senatus consulto Augustus appellatus sum* Assumes full responsibility for government: *Post id tempus auctoritate omnibus praestiti ...* Assumes title of Father of the fatherland: *...senatus et equester ordo populusque Romanus universus appellavit me patrem patriae*

35.2   **A '.** Age 76th year: *annum agebam septuagensumum sextum*

(f) Justification: Internal Controls

In justifying this schema, it is important to apply the objective criteria that Welch and Talbert have presented as necessary controls on subjective analysis. The first step is to apply the internal controls to this schema. As the preceding thematic structure demonstrates, the overall system is well balanced, with the second half of the system not only repeating the first half in a recognizably inverted order, but at the same time maintains patterns of repetition, comparison, contrast and progression of ideas. The prologue **A** and the epilogue **A'** both refer to the age of Augustus, with **A** indicating his youthfulness which marked the beginning of his achievements, and **A'** indicating the successful completion of a long life. In **B** Augustus is awarded his first magisterial honours for the initiative he demonstrated in taking on his responsibility as son to avenge the death of his parent and in the interest of the safety of the *res publica*. The accent here is on his filial *pietas* or loyalty. **B'** is a recapitulation of all the honours, both magisterial as well as ceremonial, that he had received throughout his lifetime. He is elevated here to the role of "father of the fatherland." The emphasis in this instance is on paternal *pietas* or loyalty of Augustus towards the people, and for the well-being of the *res* publica. **C** emphasises the fact that through his own efforts Augustus assumes responsibility for regaining control of the *res publica*, and in **C'** where he claims, while still maintaining full control, he hands back the control of the *res publica* to the people.

Sections **D** and **D'** refer to the dealings with foreign peoples. In **D** emphasis is on how Augustus established the supremacy of Rome through foreign military campaigns and his display of mercy and beneficence to those whom he had subdued. In **D'** the notion of dealing with foreign peoples is expanded to the fact that they became allies, and that they and rulers of other nations looked to him for protection and prosperity. **E** describes the acclaim Augustus was given in the form of military honours for securing the safety of Rome, while **E'** again expands this acclaim as coming from all of Italy, as well as from the provinces and from other nations, in establishing Rome as the leading nation. Thus the safety of all in the Roman world and beyond is assured.

Sections **F** and **F'** and also **G** and **G'** refer to his philanthropic deeds and his ability as an administrator. In **F** he responds to the crisis of food shortage by providing financial assistance and averts what might well have developed into a national catastrophe. Section **F'** again is an expansion of the image of Augustus as a provider and all at his own expense. He does not claim the booty of war nor the tributes of silver and gold that would befit his dignity as ruler. Instead, he restores these to the provinces. **G** emphasises his administrative ability in the reorganisation of government and the setting up of new laws in the interests of order and future prosperity. **G'** gives an account of the organisation and expenditure involved for the provision of. public works such as the water supply, the building or restoration of temples and government buildings, as well as the provision of lavish crowd-pleasing events such as gladiatorial shows, games, and naval displays.

Emphasis in both **H** and **H'** is on the relationship between Augustus and the citizens. In **H** the citizens' concern for Augustus' well-being is shown to be a priority. Vows are offered for his continued good health. The people pay him the highest honours by recognising him as one amongst the deities. In **H'** Augustus reciprocates showing his concern for the welfare of the citizens by bestowing grants of monies to various sections of the population as well as restoring and building sacred shrines for their benefit. **I** and **I'** form the mid-point of the *Res Gestae*. The employment of allusions to both history and myth in these sections, is rhetorically significant, in that it is intended to create the impression that a new age, the *saeculum aureum*, has been inaugurated.

There were many expressions of the *saeculum aureum* depicted in the art and architecture of the Augustan period. Zanker comments on the force of meaning which these visual images of the "new age" were meant to convey:

> The fusion of myth and history was realised in the creation of a timeless present. A concept of the future, in the sense of a further development, did not exist in this system. The *saeculum aureum* had dawned, and it was only a question of maintaining and repeating it. After a period of rapid and drastic change, Rome had arrived at a state of equilibrium, a timeless and mythically defined present. Internal harmony and external strength, fertility and prosperity, would all continue unabated, at least so long as the Julii ruled and both princeps and people made sure to worship the gods as was proper and live according to the ways of their forefathers (1988, 215).

This image of the *saeculum aureum* and its ideological intention is taken up in the middle sections of the *Res Gestae* (13; 14: 1-2). In **I** the historical fact that the gates of the temple of Janus had been closed only twice in the history of Rome before the birth of Augustus and yet three times in the space of his lifetime, are "fused" with mythological associations. The god, Janus, was regarded by the Romans as guardian of gates and doors and over beginnings and endings, and was commonly represented with two faces looking in opposite directions (*OCCL* 1989, 304; *DCM* 1988, 241). This image is surely meant to draw associations with the comprehensive vision attributed to Augustus. Mention of Augustus' victories over land and sea was intended to evoke connotations of the power of Rome extending far beyond anything achieved in the history of Rome. The mythologies associated with Augustus' achievements are not just in relation to the historical event of Actium, but rather the achievements of securing peace and stability were brought to the world at the time of his birth. As Brunt & Moore comment, "the birth of a new god inaugurated a better age" (1967, 54). The birthday of Augustus was given special prominence in the Roman calendar and it was recognised in places far beyond Rome. In approximately 9 BCE the celebration of the birthday of Augustus as the beginning of the official year of the Asiatic province was the subject of the Asiatic Council's deliberations regarding the provincial Calendar. Danker states that copies of the letter of Paulus Fabius Maximus to this effect and the accompanying documents were published in numerous cities of Asia (1982, 216).[25] The letter begins with reference to the importance of Augustus' birth:

> It is subject to question whether the birthday of our most divine Caesar spells more of joy or blessing, this being a date that we could probably without fear of contradiction equate with the beginning of all things, if not in terms of nature, certainly in terms of utility, seeing that he restored stability, when everything was collapsing and falling into disarray, and gave a new look to the entire world that would have been most happy to accept its own ruin had not the good and common fortune of all been born: Caesar. Therefore people might justly assume that his birthday spells the beginning of life and real living and marks the end and boundary of any regret that they had themselves been born (1982, 216).

The Asians responded with two decrees. Again, praise of Augustus and his achievements takes on mythological connotations:

> Whereas Providence that orders all our lives has in her display of concern and generosity in our behalf adorned our lives with the highest good: Augustus, whom she has filled with arete for the benefit of humanity and has in her beneficence granted us and those who will come after us [a saviour] who has made war to cease and who shall put everything [in peaceful] order; and whereas Caesar, [when he was manifest], transcended the expectations of [all who had anticipated the good news], not only by surpassing the benefits conferred by his predecessors but by leaving no expectation of surpassing him to those who would come after him, with the result that the birthday of our God signalled the beginning of Good News for the world because of him ... (1982, 217).

The fusion of history and mythology is also apparent in Ι'. Although there is little mention of people by name in the *Res Gestae*, in Ι' Augustus' grandsons Gaius and Lucius are given special mention and prominence. With reference to what is generally regarded as the *Ara Pacis*, Zanker draws attention to the images of the two boys who occupy a prominent position and he claims that they are depicted as "little Trojans" in a procession "composed solely of members of the imperial house arranged according to the order of dynastic succession" (1988, 217-8).[26] The inclusion of the names of the boys in the *Res Gestae*, and the statement that each had been appointed leader of the

---

[25] For the Greek text and extant fragments of the Latin version, see EJ (1976) 81-83.

[26] There is some disagreement as to whether the monument to which Zanker refers is the *Ara Pacis*. Weinstock (1960) 4-58, provides numismatic evidence as well as evidence from other literary sources which suggest that the altar dedicated to the cult of Pax was not the *Ara Pacis Augustae*. However, Brunt (1967) 54, cites the work of other scholars who provide evidence which contradicts Weinstock's claim.

younger generation was meant to convey the idea that the *Pax Romana,* inaugurated by Augustus, would continue through future generations. In his discussion of the part that Augustus' successors played in the national mythology, Zanker provides a photographic illustration of what is generally regarded as a posthumous cuirassed statue of Gaius Caesar, and draws attention to the fact that the victory that is depicted on the cuirass of the statue "is placed in a cosmic setting," which was also the case of the cuirass of the statue of Augustus (1988, 224; cf. 190). With reference to this, Zanker draws the following conclusion:

> What makes this ostensible image of Gaius as victor so interesting ... is not so much the way it is taken for granted that the young prince assumes the role of Augustus, but the allusions to the victory at Actium and the Golden Age, in the form of sea centaurs holding rudders and regular centaurs whose tails end as vines ... In other words, the new victory of Gaius assures the continuity of the well-being first created by Augustus at Actium. The old slogans of the early Augustan Age have coalesced into an ideology of victory, and the princeps' early victories are treated like heroic deeds of a mythological past (1988, 223).

In the *Res Gestae*, it is stated that the honours bestowed on the boys are in fact given to honour Augustus. The person of Augustus remains central. It would seem, therefore, that the mid-point or climax of the *Res Gestae*, is meant to convey the notion of the dawning of a new age which encompasses both past and future into an eternal present, with Augustus as the centre point.

While it is apparent that each half of the chiastic structure in the *Res Gestae* is balanced by the other in terms of theme, the content in the second half of the text is actually a consolidation or an amplification of achievements. The achievements are noted as being much more universal in their effects. As Judge observes, there is an underlining "by repetition" with reference to the frequency, scale and distribution of gifts, the amounts given to others, the various recipients, such as "whole sectors of the Roman community" and also the many sources of funds which were at Augustus' disposal (1985a, 151).

A comparison of the "data" contained in the *Res Gestae* with the "historical data" of the Augustan period presented in the writings of Roman historians such as Livy, Suetonius, Cassius Dio, orators such as Cicero and poets such as Ovid, Vergil and Horace, reveals that the author of the *Res Gestae* has not set out to give an itemised or chronological account of the events of the life of Augustus, but rather the focus is on a selection of themes related to military, civic and religious achievements, intended to emphasise that these deeds of Augustus are worthy of the highest form of praise. The author has then arranged these themes in a chiastic pattern in order to emphasise that the focus of the message of the *Res Gestae* lies in the middle sections of this text. The use of this literary convention of chiastic structure is not intended as an end in itself, but rather it is employed in order to draw out the significance of the meaning of the *Res Gestae*. It is obvious that the author of the *Res Gestae* has intentionally used and arranged the material in order to subtly and yet forcefully convey the message that the *Pax Romana* is attributed to the achievements of Augustus. It was the result of Roman victory and power.

(g) Justification: External Controls

The external controls which Talbert identifies as a check to subjectivity can also be applied to the *Res Gestae* as evidence for the chiastic pattern in the text. As previously mentioned, the chiastic structural arrangements were literary conventions used in different cultures in the ancient world. Poets of the Augustan era, for example, Vergil (70-19 BCE), Horace (65-8 BCE) and Propertius (50-approx. 19 BCE), made use of chiastic structures in their poetic compositions.[27] Talbert's understanding of R.S. Conway's conclusion from research on the *Aeneid* was that "the crowning book which Vergil placed in the centre to unite all that stand before it and all that stand after it is Book 6" (1974, 7). Talbert explains that this is consistent with the findings of Lawrence Richardson's study of narrative poetry in the Republican period: "Roman poets were following the basic compositional rules of tragedy which determined the position of the climax near the centre of the action. The climax falls near the centre and the denouement at the end" (1974, 7). Francis Cairns demonstrates that in the fourth book of Propertius' elegies, the central position is 4.6 which "deals with the most important event of Augustan history — the victory at Actium which established Augustus as undisputed master of the Roman world" (1984, 131). Cairns (1984, 133) identifies the thematic chiastic structure of the elegy in the following way:

A1	(1-10)	The sacrifice
B1	(11-14)	Prologue to the narrative
C1	(15-18)	The *monumenta* at Actium
D1	(19-26)	Prelude to the battle, disposition of forces, favour of sea-gods
E1	(27-54) (a) (b)	The epiphany of Apollo (27-36) The speech of Apollo (37-54)
F	(55-8)	The centre-piece - the battle of Actium

---

[27] See Vergil's *Aeneid* (Duckworth 1962); Propertius' *Elegy 4.6* (Cairns 1984); Horace's *Odes* (Santirocco 1986).

E2	(59-60) (a)	The epiphany of Divus Iulius (59)
	(b)	The speech of Divus Iulius (60)
D2	(61-6)	The aftermath of the battle, the flight of the enemy and the favour of the sea-gods
C2	(67-8)	The *monumenta* on the Palatine, i.e. the temple of Apollo Palatinus
B2	(69-70)	The epilogue to the narrative
A2	(71-86)	The banquet following the sacrifice

Here, as Cairns indicates, the climax is located at the centre F: 55-8, with the banquet following the sacrifice as the denouement at A2: 71-86. Both Drew (1929, 242-54) and Duckworth (1959, 225-37) identify parallel structures in Vergil's *Georgics*. These examples suggest that in the literary milieu of the Augustan period, writers consciously employed chiastic structure in their literary works. The *Res Gestae*, therefore, was no exception.

Another "external control" as a check to subjective interpretation regarding the organisation of the content contained within a document, is its counterpart in the visual art of the period (Talbert 1974, 9). Some photographs reproduced in Zanker's study of the power of images in Roman art and architecture, clearly indicate that a form of chiastic structure was commonplace in the art and architecture of the Augustan period. One such example that Zanker provides is the pediment of the Temple of Mars Ultor (1988, 196). There are three figures on each side of Mars the Avenger (Mars Ultor) who stands at the centre. The two figures furthest away from Mars, Palatin and Tiber, are reclining and facing away from him. The next two, Romulus and Roma are seated and facing towards Mars. The two figures that are nearest to Mars, Venus and Fortuna, are standing by his side and looking outwards, as Mars likewise is doing. Zanker observes:

> The strict ordering of the figures mirrors the abstract character of their message. The figures relate to each other only in their common association with Augustus (1988, 196).

The vine motif, a symbol of the *saeculum aureum*, and which is featured on the so-called *Ara Pacis Augustae*, depicts the abundance of nature with connotations of the fruitfulness and abundance brought about by the achievement of Augustus in bringing peace and prosperity to Rome. However, each of the vine clusters are arranged symmetrically (1988, 181). This would seem to suggest that the design was intended to portray the *aureum saeculum* as a time of order and perfection. According to Talbert, Duckworth "has pointed to the fact that the same structural principles underlie the architecture of the *Aeneid* and the *Ara Pacis* or Augustan altar of peace" (1974, 69).

There are six friezes of the *Ara Pacis Augustae* which are divided into two groups of three. There is a Roman half and a Julian-Augustan half, with each balancing the other. Talbert (1974, 69) provides the following diagram by way of illustration.[28]

Roman half —   a. Legend: Romulus and Remus
                  b. History: Roman magistrates in procession
                  c. Symbol: Roma

Augustan half —   a. Legend: Aeneas sacrificing
                  b. History: Augustus and imperial family in
                     procession
                  c. Symbol: Italia

City and town plans, military camps, civic and religious buildings, and theatres very often featured a symmetrical and axial design with a central focus.[29] An example is the forum of Augustus which basically followed the design of the forum of Caesar (Carter 1989, 46). Carter describes its features (1989, 50-1).[30]

> The basic idea is identical to that of Caesar: a temple on a high podium set on the long axis of a rectangle and dominating it from one end. But there is a subtle variation. Although the colonnades which line three sides of the forum are straight, there hide behind them two semi-circular recesses. These are positioned so that the axis which joins them is aligned with the line of columns which constitute the front of the temple, and thus a cross-axis is introduced which would only be perceived from the steps of the temple or from within the apses themselves ... The apses and colonnades contained two series of statues, with accompanying inscriptions, portraying the great figures of Roman history.

As Zanker points out, the poet Ovid's description of the forum of Augustus provides an indication of how the symmetrical design of this edifice would have been understood by those gazing on this structure (1988, 113):

> *Hinc videt Aenean oneratum pondere caro*
> *Et tot Iuleae nobilitatis avos;*
> *Hinc videt Iliaden humeris ducis arma ferentem*
> *claraque dispositis acta subesse viris*

> On the side he [i.e. Mars Ultor] sees Aeneas laden with his precious burden, and so many ancestors of Julian nobility. On the other he sees Ilia's son bearing on his shoulders the arms of the (conquered) general,

---

[28] Talbert refers to the study of Jocelyn C. Toynbee, "The *Ara Pacis* Reconsidered and Historical Art in Roman Italy." *Proceedings of the British Academy* 39 (1953) 67-96. See also Zanker's discussion and photographic illustrations (1988) 157-61; Richardson's discussion regarding the notion of *imperium* which the design of the Forum of Augustus exhibited (1991) 9.

[29] On Ancient Roman town planning and architecture see Barton (1989).

[30] See also a reconstruction drawing in Zanker (1988) 113 and ground plan, 194.

and the splendid records of action (inscribed) beneath the (statues of the) men arranged in order (Ov. *Fast.* v. 563-6).[31]

Military camps were also constructed on symmetrical lines. In his account of the organisation of the Roman army Josephus, writing in the latter half of the first century CE, describes the camp construction in the following way (*BJ* III. 79-84):

> The interior of the camp is divided into rows of tents. The exterior circuit presents the appearance of a wall and is furnished with towers at regular intervals; ... In this surrounding wall are set four gates, one on each side ... The camp is intersected by streets symmetrically laid out; in the middle are the tents of the officers, and precisely in the centre the headquarters of the commander-in-chief, resembling a small temple.

Bartlett (1985, 118) points out that in this account Josephus may have been influenced by a similar passage from the historian Polybius who had also described an account of the construction of a Roman camp in the second-century BCE. It would seem then that the design of the camp had remained on much the same lines long before and long after the life time of Augustus. It is, however, interesting to note the attention to the symmetrical pattern which had prevailed over this time.

The symmetrical design was not restricted to public or official art and architecture. A terra-cotta relief plaque (Zanker 1988, 184), a silver krater (1988, 185), the decoration on a marble table leg (1988, 184; 270) are examples of the symmetrical design used in the private sector during the Augustan period. Numismatic iconography often employed symmetrical design in its representation of images of public buildings or symbolic motifs.[32] Unlike official Roman poetry which was available mainly to the literate elite, coinage reached every sector of society. As was the case with inscriptions, it was a powerful medium through which mass consciousness could be shaped.

A third external control for judging whether a piece of literature might contain chiastic structure is to ascertain if the technique of chiasmus is indigenous to the cultural mentality (Talbert 1974, 9). As has been demonstrated, the attention to symmetry of themes, images and ideas in literary works, and visual expressions of themes, images and ideas in art and architecture in the Roman world suggest that balance in literature and artistic styles was part of the world-view from which peoples living in the ancient world found expression and produced meaning. This way of viewing the world may be contrasted with that of the late 20th century and the way people of this century, particularly in the western societies, express a world view in literature, art and architecture, that tends towards being open-ended rather than seeking denouement, that

---

[31] Translation by Judge (1985a) 92.
[32] There are numerous studies illustrating Roman coin types, but see Sutherland (1976 & 1987); Mattingly (1923); Grant (1969); Oster (1982); Zanker (1988).

consciously expresses ambiguity and diversity rather than balance and symmetry, and engages in lateral rather than circular approaches to problem solving.

The *Res Gestae* as a Universal Message

The discussion of the *Res Gestae* has demonstrated that the inscription was intended to convey a universal message for a universal audience. The deliberate choice of a chiastic structure for the *Res Gestae* was to emphasise the major message of the text. The new age had dawned, peace and prosperity were assured. Freedom was restored to the people. All this had occurred because of the actions of the man, Augustus. The appelation *pater patriae* was not just an honorific title, but a political statement which left no doubt as to who held the dominant power in the Greco-Roman world (Heuss 1975, 95). As long as each successive leader of the "restored" republic drew on the tradition which Augustus had firmly established, Rome would continue to remain the supreme force within the Mediterranean world and beyond.

Just what message or messages people in the ancient Mediterranean world drew from the *Res Gestae* would have depended very much on what specific aspect arrested their attention at any one time. As with any text, work of art, literature or inscription, the message would have generated multiple meanings, not just one meaning, and which would have depended, of course, on the hermeneutical perspective of the reader. How people appropriated the message of the text to their world view would have depended on their experience of Rome's intervention directly or indirectly in their lives. Whether or not the ordinary person would have been bothered with the details in the inscription, or even whether some people could read it at all, nevertheless the inscription in itself would have been iconographically significant. This means that the inscription would have generated its meaning of power in the ancient Mediterranean world in much the same way as other inscriptions and monuments throughout history have signified and continue to signify a specific ideological perspective.[33]

Besides the form of the inscription, other elements in the text of the inscription would have conveyed the sense of power that emanated from Rome. The use of the first person would have placed the *Res Gestae* in the same league as other eminent inscriptions, and evoked cultic connotations. The emphasis on setting precedents would have been designed to appeal to the citizen's sense of belonging to a leading nation. The mention of large numbers would have served to emphasise that the achievements were on a mammoth scale, and would have conveyed an impression of Rome's strength.

---

[33] Some examples are the Magna Carta of 1066, the American Statue of Liberty, the White House, the Kremlin, to name but a few.

The emphasis on the themes of *libertas, victoria, pax, clementia, honos, iustitia, fides* and *pietas* would have promoted the ideology of freedom for which all peoples yearned. Allusions to great mythological figures of the past, both explicitly, for example Janus, and implicitly, such as Aeneas, would have inspired confidence that their freedom was somehow linked into a cosmic reality.

Since the inscription was set up in locations which had cultic significance, it would have been natural for the people to identify with the inscription religiously as well as politically. The *Res Gestae* therefore reflected the new form of Government that Augustus had developed and promoted. It attempted to establish the ethos for future government administration.

The *Res Gestae Divi Augusti* therefore, was to be a permanent reminder to the people of what had been achieved, and by extension of just what should be preserved in future generations. Its message was that *libertas* had been won on behalf of the people. It was the responsibility of future generations to protect it.

CHAPTER THREE

The Concept of Freedom under *Pax Romana*

The Concept of *Libertas* in the Roman World

(a) *Libertas* as a Republican Concept

In writing his history of Rome, Livy begins his account in the second book, by stating that the theme of his work is the "new liberty (*libertas*) enjoyed by the Roman people, their achievements in peace and war, annual magistracies, and laws superior in authority to men" (*Livy*, ii. 1. 1).[1] He further explains that "this liberty (*libertas*) was the more grateful as the last king had been so great a tyrant" (*Livy*, ii. 1.2). Livy interprets the expulsion of the last of the Tarquin kings from Rome as an event that had brought an end to autocratic rule which had spanned some two hundred and forty-four years (*Livy*, 1. 60. 4). The overthrow of regal power meant, at least theoretically, that the people held the power, and in this new found freedom which they fiercely guarded, they could be in control of their own destiny (*Livy* ii.1.9; ii.2.5; ii.15.3). *Libertas* thus became a political catchword of the Roman Republic.[2] Livy began writing his history in approximately 27 BCE (Foster, 1967, xi) He was therefore a contemporary of Augustus and seems to have been on amicable terms with him (1967, xi).[3] During his life-time Livy would have been well aware of the struggle for power that had occurred amongst the various factions and which had finally resulted in Augustus' rise to power. It is a matter of speculation as to whether Livy, in beginning his history at this time, was endeavouring to call attention to the fact that Roman society was in danger of reverting to a form of regal rule or whether he viewed Augustus' actions as a positive step towards the restoration of the Republic.

It is to the events of finally securing the safety of Rome in 27 BCE to which reference is made in the closing lines of the *Res Gestae*. Here it is stated that although it was with the consent of all the citizens that Augustus had been placed in full control of the state, he nevertheless had transferred the *res publica* from his control into the hands

---

[1] See also Tac. *An*. n i.1.

[2] The word "republic" is used here to distinguish the Roman political period from that of the regal period. It does not refer to a political constitution that has parallels with modern day understandings of the term. For a very helpful explanation of various renderings of the term in Roman antiquity, see Judge, "Res Publica Restituta: A Modern Illusion" (1985a).

[3] Foster refers to *Livy* iv.xx.7.

of the senate and the people of Rome (*R.G.* 34.1). The insistence is that Augustus' actions had been consistent with the republican notion of *libertas*.

Although *libertas* was considered to be a political catchword of the Roman Republic, in fact it could often mean different things to different people (Brunt, 1988, 283).[4] Fears claims that in the politics of Rome, the term was "eminently malleable, capable of invocation by all factions" (1981, 872). He provides the following examples (1981, 872-3):

> Tiberius Grachus spoke of *Libertas* and the expulsion of kings; his political opponents assassinated him for the sake of *Libertas* ... For his followers, Sulla was a saviour and a new founder of the *res publica* and its constitution. For his opponents he was a tyrant and his new order a tyranny which sought to destroy that pillar of *libertas*, the tribune's power ... Cicero could be viewed as both saviour and destroyer of *libertas publica* ... Cicero himself hoped to be honored as *liberator* for his role in saving the republic from Catiline. His political opponents judged his actions in a different light. They called him king and tyrant ... The armies of Pompey and Caesar fought each other in the name of *Libertas* ... it was also in the name of *Libertas* that Caesar was assassinated.

Ancient literary sources have tended to present the notion of *libertas* from the perspective of the aristocratic class. However, there is evidence which attests that the term *libertas*, could likewise reflect "the interests and concerns of the common people as well as the feuding oligarchs" (Brunt 1988, 282). Since, as Brunt (1988, 283) explains, "the liberty or liberties of the aristocracy and of the plebs were not always congruent with each other," any study of the meaning of the term *libertas* in the Roman world, has to take into consideration how various sectors within the society understood the term, and how it was appropriated to their respective situations.

(b) *Libertas* as a Civic Concept

In the same way that the English word "freedom" comprises "two different concepts, namely "freedom from" and "freedom to," neither of which admits to any but general definitions," so also does the Latin word *libertas* (Wirszubski 1950, 1). Basically, the term *libertas* defines the status of the person who is not a slave. In other words, it denotes the status of the person who is a *liber* (1950, 1). In Roman law, the slave did not have rights and was subject to the domination of others, whereas the free person was capable of possessing rights and was not subject to domination (1950, 1). Brunt claims that the same thing can be said of the equivalent Greek term *eleutheria*. He explains that even though in both Rome and Greece there was no single idea of

---

[4] Starr (1952) 1-16, also makes this point.

freedom, there is evidence which suggests that "to a very large extent the same range of meanings or applications is to be found in the thought and practice of both Romans and Greeks" (1988, 283). For both Rome and Greece, freedom was primarily understood as "the legal status opposed to slavery" (1988, 283). There is, however, a fundamental difference between the Roman concept of freedom and the Greek concept of freedom. In the Roman Republic and the Early Principate, freedom was considered not as a person's innate right, but rather as an acquired civic right which was granted only by the laws of Rome (Wirszubski 1950, 3-4). The concept of *libertas* therefore, carried with it the notion of restraint. Some scholars have contrasted this with the Greek word *eleutheria* which has connotations of licence and carries with it the idea that people had the right to do and live as they wished (Brunt 1988, 282). Wirszubski claims that "the Roman Republic never was, nor, on the whole, was meant to be, a democracy of the Athenian type," and that "*eleutheria* and *parrhesia* as its chief expressions appeared to the Romans as being nearer licentia than libertas" (1950, 13). It would appear obvious, that the Roman understanding was that "genuine libertas can be enjoyed only under the law" (1950, 7). In contrast to the Stoic definition of abstract freedom with its emphasis on the "subjective free will of the agent," the Roman understanding of *libertas* was "the objective right to act" (1950, 8). It was understood in terms of social relations and social responsibility rather than in terms of the individual's autonomy (1950, 8).

(c) Status and *Libertas*

The basis of Roman law provided for equality before the law and the assurance of the fundamental political rights of its citizens. However it did not "preclude differentiation beyond this sphere" (Wirszubski 1950, 15). Equality before the law did not necessarily mean "equality of political rights enjoyed by all the citizens" (1950, 13). Nor did it mean that all citizens had the right to govern (1950, 14). In explaining the distinction, Wirszubski states that while all citizens nominally had the right to govern, its actual exercise was subject to the degree of *auctoritas* and *dignitas* of the citizen (1950, 14). The Romans accepted that the concept of *libertas* and *dignitas* were not mutually exclusive, provided all rights of the people were respected and upheld. However, when appeals were made to one at the expense of the other, the ensuing result was tension and conflict. The reasons such situations arose was because "socially and economically the Roman society was not homogeneous, and there was nothing to prevent the nobles from identifying dignitas with the distinctions and preserves of their own class" (Wirszubski 1950, 16). The nobles claimed *dignitas* as a natural right which sprung from their ancestral connections, and also on the basis of the offices they had held. These claims often caused discontent among the populace at large, and forced citizens to assert and safeguard their rights against the excessive claims of *dignitas* by those whose power might adversely affect the freedom of the citizens or of the State (1950, 16-7). Ramsay MacMullen (1986, 512-524) cites a number of examples of social interaction in the ancient world as evidence of how the concept of *dignitas* reinforced within the society the notions of superiority and inferiority, insiders and outsiders.

(d) Slavery and *Libertas*

In Roman society slaves could lay no claim to equality before the law. For the most part, any privileges they might be given depended on the arbitrary will of their owners. They were "in almost all respects a piece of property, to be brought and sold, given away, or bequeathed, like any other animal"(Brunt, 1988, 284). Any children (*liberi*) of the slaves automatically became the property of the slave owners, and were subject to the *pater familias*, the head of the household. Like the slaves, the *liberi* were not able to own property, and could be bought and sold or handed over to an aggrieved party as compensation in civil disputes. Brunt explains that although the *liberi* were subject to another's domination, they did enjoy more freedom than slaves or those who had been freed because they were under the power of their *pater familias* and thus they possessed rights and incurred the obligations of citizens (1988, 287). It also meant that they could hold office, serve in the army and marry, and that their children were considered to be of free birth (1988, 287). Those who were bonded in some way, that is the sons of those who had been handed over to the ownership of others, those who were in servitude to their creditors as well as those who had contracted to serve as gladiators were all free to marry and to seek protection from those magistrates who might act arbitrarily against them. It was possible for the *liberi*, the *filius in mancipio*, the *addictus* and the *auctoratus* to be given the title of free birth once the conditions of their bondedness were removed. However, the slave who was granted manumission was given only limited rights as a citizen (1988, 287). Brunt claims that although there were thinkers who "asserted that all men were born free, and that slavery was unjust as an institution," the abolition of slavery was never seriously proposed because it was "deeply rooted in the economic organisation and traditions of the Graeco-Roman world"(1988, 289).

In both the Greek and Roman understanding of freedom, whole communities could also be regarded as free or not free (1988, 291). Brunt points out that "a state could be regarded as free if it were not subject to the rule of another state, or if the citizens had rights against their own rulers and were not enslaved to their despotic will" (1988, 291). He explains that both the Greeks and the Romans considered that any people or nations "who were subject to the arbitrary will of a single man or a small group of men were held to be deprived of their freedom" and that their situation was considered to be the same as that of slaves. The Greeks thus considered the subjects of the absolute Persian king as his slaves, while for the Romans, the notion of *libertas* was considered incompatible with *regnum* and the *dominatio* of a faction (1988, 291). Freedom associated with communities could refer to either their relations to other states or nations, or to the internal organisation of the community, and in both cases freedom was a matter of degree. Although the citizens of some communities were guaranteed some rights by law, their freedom increased in accordance with further rights they could acquire. For the citizens of both Athens and Rome, national freedom consisted in being independent of foreign rule (1988, 292). The independence of a state, therefore, ultimately "rested on power" (1988, 292).

Rome's freedom was attained through the conquest of other nations and was maintained through the power and control it was able to exert over other nations. In its dealings with other nations, states or cities, Rome believed that it had the right to grant freedom in varying degrees to those who had become subject to the power of Rome. It was often to Rome's advantage to respect the freedom of cities under its domination by making treaties with them. Rome granted them certain rights and privileges, and at times ensured that the citizens were not subject to arbitrary interference from Roman officials (1988, 293). An example of how Rome regarded the status of other peoples with whom it had made treaties, is to be found in the statement of Proculus, a jurist of the first century CE:

> For this provision is added so that it should be understood that one of these peoples is superior, not that the other is not free: just as we understand that our clients are free, although they are not equal to us in influence, rank or power, so it is to be understood that those who are required courteously to uphold our majesty are free.[5]

Of course any rights and privileges granted to other peoples were revoked if the cities rebelled against Rome in any way, and they consequently suffered a curtailment of freedom. Whatever the degree of freedom subject nations enjoyed, they were left in no doubt as to who was in control. Brunt cites the complaint of the ambassador of the free citizens of Archea who "remarked in 184 that their treaty afforded them no security, since *imperium* belonged to Rome" (1988, 294).[6]

---

[5] Rich (1990) 117.
[6] Reference here is to Livy xxxix. 37. 13: *Specie, inquis, aequum est foedus: re apud Achaeos precarialibertas, apud Romanos etiam imperium est.*

(e) Government and *Libertas*

Government of Rome under the Republic was carried out, broadly speaking, by three main bodies, namely, the People, the Senate and the Magistrates. In theory the Assembly of the people was the ultimate source of power. It "elected the magistrates, enacted or repealed laws (*leges*), and, in the capacity of *iudicium populi*, confirmed or annulled sentences of death or flogging passed on Roman citizens in the courts of criminal justice" (Wirszubski 1950, 18). However, these powers were somewhat circumscribed as Wirszubski explains:

> Any Assembly to be lawful had to be convened and presided over by a competent magistrate ... the Assembly could not on its own initiative propose candidates for public office, nor introduce bills and motions, nor put before the magistrate any questions. The People had to listen to what they were told, and to cast their votes according to the motion (*rogatio*) introduced by the magistrate ... The citizen had a vote, but he had no right to make his voice heard (1950, 18).

The Senate was the official deliberative body in Rome, but it too, was also convened and presided over by a magistrate. Although allowed to speak on matters of public affairs, a senator's right to speak was subject to the discretion of the presiding consul. The Senate acted as the advisory body of the Executive which consisted of magistrates, consuls and tribunes. In theory the Executive was supposed to consult the Senate before undertaking any action, but in practice this depended on the power of those in the Senate at any one time. Wirszubski points out that the "striking feature of the Executive in the Roman Republic was the vast extent of its powers and its prerogatives" (1950, 21). He states that the "mandate of the consuls was irrevocable before expiry; they were unimpeachable during their term of office; they commanded unconditional obedience, and possessed judicial and coercive powers" (1950, 21-2).

The office of tribunate was only open to the plebians, although it was generally the plebian nobles who attained office. The role of the tribune was to protect the citizen who had been wronged and to uphold the freedom of the citizens. According to Lacey & Wilson, the tribunes "were originally not magistrates, but had represented the common soldiers before their commanders while on campaign" (1970, 6). However, over time they assumed more and more power in which they virtually were able to control the meetings and decisions of both the consuls and the Senate. It is important to note that the ordinary citizen did not have automatic right to the help of the tribune. While it was the citizen's right to appeal against any violation of political rights and freedom, it was the tribune's right to either intercede or refuse to intercede on behalf of the citizen (Wirszubski 1950, 26-7). In effect, this meant that the tribune was able to exert power over the citizen.

In order to protect the citizens and the State from being totally dominated by too strong a government, a system of checks was designed in order to limit both the length of time the Executive could hold office as well as the exercise of its powers. Both *imperium* and *potestas* were granted for only one year, after which they automatically expired (1950, 22). All magistracies consisted of two or more colleagues of equal status. Each could act alone, but each also had the power to veto the decisions and actions of other magistrates. The practice of *intercessio* was able to be used effectively by the tribunes, because they held greater power in respect to other magistracies and ostensibly could hold in check the *imperium* of the consuls.[7] Thus, as Wirszubski explains, both the institution of limited tenure and collegiality of office were designed to ensure political freedom (1950, 22-3). Its actual practice was another matter. The smooth working of government depended on the goodwill and co-operation of all concerned. However, in a society in which *dignitas* determined power and privilege, and in which the limits of office were not clearly defined, the way was wide open for the ambitious and unscrupulous to misuse the powers of office in order to further their personal ambitions.

(f) *Libertas* and Power

During the century or so before the collapse of the Republic and the beginning of the Principate, the power of the Senate began to increase. Although the people were technically supposed to be consulted on matters pertaining to the state, particularly on matters of war, the people "could be induced to follow senatorial policy" (Wirszubski 1950, 32). The tribunes gradually became allied to the ruling class rather than championing the causes of the under-privileged, with the result that the centre of power was gradually transferred to the advantage of the Senate (1950, 33-4). Although, the senate acted as the ruling body, "the counsels of the Senate itself were swayed by a comparatively small group of the *nobiles*, the aristocracy of office, prominent among whom were the consulars to whom the procedure of the Senate gave practical advantage" (Wirszubski 1950, 33).

Wirszubski (1950, 38) cites evidence from Sallust which attests to the growing powers of the nobles which extended from holding chief magistracies to that of commanding military forces, the governing of the provinces, control of the treasury and the law-courts. He further explains that "although *nobilitas* originally meant distinction through service and merit, not true blood, and as such its ranks could not, in theory, be

---

[7] *Intercessio* was the right of a member of the magistracy to oppose any action undertaken by either a colleague of equal standing or of someone of lesser rank. See Wirszubski (1950), 22.

closed, it hardened into an exclusive, arrogant, and complacent clique, jealous of its possessions, and determined to retain its power and to perpetuate its rule. Their *dignitas* came to mean reckless and unjust domination" (1950, 38). In contrast were those who objected to the dominance of the nobles. Among these "were many of the dispossessed, who longed for economic security; many of the plain citizens, who longed for an efficient and civil government; the more ambitious members of the rising Equestrian Order, who longed for political power; and such aristocrats as had fallen on evil times, or were for some reason or other at variance with those in power, and longed for *dignitas*" (1950, 39). Within the society two specific groups emerged namely, the *Optimates* who were the ruling oligarchy, and the *Populares* whose composition was made up of a variety of people who championed reform, civil rights and a greater share in the government of the state. Naturally there was great rivalry between the two groups. Both asserted that their cause was to champion the freedom of the state, but in reality the motive that drove each group was the struggle for power and control over public affairs.

Amongst the many issues of contention was that over the granting of extraordinary executive powers, which could be either a special office conferred by a special law, or that of an office exercised contrary to the existing rules or as a dispensation from those rules (1950, 61). Wirszubski states that it was in the interests of the Senate and the ruling class to oppose any situation which could put their respective power in jeopardy (1961, 62). They were more inclined therefore, to uphold the *status quo* and reject changes to the tenure of offices.

The expansion of the Roman frontiers necessitated the deployment of armies which were drawn for the most part from the *populares* and the *plebs urbana*. As the army provided a source of financial income for the soldiers, it was to the soldiers' advantage to pledge allegiance to their commander who held *imperium*. The soldiers also looked to their commander for land grants after their discharge from the army as a reward for their loyalty to his command. Brunt draws attention to the fact that "Sulla, Pompey, Caesar, the triumvirs, and Augustus himself, all owed their power to their troops, and it was primarily by enriching them, and especially by promises and grants of land, that they secured their allegiance" (1988, 77). Commanders of armies were granted extraordinary powers, and were often accused by the senate of seeking *regnum*, a term which was considered incompatible with that of *libertas*. Pompey, Caesar and Augustus all received long-term commands from the people. Brunt points out that those holding these commands were not answerable to the senate, and they could build up military power "to put pressure on the senate or to defeat it in armed conflict" (1988, 18). It was the granting of these extraordinary commands, as Brunt observes, that enabled Augustus to acquire control of the provinces where most of the legion's were stationed, and through which he was able to continue his military exploits (1988, 18).

Consequently, this led to the situation where "*imperium* once again came to be truly monarchical, irresponsible, and unchecked" (1988, 18).

Roman imperial expansion created a wide gap between the rich and the poor. Although those recruited into the army as soldiers would have profited to some extent from the booty of warfare, they were often forced to leave their own small farm holdings for lengthy periods of time with the result that these farms fell into disuse and debt. The rich, however, being furnished with the larger share of the profits of war, were able to acquire large estates and secure numbers of slaves to work the land. The dispossessed drifted to the cities or towns in search of a livelihood, but often without much success. Thus there existed, at least in Rome, a great mass of urban poor who lived in squalor and without means of support.[8]

As the ability to hold power depended on wealth or its acquisition, there was also a gap between those who had the power to act and those who did not. Those without power came more and more to depend on those who held power. As a result the ordinary citizen, and particularly those without means, tended to pledge their support to those who would be the more likely to provide for their welfare and interests. The leaders of the factions were obviously able to use this situation to their advantage.

The Term *Libertas* in the *Res Gestae*

The word *libertas* in its abstract and political sense is used but once in the text of the *Res Gestae*, and appears in the opening lines:

> *Annos undeviginti natus exercitum privato consilio et privata impensa comparavi per quem rem publicam a dominatione factionis oppressam in libertatem vindicavi* (I c.1. 1-3)

> ἐτῶν δεκαεννέα ὢν τὸ στράτευμα ἐμῇ γνώμῃ καὶ ἐμοῖς ἀναλώμασιν ἡτοίμασα, δι' οὗ τὰ κοινὰ πράγματα ἐκ τῆς τῶν συνομοσαμένων δουλήας ἠλευθέρωσα (I c. 1. 1-4)

> When nineteen years old, I raised an army, by my private decision and at private expense, by which I vindicated the liberty of the *res publica* when it was suppressed by the domination of a faction.

In commenting on this opening verse, Wirszubski suggests that it may well be that "Augustus did not write the first sentence with the view of establishing himself as the restorer of freedom," but rather with a view to justifying his action of taking up arms

---

[8] See Lenski's important discussion on the nature of the state, ruler and social inequality in the ancient world (1966) 210. Also Carney (1975) 183-4.

against Antony, which in other circumstances would have constituted treason (1950, 101-2). In arguing this position, Wirszubski claims that the opening sentence has to be seen in the light of the events "in late 44 and early in 43 B.C ... and not in the light of the year 27 B.C." (1950, 102). He states that the reference here is to the battle at Brundisium in 44 BCE, and not to the events of Actium and its aftermath. He draws attention to the fact that the opening lines of the *Res Gestae* in fact echo the words used on a number of occasions by Cicero in his speeches in the Senate when he both justified and praised the action taken by Augustus.[9] Thus Wirszubski claims that Augustus is doing nothing more than re-emphasising "that he strictly observed the constitution" and that the beginnings of his politcal career were legal (1950, 103). According to Wirszubski, the words *vindicatio in libertatem* in the opening lines of the *Res Gestae* were well worn republican clichés which had little effect other than denoting "a public-spirited intention and little, if anything else" (1950, 104).

Ramage does not entirely agree with Wirszubski. While he concedes that the words were an "often-repeated republican formula," he argues that Augustus sets out to deliberately convey the notion of republican connotations, and that the opening lines are a "rhetorically emphatic statement whose effectiveness is enhanced by three formal phrases in which the key words produce solemn and resounding tones" (1987, 66-7). Ramage claims that in the context of the opening lines, the word *libertas* is highly significant in that "it is the precursor—one might even say the prerequisite (1.2: *eo* [*nom*]*ine*)—for establishing normalcy in government. Once it has been won back, senate, people, consuls, and Octavian begin behaving in a sane and sensible way of the free republic" (1987, 67).

The interpretation that Judge places on these opening lines of the *Res Gestae* is somewhat different from the view that Ramage espouses. According to Judge (1985a, 135), Augustus is not only attempting to justify the legitimacy of his rise to power but is also emphasising the honours bestowed on him because of the actions he took to protect the liberty of the *res publica*. Judge explains that the words in the first verse are "loaded political terminology" which "is balanced by the strictly legal expression" in the following two verses of the text (1985a, 135). He claims that "the essential truth is plainly stated that the private act was publicly endorsed, and no one could say that Augustus had hidden his revolutionary origin" (1985a, 135). Judge argues that Augustus seems to be preoccupied with the problem of legitimacy which hung over his political career and states that the first verse in the *Res Gestae* "constitutes a preliminary *exemplum virtutis*, to be balanced and echoed in the conclusion 34. 1"(1985a, 135). Judge explains that these words echo "the same array of themes" that can be found in former tributes to political leaders who acted on behalf of the liberty of the *res publica*,

---

[9] See Cic. *Phil*. iii.2.1-5; iv.2.4; v.16.42-45.

and that Augustus "safely displays his usurpation in terms familiar to public admiration" (1985a, 135).

The significance of the word *libertas* in these opening lines of the *Res Gestae* becomes apparent, however, if viewed in the light of the genre of the *Res Gestae*, namely encomium. In the structure of encomium, the prologue (προοίμιον) "indicates the importance of the person or thing being praised" (Hester 1991, 296). In other words, it introduces the theme of the encomium. In his use of the phrase *rem publicam a dominatione factionis oppressam in libertatem vindicavi* in the opening lines of the text, the tenor or motif for the whole of the *Res Gestae*, is deliberately established.[10] It is is the "prelude" to the main message which the climax of the chiastic structure of the *Res Gestae* (13;14:1-2) emphasises, namely the restoration of the new age of peace and freedom. From the outset Augustus wants to be remembered and thus honoured and praised for the way in which his actions against "a tyrannical faction" had brought liberty for the whole of the Roman people. The remainder of the text of the *Res Gestae* explains how, through the deeds and achievements of Augustus, the Roman world was able to continue to live in a state of *libertas*. The closing verses (34:1-35:2) form the epilogue (ἐπίλογος), and constitute "a statement about the restoration of the government to the Senate and the People of Rome, and the honours conferred on Augustus in recognition of that service" (Wirszubski 1950, 100). In other words, this statement is intended to remind the reader that *libertas* has been restored.

The chiastic structure of the text indicates that the opening lines of the *Res Gestae* and the closing verses can be bracketed together, and are thus intended to be rhetorically emphatic. The opening lines and closing statements (34.1-3) of the *Res Gestae* refer to events occurring between 44 and 27 BCE, during which time Augustus having defeated the "faction" elements, had "extinguished the civil wars" and restored the *res publica* "into the discretion of the senate and the people of Rome" (*RG* 34.1). The opening phrase *rem publicam a dominatione factionis oppressam in libertatem vindicavi* would have evoked for those readers familiar with senatorial speeches, the connection with the praise which Cicero had proclaimed in the Senate in reference to Octavian's defeat of Antony:

> "Caius Caesar, a young man, or rather almost a boy, but one of incredible, and, as it were, god-like intelligence and courage, at the very time when Antonius' frenzy was at its greatest heat, and when his cruel and deadly return from Brundisium was dreaded, while we were not asking for, or thinking of, assistance, nor even hoping for it, for it seemed impossible, collected a very stout army of the invincible class of veterans, and lavished his patrimony— though I have not used the proper phrase; for he did not lavish it, he invested it in the salvation of the State. And although we cannot recompense him to the extent our debt to him

---

[10] See commentary in Brunt & Moore (1967) 38.

requires, yet we should feel a gratitude the greatest our hearts can
conceive. ... From this calamity Caesar on his own initiative—it could
not be otherwise—has freed the state." (*Phil*. iii. 2.1-5).

Chapters 13 and 14 of the *Res Gestae* which as has been demonstrated form the climax
of the text, reinforce the notion of *libertas*. The *aureum saeculum* has been inaugurated.
The notion of *libertas* has now become synonymous with the *Pax Romana*. Ramage
(1987, 71) notes the connection between *libertas* and *pax* in the coin issue com-
memorating the victory of Augustus:

> In the case of the coin, while the restorer of *libertas* is celebrated on the
> obverse, the message of the reverse is more important for Augustus'
> purposes. Here Peace appears holding a caduceus in her right hand and
> standing on a sword. A cista mystica with a snake emerging from it
> appears to her left and the whole is surrounded by a laurel wreath. With
> the obverse, then, the emperor may be announcing himself as the restorer
> of *libertas*, but on the reverse he suggests how this was done and points
> to its ramifications. He has achieved his goal through Victoria (laurel
> wreath) and this has brought peace (*pax*) and prosperity (*caduceus*).

Ramage cites two instances where Cicero had made a direct connection between *libertas*
and *pax*, namely *Phil*. 1. 32 *(quia libertatem pax consequebatur)* and 2.113 *(pax est
tranquilla libertas)*

It would seem that the notion of libertas in the first verse of the *Res Gestae* is
intended to be taken as "the republican phenomenon" as Ramage suggests. (1987, 68).
However, Ramage, following Wirszubski (1950, 97-123), points out that this was "not
necessarily to be taken as the true Augustan freedom," and argues that "references in
the *RG* tend to confirm this and at the same time show how Augustus adapted the idea
for his own purposes" (1987, 68). The interpretation of what this freedom meant and
how it was able to be maintained throughout the Roman world during Augustus'
lifetime is spelled out in actual terms throughout the *Res Gestae*. While appealing
initially to the republican connotation, it was in effect a new expression of the meaning
of freedom.

The Concept of Freedom in the *Res Gestae*

An analysis of the text of the *Res Gestae* clearly shows that the freedom that was
claimed to have been brought to the Roman world by Augustus was very much bound
up with the position of power he was able to secure for himself and for Rome through
military conquest. Augustus was able to boast that freedom from wars and major unrest
was won initially through his *imperium* in the suppression of faction elements, and was

maintained throughout his life by means of his *auctoritas* in his control of the affairs of the *res publica*. What Augustus was able to use to his advantage was not so much the republican notion of freedom, as Ramage claims, but rather the very organisation of the system of republican government. It was through this means that he was able to secure and maintain control over the Roman world, and so bring about a state of peace which was in reality largely an absence of the factional wars that had plagued preceding generations. Throughout the text of the *Res Gestae* emphasis is placed on the fact that in spite of the extraordinary powers of office Augustus was granted from time to time, the offices he did secure were in accordance with the republican notion of government. In particular emphasis is on the legality of the tribunician power with which Augustus was invested some thirty-seven times. However it becomes obvious to the reader of the *Res Gestae* that it was the very office of *tribunicia potestas* with its intended major function of protecting the freedom of the citizens, that was in effect, the means through which Augustus was able to take full control over the Roman world.

As already mentioned, the *Res Gestae* is not set out as a chronological enumeration of the events and achievements of Augustus' life. The enumeration of achievements in the *Res Gestae* is organised in such a way that specific events, deeds and expenses are grouped together for rhetorical effect. The account of the achievements shows a development from the specifics of "overcoming the faction element" that had threatened the republic of Rome (*RG* 1.1) to the assertion of the universality of Rome's domination of the world (*RG* 35. 1). According to Aristotle (*Rhet.* I. ix, 33) achievements constitute the major component of an encomium. In the *RG*, the emphasis on the achievements of Augustus, is therefore intended to draw admiration and praise from the readers and also to convince the readers that the reign of Rome had secured for them their peace and freedom.

It has been pointed out in the previous chapter that various divisions of the text have been proposed by scholars in an attempt to analyse the text of the *Res Gestae*, and to draw out its inherent message. However, for the purpose of identifying the theme of *libertas* that is evident in the text, another perspective regarding the division of the text is warranted. There are five instances in the text of the *Res Gestae* in which Augustus explicitly refers to the tribunician power that he held, namely 4.4; 6.1, 2; 10.1; 15.1,2; 34.1, 3. A comparison between the Latin and the Greek texts of the *Res Gestae* reveals that in all instances where reference is made to the tribunician power, the Latin term *tribunicia potestas* is rendered in the Greek text as δημαρχικὴ ἐξουσία. It would seem that the term δημαρχικὴ ἐξουσία is the standard Greek translation for the Latin term *tribunicia potestas* as it not only occurs consistently in the *Res Gestae*, but is also to be found in other documents with reference to the title of the *triumvirate*.[11] The

---

[11] See reference to ἐξουσία in Mason (1974) 44, 133.

edicts of Augustus and the Senate of 7-6 BCE and 4 BCE all contain the Greek term δημαρχικὴ ἐξουσία. For example, the first edict begins with the pronouncement (EJ, 139):

αὐτοκράτωρ Καῖσαρ Σεβαστὸς ἀρχιερεὺς δημαρχικῆς
ἐξουσίας
ἑπτακαιδέκατον αὐτοκράτωρ τεσσερασκαιδέκατό λεγει …

The edict of Augustus to the Jews and quoted by Josephus, again contains the official salutation in Greek:

Καῖσαρ Σεβαστὸς ἀρχιερεὺς δημαρχικῆς ἐξουσίας λέγει
(*AJ* xvi. 162-5).

A letter from Tiberius in 15 CE likewise contains the Greek terminology δημαρχικῆς ἐξουσίας in the official greeting (EJ 147).

Τιβέριος Καῖσαρ θεοῦ Σεβαστοῦ υἱὸς Σεβαστὸς
δημαρχικῆς ἐξουσίας…

(a) *Tribunicia Potestas* and δημαρχικὴ ἐξουσία

The Latin terminology, *tribunicia potestas*, and the Greek terminology, δημαρχικὴ ἐξουσία, would have been immediately clear to the first century Latin or Greek reader as political concepts. The Greek word ἐξουσία comes from the verb ἔξεστιν meaning "it is free" (Foerster 1964, 560). Accordingly it can denote "that an action is possible in the sense that there are no hindrances or that the opportunity for it occurs" (1964, 560). It can also mean "that an action is not prevented by a higher norm or court" (1964, 560). Foerster identifies five perspectives from which the word ἐξουσία can be understood. Firstly as early as the time of Euripides "ἐξουσία … denotes "ability to perform an action" to the extent that there are no hindrances in the way, as distinct from δύναμις in the sense of intrinsic ability" (1964, 562). A second understanding of ἐξουσία is that of "the possibility granted by a higher norm or court, and therefore the right to do something or the right over something" (1964, 562). According to the context, as Foerster explains, it can mean "authority," "permission," "freedom" (1964, 562). Used in this sense it refers to "the possibility of action given authoritatively by the king, government or laws of a state and conferring authority, permission or freedom on corporations or in many instances, esp. in legal matters, on individuals" (1964, 562).

An important aspect that Foerster (1964, 562) notes is that translations of ἐξουσία "express different sides of the one term which in itself denotes only the possibility of action." Thus, as he demonstrates with reference to classical Greek literature, ἐξουσία can be used "of any right (permission, freedom etc) in the various relationships similar to and guaranteed by national institutions, e.g., the rights of parents in relation to children, of masters in relation to slaves, of owners in relation to property and of individuals in respect of personal liberty" (1964, 562). A third point to which Foerster draws attention is the difference between δύναμις which denotes external power and ἐξουσία which denotes "the power displayed in the fact that a command is obeyed, i.e. the power to pronounce it" (1964, 563). Fourthly, ἐξουσία can also denote the Stoic sense of moral power, for example "Diog. L., VII, 121: Only the wise man is free" (1964, 563). While ἐξουσία can be used "in the sense of self-asserted freedom … or caprice" it "does not alter the fact that ἐξουσία is mostly used in the context of legal order" (1964, 563). Lastly, Foerster points out that there are also derived meanings such as "authoritative position," "office of state," "office-bearers" and "rulers" (1964, 563). It would seem that on the basis of this study of ἐξουσία the sense of "freedom to act" is the fundamental understanding of this word.[12]

The Latin word *potestas* likewise conveys the sense of the power or freedom to choose, decide or act. According to Lewis and Short (1951, 1408) *potestas* is derived from *possum* and the general classical meaning is the "ability or power of doing anything."[13] The *Oxford Latin Dictionary* (1977, 1417) provides eight basic categories reflecting the meaning of *potestas*:

1. Possession of control or command (over persons or things), power
   (b) in political or military contexts, (c) in legal or quasi-legal contexts
   (d) power over life and death (e) personified as a deity.
2. Command, control (of faculties, emotions etc.).
3. A person of power, office, magistracy; also jurisdiction, authority.
4. A person possessing power or influence, (b) spiritual power.
5. The power (of doing something), chance, opportunity, right.
6. Opportunity to choose, decide, power of choice, discretion, control.
7. Physical or mental power.
8. Force, function of a word or law.

It must be remembered, of course, that in identifying the meaning of Latin words, the modern Latin dictionary draws its references from a wide variety of contexts with

---

[12] Likewise ἐξουσία as "freedom of choice," "right to act," *GEL*, 277-278. Also "power of choice," "liberty of action" noted as primary meaning (cf BGU IV. 1158[13] [9 B.C.]) *VGT* 225. Also *PGL* (1961) 502, "of individual's power of choice."
[13] According to *DELL* (1959) 528, *potestas* refers particularly to political power.

respect to place, function and time. Naturally the meaning of *potestas* is adapted and used at the discretion of the writer or speaker according to its appropriate and accepted terminology. Nevertheless the meanings which the *Oxford Latin Dictionary* attributes to the word *potestas* can be equated with the meanings that are attributed to the Greek word ἐξουσία (Foerster 1964, 560). A further example of the parallel meaning is provided in the *Thesaurvus Linguae Latinae*, in which the word *potestas* is given as being synonymous with the Greek word ἐξουσία (*TLL* 1980, 301).

The concept of the Latin term *triumvir* with its connotation of the exercise of the power of government on behalf of the people, and which theoretically was the voice of the people, is conveyed in the Greek word δημαρχική. According to Larsen (1973, 45), the word δημαρχική "refers to a state or government in which the power (*kratos*) is wielded by the *demos*." Theoretically, it conveys the sense that the people have the power to rule.

An analysis of each of the instances of *tribunicia potestas* and its Greek translation, δημαρχικὴ ἐξουσία in each of the respective contexts within the *Res Gestae* reveals that the intention of the author is to emphasise how Augustus, in maintaining the office of *triumvir*, had acted as the voice of the people and for the good of the people. The claim by the author of the text is that the actions that Augustus carried out by virtue of his office, were geared to this end and were legally justified.

(b) Augustus and Tenure of Office

The first reference to the tribunician power is found in *RG* 4.4

> *Consul fueram terdeciens, cum scribebam haec, et eram septimum et tricensimum* **tribuniciae   potestatis**....
>
> Ὑπάτευον τρὶς καὶ δέκατον, ὅτε ταῦτα ἔγραφον, καὶ ἤμην τριακοστὸν καὶ ἕβδομον δημαρχικῆς ἐξουσίας.
>
> At the time of writing I have been consul thirteen times and am in the thirty-seventh year of **tribunician power**

Having established the circumstances that had led to his success in delivering Rome from potential despotic rulers and that of avenging his father's death (*RG* 1.2-2.1), the list of Augustus' achievements begins in 3.1 with a statement of the military record of his life. At the outset this is described in global terms. The magnitude of claims draws attention to what the author wants the reader to notice, namely Augustus' charismatic qualities as a leader, and whose mission it was to establish stability and peace throughout the Roman world. Although military achievements are here brought to the reader's notice, the emphasis, as Judge (1985a, 137) states, is on "the winding down of the wars rather than on the military feats as such." This is then followed by an enumeration of the honours that were bestowed on Augustus for this service to the people of Rome. Emphasis is on the fact that these honours were granted to him through the decrees of the senate which acted as the legitimate body on behalf of the populace as a whole. The section (4.4) concludes with the statement that Augustus had held the tribunician power some thirty-seven times. Hence it seems that Augustus wants it on record that although holding this office for such a long period was unprecedented, nevertheless in the circumstances it was fitting and proper given the fact that he was able to accomplish great things for Rome through this long tenure of office.

(c) Civic Leader

The section from *RG* 5.1 to 9.2 forms the context for the specific reference to the second mention of tribunician power which occurs in 6.1-2.

> senatu populoque Romano consentientibus ut curator legum et morum
> **summa potestate** solus crearer...Quae tum per me geri senatus voluit,
> per **tribuniciam potestatem** perfeci.

> τῆς τε συνκλήτου καὶ τοῦ δήμου τῶν ʾΡωμαίων
> ὑμολογούντων, ἵνα ἐπιμελητὴς τῶν τε νόμων καὶ τῶν
> τρόπων ἐπὶ μεγίστη ἐξουσίαι μόνος χειροτονηθῶ...
> ʾΑ δὲ τότε δι᾽ ἐμοῦ ἡ σύνκλητος οἰκονομεῖσθαι ἐβούλετο,
> τῆς δημαρχικῆς ἐξουσίας ὧν ἐτέλεσα.

> the senate and people of Rome agreed that I should be appointed
> supervisor of laws and morals without a colleague and with supreme
> **power** ... The measures that the senate then desired me to take I carried
> out in virtue of my **tribunician power.**

In this section attention is drawn to the fact that Augustus' actions as a civic leader ensured that the people could continue to live in a state of freedom. He is also emphasising that the accolades he received were bestowed on him by the senate and people and again that the offices he held and the actions he had taken were legitimate. The section begins (*RG* 5.1) with the statement that Augustus had refused the dictatorship which the senate and people had wanted him to assume. While it is somewhat difficult to judge his motives for the refusal of this office it would seem that the role of dictator was fraught with the possibility of being usurped by another as had happened to Pompey and Caesar. On commenting on Augustus' reluctance to be named as dictator, Cassius Dio (54.1) makes the following telling remark:

> He knew that the authority and the honour he already possessed raised him above the position of past dictators, and he was rightly on his guard against the jealousy and hatred which the title would provoke.

The measures that Augustus would have been able to execute in the role of dictator would also have been circumscribed to a large extent by the decrees of the senate or by the opposition of enemies from within the senate, which he knew only too well. As a member of the senate Augustus would have been in a much better position to ascertain any contentiousness against his actions.

Augustus' ability as an administrator is highlighted with the point made that in the great famine he was able to take charge of the corn-supply and could claim that "I delivered the whole city from apprehension and immediate danger at my own cost and by my own efforts" (*RG* 5.2). The claim of Augustus here is that the people looked to him for their well-being and basic food supply. The implication is that the people were freed of the worry of not having sufficient basic food as he was in control. In fact for anyone to have control over the grain supply was to have ultimate control over the distribution of this basic resource, as well as the power to determine who would be given access and who could be denied access to the grain supplies. Control, of course meant power. As Moxnes (1988, 27) points out, in the Greco-Roman economy in the first century the central concern was to be able "to have power to control the economic system and to expropriate the surplus." The situation always had the potential to be used as a bargaining or a punitive measure by those in control if the situation warranted it. Those who accepted Augustus' administration could in effect be guaranteed access to the resources. Therefore all could look to him for their basic sustenance and needs.

In 5.3 -6.2 there is an enumeration of the offices he was asked to accept, but again he emphasises his refusal of any office that was not in accordance with republican principles. Yet in 7.1-3 he makes mention of his ranking as *principatus senatus* and lists his membership in the priestly colleges. Through all of these offices he was able to considerably influence the legislation and the cultic practices of the state. In holding a number of offices at a high level he was able to influence policy in accordance with the legitimate functions that properly pertained to those offices. A description of the way Augustus reorganised the magistracy and the nation is emphasised in 8.14. He introduces a sense of order into the organisation of the Roman nation by carrying out a census of the people, performing a *lustrum* from time to time in which more people were registered as Roman citizens, and passing laws that were designed to raise the moral standards of the nation. Again one gets the sense of the power and control that Augustus had in all of these measures.

Since, as Brunt (1967, 52) states, the well-being of the nation was seen as being dependent on the well-being of the leader, it is appropriate that there is mention of the institutionalisation of vows and sacrifices for Augustus' health and for which the ordinary citizens both communally and individually had adopted as a cultic practice. The safety of the people was bound up with the degree of his sanctity, that is, his god-like qualities. Although he was given supreme power to govern, he insists that all of his actions were carried out by virtue of the tribunician power with which he was vested by the people.

(d) Religious Leader

In the section *RG* 10 Augustus states that his name was included in the hymn of the Salii and that he was at this time prevailed upon to take upon himself the tribunician power for life.

> Nomen meum senatus consulto inclusum est in saliare carmen, et sacrosanctus in perpetum ut essem et, quoad viverem, **tribunicia potestas** mihi esset, per legem sanctum est.

> Τὸ ὄνομά μου συνκλήτου δόγματι ἐνπεριελήφθη εἰς τοὺς σαλίων ὕμνους· Καὶ ἵνα ἱερὸς ὦ διὰ βίου τε τὴν δημαρχικὴν ἔχω ἐξουσίαν νόμῳ ἐκυρώθη.

> My name was inserted in the hymn of the Salii by a decree of the senate, and it was enacted by law that my person should be inviolable for ever and that I should hold the **tribunician power** for the duration of my life.

Being included in the hymn of the Salii meant that Augustus was regarded as one amongst the deities that guarded Rome.[14] As Rome's guardian the safety of the people was also bound up with the personal sanctification of Augustus. The statement in 10.1 is intended as a preface to what follows in sections 10.2-14.2. Honours were bestowed on him for his work in establishing peace throughout the "whole empire of the Roman people" (*RG* 13.1). Altars were erected in various places in order that his achievements in this regard would be remembered and celebrated. Again emphasis is on the universal support celebrated annually through ritual sacrifices. Peace was secured by victories. A new golden age had dawned.

---

[14] See also Lattke (1991, 89f and 55.

(e) Benefactor

Section 15 marks a shift in emphasis. Having completed the list of honours that were bestowed on him, he turns to the *impensae* as an example of his achievements on behalf of the people.

> et **tribunicia potestate** duodecimum quadringenos nummos tertium viritim dedi ...**Tribuniciae potestatis** duodevicensimum, consul XII, trecentis et viginti millibus plebis urbanae sexagenos denarios viritim dedi.

> καὶ δημαρχικῆς ἐξουσίας τὸ δωδέκατον ἑκατὸν δη–
> νάρια κατ᾽ ἄνδρα ἔδωκα... Δημαρχικῆς ἐξουσίας ὀκτω–
> καιδέκατον, ὕπατος δωδέκατον τριάκοντα τρισὶ μυριάσιν
> ὄχλου πολειτικοῦ ἑξήκοντα δηνάρια κατ᾽ ἄνδρα ἔδωκα.

> in the twelfth year of my **tribunician power** I gave every man 400 sesterces for the third time... In the eighteenth year of my **tribunician power** and my twelfth consulship I gave 240 sesterces apiece to 320,000 members of the urban plebs.

Sections 15-24 contain references to the various endowments Augustus lavished on the people of Rome. This is prefaced in 15. 1, 2 with the fact that it was in the twelfth year of his tribunician power and again in the eighteenth year of his tribunician power when he distributed his wealth to the people on a grand scale. The message conveyed here is that Augustus was acting as the benefactor of the people by providing for their well-being. The amount of wealth he had amassed is also emphasised here. In the Roman world, the amount of wealth was indicative of one's degree of *dignitas* which in turn denoted the respect and honour he would have won from the people. By virtue of his *dignitas* and the benefits he was at liberty to distribute, Augustus was able to win acclaim and allegiance from the people. As benefactor he bound the people to him and in effect could exercise control over their lives.

(f) Transference of Power

The final reference to the power of Augustus occurs in *RG* 34. 1-3. The statement here amounts to what may be termed as the denouement of the *Res Gestae*:

> In consulatu sexto et septimo, postquam bella civilia extinxeram, per consensum universorum potitus rerum omnium, rem publicam ex mea **potestate** in senatus populique Romani arbitrium transtuli ... Post id tempus auctoritate omnibus praestiti, **potestatis** autem nihilo amplius habui quam ceteri qui mihi quoque in magistratu conlegae fuerunt.

Ἐν ὑπατείηαι ἕκτη καὶ ἑβδόμη μετὰ τὸ τοὺς ἐνφυλίους
ζβέσαι με πολέμους κατὰ τὰς εὐχὰς τῶν ἐμῶν πολειτῶν
ἐνκρατὴς γενόμενος πάντων τῶν πραγμάτων ἐκ τῆς ἐμῆς
ἐχουσίας εἰς τὴν τῆς συνκλήτου καὶ τοῦ δήμου τῶν
Ῥωμαίων μετήνεγκα κυριήαν...'Αξιώματι πάντων διήνεγκα,
ἐξουσίας δὲ οὐδέν τι πλεῖον ἔσχον τῶν συναρξάντων μοι.

In my sixth and seventh consulships, after I had extinguished civil wars, and at a time when with universal consent I was in complete control of affairs, I transferred the republic from my **power** to the dominion of the senate and people of Rome... After this time I excelled all in influence, although I possessed no more official **power** than others who were my colleagues in the several magistracies.

In spite of all that he had achieved and all he had bequeathed to the people, Augustus is reiterating that his achievements were able to be actualised because he had acted in accordance with republican principles and ensured that the people shared in the power. The inference here is that both he and the people had the power to act. He it was who exercised leadership on their behalf because of his *auctoritas*, and even though the people by universal consent wanted him to be dictator he insisted that they in fact share in government. This magnaminity would have won him popularity, acclaim and the allegiance of the people.

(g) Augustan Freedom

While the opening lines of the *Res Gestae* introduce the theme of *libertas* in legal and political terms, it is in the closing lines of the text where the nature of freedom is brought to the attention of the reader. It is at this point that the reader becomes aware of the difference between what Ramage describes as "the republican phenomenon" and "true Augustan freedom" (1987, 68). The title of *pater patriae* was intended as a fitting expression of how the relationship that existed between Augustus and the citizens of Rome was regarded. Just as the term *pater familias* denoted that the life force or genius of the family resided in and emanated from the head of the household, so did the title *pater patriae* which was conferred on Augustus, signify that the genius or life force of the Roman people resided in and emanated from Augustus. According to Grant the appellation *pater patriae* "was the culmination of his honours, and the crystallisation of the *auctoritas* which was the moral and executive basis of the new *régime* (1969, 319). Edwin Judge spells out the implications of this title (1985a, 171):

the new title subjects everyone to a form of dependence, and elevates Augustus to a form of control, that is more simple, fundamental and universal than any of the bonds that hold together the organs of the state. In the last resort the position of Augustus is paternal, and founded upon personal and community relations rather than legal ones.

While Augustus regarded himself as one amongst the people and as such considered himself subject to the law as was every Roman citizen (*RG* 6.1-2; 8.5), the title *pater patriae* in fact put him above the law. The checks and balances that theoretically would have ensured the distribution of powers under the law in the Republic, in the last analysis were ineffective when *potestas*, *dignitas* and *auctoritas* became concentrated in the leading citizen. His sway of influence extended, not only over the citizens of Rome itself, but over all the peoples who came under the domination of Rome (*RG* 23-33). As J. Rufus Fears observes, the bestowing of the title *pater patriae* on Augustus "had significance far beyond the honorific" (1980, 109). Fears explains that it signalled

the collapse of a commitment to collective authority, with its demands for collective decision making and its concomitant anxieties and political strife, all hallmarks of the vivid civic life of the Greek polis and the Italic city state. It bespoke a society eager to seek refuge and final salvation in a great father figure, who could nourish and foster all who came to his bosom, relieving them of all anxiety, all responsibility, and all necessity for decision (1980, 109).

This state of affairs continued not only throughout the long years of the reign of Augustus, but extended to that of the reign of his successors throughout the period of the Roman empire.

In a system of government in which access to the leading citizen was mediated through the organ and offices of the state, the expression of the benevolent power of Augustus would have had little direct observable effect on the ordinary person except in so far as it secured their allegiance to him. However it was those who held *imperium* in one way or another in the structures of government, whether this was in Rome itself or in the provinces throughout the Roman occupied world who had the most to gain by courting the favour of the ruler of Rome. They also had much to lose in not complying with the wishes of Rome. Although Augustus states emphatically that he did not seek divine status and the special privileges that his subordinates were wanting to confer on him, he nevertheless concurred with the wishes of the people when they wanted to pay tribute to him in some form, if in fact these tributes were consistent with Republican tradition. Both ancient and modern commentators have remarked on the genius of Augustan administration in allowing various colonies and provinces to continue their traditional ways of societal organisation and administration wherever this did not appear as a threat to Roman government. In this way, Augustus was able to appease the people, or more correctly appease those who held the power, and win from them allegiance to the rule of Rome.

In spite of Augustus' insistence that his reign was based on the republican tradition, it was as Fears points out, a military monarchy, which rested "upon an autocrat's control and the finances and military forces of the commonwealth" (1981, 805). However as Fears continues to explain, the victories that were achieved through him were portrayed as evidence of more than just the conquest of other peoples. The propaganda surrounding Augustus' victories, whether articulated through the media of architecture, poetry, coinage, inscriptions or civic ceremonials, emphasised the "creative act" of Augustus in inaugurating the restoration of peace and prosperity. His actions were intended to be regarded as "essential proof of the supernatural gifts of Augustus and of the divine sanction which blessed his achievement" (1981, 806). As the League of Asian Cities testified in 9 BCE, Augustus' achievement of bringing peace to the world was hailed as "nothing less than the salvation of the entire human race" (1981, 806). Fears draws attention to the numismatic evidence portraying the theme of *Victoria Augusta* that was promoted not only by Augustus but by successive rulers of the Roman empire down to the time of Constantine (1981, 812). *Pax* and *libertas* were very often portrayed as being intimately linked with *victoria, salus, concordia* and *securitas*. According to Fears, the ideology of victory promoted by the rulers "conveyed far more than the mere fact of military triumph. It characterized a conception of the social order in which the well-being of the people was seen to reside entirely in the figure of a charismatic monarch (1981, 815).

As first among equals, Augustus held the reins of power, and for the citizens of Rome freedom became, not the freedom of the restored Republic, but freedom from arbitrary rule. It was this concept of freedom which in effect set the tone for the appeals to freedom that subsequent rulers of Rome adopted (Hammond 1963/ 64, 93-113). Throughout the Roman world in the first century CE this concept of *libertas* in one way or another was reflected on the coinage of the various emperors, and the distribution of coinage amongst the populace served to reinforce the notion that ultimately their freedom rested in the hands of the ruler of Rome.

The Non-elite in Ancient Mediterranean Society

Ancient literature that reflects the social situation of the Roman world in the first century CE, has mainly focussed on the world of the ruling class which comprised about two per-cent of the total population.[15] The concentration of this literature has generally been biased towards such political matters as the lives and fortunes of the imperial regime, victories in wars, legislative and government matters, as well as the career paths of the ruling class. Little of the ancient literature has directly provided information concerning the way in which the general population fared. As the other 98 percent of the population also shaped the events of history, it is important that historians also focus on this sector. Because information regarding this area is sparse, modern inquiry has to resort to "reading between the lines" of the available literature that reflects the views and perspectives of the ruling class, and also to draw on evidence from cross-cultural studies provided by scholars such as Lenski (1966) and Carney (1975). The research undertaken by both Lenski and Carney has provided an important if a somewhat broad picture of the nature and composition of populations in ancient societies.

The Roman world of the first century can be categorised as a pre-industrial agrarian society, or what Borg terms a "peasant society" (1994, 101). Within this society there were essentially two major divisions, the elite and the peasants. Gottwald (1993, 6) identifies the elite as "the dominant tribute-imposing class," and the peasant class as the "dominated tribute-bearing class." Lenski identifies nine classes that span these two divisions. Included in the elite sector, which comprised about ten per-cent of the population, were the ruler and the governing class, the service groups or what Lenski terms as the "retainer" class consisting of soldiers, bureaucrats, scribes and *publicani*, the merchant class and the priestly class. The second division comprising about ninety per-cent of the population, included the agriculturalists, artisans, the unclean and degraded classes, and those who were considered as being expendable.

Borg explains that the difference between the peasant society and previous horticultural societies lay in its socio-economic organisation which basically was "the emergence of centralised forms of government." Another distinctive feature was the development of cities which was "made possible by greater agricultural production," and which led to the development of "city-states, nations and eventually empires" (1994, 101). According to Lenski there also emerged an "unequal distribution of power, privilege and honor" which resulted "largely from the functioning of their political systems" (1966, 210). In other words, as Lenski (1966, 210) explains, "in

---

[15] This estimate is based on Lenski's study of populations in agrarian societies in general terms (1966, 219). The Roman world that spans the lifetime of Augustus and his successors in the first century CE can be classified as an agrarian society.

these societies the institutions of government are the primary source of social inequality."

Lenski (1966, 210) also makes the point that an understanding of the distributive process operative in such a society in the ancient world and the consequences for the non-elite in that society, has to be gleaned from the perspective projected by the elite. He explains:

> For them, the state was not merely an organisation which defined and enforced the rules in the struggle for power and privilege. It was itself one of the objects of the struggle. In fact because of the great powers vested in it, it was the *supreme prize* for all who coveted power, privilege, and prestige. To win control of the state was to win control of the most powerful instrument of self-aggrandizement found in agrarian societies. By the skilful exercise of the powers of the state, a man or group could gain control over much of the economic surplus, and with it at his disposal, could go on to achieve honor and prestige as well. As a consequence, the one who controlled the state would usually fight to preserve his control, while others would strive either to curry his favour and thus share in his good fortune, or would seek to displace him.

Records of military campaigns bear witness to this constant struggle to maintain power. As Lenski (1966, 211) observes, the interests of the common people were not taken into consideration in such campaigns other than perhaps to reward them for their loyalty if victory was achieved. Wars were generally undertaken to enhance the personal power of the ruler or ruling classes or to protect their interests from warring neighbours. Likewise internal factional struggle for power was based on political advantage rather than on principles of justice and protection for the population as a whole.

Such a society, according to Carney (1975, 93), produced "structured immobility." In the Roman dominated world of the first century, family connections generally counted before ability. Any upward mobility was generally only available through warfare and service under the patronage of an autocrat, military leader or landowner. The elite class, however, depended on the labour of the peasant class which was predominantly based on agriculture and which served to furnish the elite with the means for wealth, power and prestige. The wealth of the elite was derived from two sources, either booty obtained in war or from the peasant population in the form of land rent and taxes. Borg maintains that in the Mediterranean world of the first century CE, "generally about two-thirds of the wealth generated by agriculture ended up in the hands of the urban elites. The remaining one-third was left for the other 90 percent of the population, the rural peasants who were, of course, the primary producers of wealth" (1994, 102). The peasant group gained very little from their taxed contributions. Any public administration of the money tended to be spent on the building of palaces, temples and government centres. The construction of highways and bridges were generally intended for the deployment of armies and the journeys of government officials and their retinue, as well as for the transportation of food supplies and luxury items to the major city centres. For the most part the revenue extracted from the peasant class served to increase the personal wealth of those among the elite. As Carney points out, "conspicuous consumption was prized as the mode of living proper to a man of importance" (1975, 97).

The goal in life for the peasant male was self-sufficiency in providing for his family and livestock, and ensuring that there was enough seed for future harvests (Carney 1975, 99). According to Carney there was not a lot of solidarity amongst the peasant class. Prosperity often aroused suspicion that it was gained at the expense of some other person's misfortune. Rather than risk ostracism those in the peasant class tended to keep expectations and aspirations fairly low. There were times, though, when individuals would try to establish some form of client relationship with the elite as a way out of their cycle of poverty, but as Carney (1975, 100) points out, this only served to validate and reinforce the high status of the elite and the low-self-esteem of the peasant.

On occasions members of the elite encouraged the upward mobility of certain people from the peasant class in a patron-client relationship in order to protect or increase their own positions amongst their elite colleagues. Carney (1975, 94) points out that the consequences for the peasant class was that any leadership potential amongst the peasant class was incorporated into the dominant class, leaving the minority groups without natural leaders who might help awaken in the peasant groups a consciousness of their needs and interests:

> leaching off the leadership potential of the out-groups and incorporating it into (and thus consolidating) the dominant group. Thus bereft of their natural leaders, out-groups and minority groups proved unable to awaken to consciousness of, or to assert, their group interests. Patronage virtually precluded the emergence of class consciousness.

Evidence from the sources of ancient Roman literature suggests that amongst the non-elite there was little concerted effort on their part to improve their situation because of the difficulty in challenging political structures that undergirded the society. In spite of the rhetoric surrounding the benefits of the *Pax Romana* concerning the freedom and general well-being of Rome's citizens, the political reform of which Augustus boasted did little to radically alter the plight of the peasant sector of society or to alter the notion that power, privilege and prestige were the prerogative of the elite.

In a world where freedom was regarded as being commensurate with the degree of power that a person or nation was able to secure, the propaganda of *libertas* in whatever form it was presented, had little meaning for those in the peasant sector of the society who had little power to alter the course of their lives.

Reactions in the East to the Freedom of the *Pax Romana*

Whenever a society is overpowered by another or by what Price calls "an intrusion of authority" into its world, a system of adjustments has to take place in order for the subjugated people to come to terms with the change of events and alterations to their lives (1984, 247). As the expansion of Roman influence in the ancient world infiltrated north, south, east and west, the peoples whom Rome subjected through military might responded to the power of Rome in different ways. While it is true that Rome held the balance of power and exacted a submissive response to that power, it is perhaps somewhat too simplistic to judge the situation in black and white terms as one in which the people of the time generally regarded Rome as the oppressor and those nations under its sway as the oppressed. While there were those who strongly objected to Roman presence and Roman ideology which had been foisted on them, for the most part the official policy of many nations, and which many of the people were either inclined or forced to follow, was that of accommodating to this external authority. In responding in this way, not only was their safety assured, but their status and own spheres of power could be safeguarded or enhanced in their own local political circles. The ways in which each nation or city-state responded to Roman rule depended not just on the level of aggression by which Rome had entered their world, but also on the circumstances and structures relating to their own traditional social, religious and political customs.[16]

Two substantially different responses to Roman intrusion into their worlds were that of the inhabitants of the Greek cities of Asia Minor and that of the Jewish people in both Palestine and the Diaspora.[17] The reasons for citing these as examples are twofold. Firstly in both cases the responses and reactions to Roman authority in the ancient world are richly documented and hence provide valuable insight into the political and social responses to the *Pax Romana*. Secondly both cultural contexts were the seed bed out of which the Gospel traditions of first century Christianity developed, and the responses to Roman authority would have had some bearing on the way in which the first century Christians expressed their reaction to the authority of Rome and experienced the subsequent implications of this reaction.

---

[16] As an example of the extensiveness of Roman incursion into the world of many communities see Lily Ross Taylor (1931) 267-283, who cites numerous places in Roman occupied areas where records indicating divine honours bestowed on Caesar, Antony and Augustus in their lifetime have been located. She states that inscriptions from Rome have not been included, and at the time of the publication of her work, modern collections in the east were not easily accessible.

[17] Following Price (1984) 1, Asia Minor is taken to be equivalent to modern Turkey. It comprises the regions of Bithynia, Pontus, Cappadocia, Galatia, Asia, Lycia, Pamphylia, Cilicia and Syria. Following Smallwood (1981) 1, Jewish territory in general refers to what eventually became known as Palestine. It included the regions of Judaea, Samaritis, Idumaea, Galilee and Peraea.

(a) Official Greek Response to Roman Rule in Asia Minor

The Romans had been drawn into the affairs of the different regions and diverse ethnic groups in Asia Minor in various ways from approximately 190 BCE. When Attalus III bequeathed the kingdom of Pergamum to Rome in 133 BCE, Aristonicusa, a pretender to the throne, led a revolt "which lasted three years before it was quelled by combined forces of the Greek cities, the Romans, and the kings of Bithynia, Pontus, and Cappadocia" (Broughton, 1975, 505). This revolt sparked large scale unrest among the people of Asia Minor and in particular between the city and rural sectors. With the suppression of these revolts "Asia became incorporated into the systems of the Roman empire, systems which brought about a transformation in the social, political and economic circumstances of the province" (Trebilco 1994, 293). Even with Rome's involvement in the area at this time, unrest and insurrection were not altogether quashed. The next hundred years in the history of Asia Minor was one in which revolts, insurrections and large scale wars occurred frequently. Although there were attempts at securing peace through various treaties throughout this period, by 31 BCE, when Octavian defeated Antony at Actium, the region had been reduced to economic poverty and its population depleted and war weary. Octavian's victory signalled "the finality of Roman Rule" and was welcomed by the Greek world (Macro 1972, 659).

Autonomy and freedom were regarded as the hallmark of the Greek *polis* and basic to its system of political organisation. With the advent of Roman expansion into the eastern regions of the Mediterranean world, the people of Asia Minor had to come to terms with a system of authority which was "external to the traditional structures of the city" (Price 1984, 1). One of the major ways that the Greek world dealt with the incursion of Roman rule was to incorporate it within their traditional divine ceremonial contexts, or system of ruler cults (1984, 237). When they became subjects of the Roman empire, the Greeks drew on their own ancient rituals to honour their new rulers through the institution of imperial cults (1984, 238). The imperial cults were intimately linked with the political relationships between ruler and subjects. As well as honouring the new ruler, imperial cults were very often linked to diplomatic approaches to the ruler (1984, 242).

Requests for privileges as well as other concerns were frequently associated with offers of cults, and imperial priests often acted as ambassadors to the emperor (1984, 244). The imperial cult was thus "a major part of the web of power that formed the fabric of society" (1984, 248). It not only established and structured the relationship of power between the ruler of Rome and the Greek populace but it "enhanced the dominance of local élites over the populace, of cities over other cities, and Greek over indigenous cultures" (1984, 248).[18]

A significant example of an adaptation of their traditional cultic culture by the Greeks in acknowledging the power of their new rulers, was the institution of an imperial cult to Roma which was in reality "the deification of the power of the Roman state" (Mellor 1981, 966). According to Mellor, it was through the deification of Roma that "the Greeks were able to include the new colossus in the West in their traditional diplomacy. The worship of Roma could be used to convey a wide spectrum of political attitudes: admiration, gratitude, flattery, wariness and sheer terror" (1981, 958). As well as incorporating the goddess Roma into their cultic rituals, the Greeks also retained their Hellenistic practice of honouring individuals who had acted on their behalf as rulers, benefactors or liberators (1981, 976).

During the reign of Augustus, Asia Minor, strictly speaking, was under the administration of the Senate, not the ruler of Rome. However, the people of Asia Minor tended to regard Augustus and not the Senate as their ruler (Magie 1950, 446). Trebilco suggests that the reason for this may have been that Augustus instituted a number of reforms which increased the prosperity of the cities, and the people felt thus bound to him as their benefactor (1994, 298). It may also have been due to the fact that in pledging their allegiance to a person rather than to an office with its possible change of personnel, the people may have felt more confident regarding the security of their future. When Augustus visited Asia Minor in 29 BCE the people were left in no doubt as to who was the distributor of benefactions. The country had undergone substantial devastation because of the wars that had taken place there. Those city-states which had opposed him were duly punished through the levying of taxes and deprivation "of the limited authority over their citizens which had hitherto rested with their assemblies" (Cassius Dio LI 2, 1). However, those who had been loyal to him were duly rewarded with the granting of certain freedoms. Little by little as city-states became aware that in pledging their allegiance to Augustus their security and prosperity would be assured, those who had opposed Octavian soon became his supporter. Benefactions such as the granting of freedoms, the restoration of revenues and the return to all the temples in Asia of the precious ornaments which had been seized by Antony (*RG* 24, 1) would have evoked admiration and gratitude from the people.[19]

Because of the new freedom, peace and stability he had brought to the populace, Augustus was identified in some places with Zeus as either the Liberator or the Olympian or the Guardian of the city, as well as with Apollo in the aspect of

---

[18] See also Gill and Winter (1994) 79-103, particularly Winter's discussion (93-103), where he provides an overview of the rapidity with which the imperial cult spread in the East.

[19] As an example of patron/client networks and their promotion of influence and power, see Holland Hendrix (1992) 41-58.

Liberator.[20] Cultic rituals became an expression of their support and loyalty. Initially Augustus was loathe to accept the worship of his person perhaps because of the criticism that would have been levelled at him by the Senate in Rome for deviating from Republican principles. However he was open to a compromise in order, at least ostensibly, to show respect for the traditions of the subject people as was his policy, and to allow them expression of their traditional cultic rituals. Thus he permitted his name to be linked to that of Roma in cultic rituals (Magie, 1950, 471). The Koinon of Asia, the Koinon of Bithynia and the Koinon of Galatia all built temples to Roma and Augustus (Mellor 1981, 977-80). Mellor explains that "the high cost in building a temple limited them to wealthier cities" (1981, 981). This meant that less wealthier regions were inclined to incorporate the honouring of Roma and Augustus into their local festivals, and in specific dedications of cities, towns, buildings and statues. It was this combination of honouring the ruler and worshipping the goddess Roma that eventually led to the practice of emperor worship in later times.

The renaming of cities and towns was another strategy the Greeks employed to honour the Roman ruler and it also served as another subtle propaganda ploy on the part of the leaders of a city or town, in ensuring that the authority and person of the Roman ruler was kept before the people, and that the leaders would be acknowledged by the Roman ruler for their loyalty to his authority. Many cities were renamed Caesarea or Sebaste, for example, Sebaste in Pontus, Sebaste-Elaeussa in Cilicia, Caesarea which replaced the Cappadocian capital of Mazaca and the harbour capital of Iol-Caesarea established by Juba II of Mauretania (Jacobson 1988, 395-6). Those emperors who succeeded Augustus likewise were honoured with the dedication of cities to their name. As examples, Macro (1972, 672) identifies places such as Philadelphia which was changed to Neocaesareia, and other locations such as Sardis, Hyrcanis and Mostene "all became Caesareia, out of deference to Tiberius who aided them after the disastrous earthquake of c. A.D. 17."

In response to the demonstration of allegiance to his leadership, Augustus in turn rewarded the people by organising a system of taxation and levies on a more systematic basis, and allowed the communities to determine the amounts to be collected. The increase in the prosperity of the communities gave those communities a more definite position in the organisation of the empire and led to the development of urban life and the dissemination of Hellenism throughout the empire (Magie 1950, 471). However, the status of freedom possessed by the cities was not without certain conditions. In many cases cities were given the freedom regarding their local administration, and they were allowed to elect their own officials and make their own laws. But even free cities

---

[20] Whitehorne (1992) 8, states that '[T]he customary oath formula in Augustan times is by the emperor as Zeus Eleutherios, καῖσαρ Αὐτοκράτωρ θεοῦ υἱὸς Ζεὺς Ελευθέριος Σεβαστός in various permutations."

were required to make regular payments to the treasury in Rome. If at any time they allied themselves with an enemy of Rome their treaty with Rome was automatically cancelled and they could lay no claim to any former rights. Any reinstatement of their status, rights and privileges which they might subsequently seek from Rome was only granted if Augustus chose to show clemency towards them. Freedom, as Magie states had become practically dependent on Rome's favour (1950, 474).[21] The setting up of Augustus' *Res Gestae* by officials of Rome and in places of public ritual and community gathering would have been intended to keep this very notion alive in the minds and hearts of the populace of Asia Minor.

(b) Official Jewish Response to Roman Rule

Just as the concept of freedom was fundamental to the political ethos of the Greek world, so too was the concept of freedom fundamental to the political ethos of the Jewish world. Throughout their history as a people, the themes of their exodus from Egypt and of their return from exile in Babylon were celebrated and ritualised by Jews whether they resided in Palestine or resided as minority groups in other areas of the Mediterranean world.[22] They looked to Yahweh, their God, as the liberator who had rescued them from the slavery of Egypt and who had also brought them back from captivity in Babylon when the Persian king, Cyrus, conquered Babylon in 538 BCE. Through religious ritual, they invoked the power of Yahweh to free them from the oppression of their powerful neighbours and vigorously strove to maintain their autonomy as a nation. However when the Jews of the Palestine region were eventually made subject to Rome through conquest, the Jews initially responded with compliance and acquiescence to Rome's authority. This sort of attitude and behaviour was very evident in the official Jewish response towards the power that Rome wielded long before the inauguration of the *Pax Augusta*. Almost one hundred years before Pompey's conquest of Syria in 63 BCE, Judaea had sought allegiance with Rome as testified in 1 Maccabees 8:1-32.[23]

> Judas had reports about the Romans: that they were renowned for their military power and for the favour they showed to those who became their allies, and that any who joined them could be sure of their friendship and strong military support ... So Judas chose Europolemus ... John ... and Jason ... and sent them to Rome to make a treaty of friendship and alliance, in order that the Romans might rid them of foreign oppression,

---

[21] Also, Weinstock (1960) 45: "submission guaranteed peaceful life and the Romans liked to stress this point."

[22] Palestine is here used to denote Jewish territorial regions in the ancient world.

[23] See also Josephus (*AJ* xii. 414-9).

> for it was clear that the Greek empire was reducing them to abject slavery.
> The envoys made their journey to Rome ... and when they came into the
> senate house they spoke as follows: "Judaeus Maccabaeus, his brothers,
> and the Jewish people have sent us to conclude with you a treaty of
> alliance, so that we may be enrolled as your allies and friends."

Mary Smallwood points out that even though the Jews pledged unconditional loyalty to Rome with promises of offering help to Rome when required, Rome did not consider its obligations to the Jews in the same way (1981, 6-7). In fact, as Sara Mandell (1991, 218) observes, it is more than probable that the Maccabees and the ἔθνος were unaware that the treaty they thought they had established with Rome was not considered as such by the Romans. The Romans would have regarded it as a diplomatic offer of friendship, and were thus not bound to legal obligations. In Mandell's view, "Rome served her best interest when she fostered the illusion that diplomatic initiatives were in fact treaty conventions, thus permitting those to whom these instruments were granted to retain an illusion of sovereignty" (1991, 218).

Between the setting up of the treaty and Pompey's march into Syria in 64 BCE, the Romans did relatively little to intervene on behalf of the Jews in the various skirmishes and battles with neighbouring enemies in which the Jews were embroiled. Gradually the treaty lapsed because it was of little practical value to either Rome or the Jews. Although there were times when the Romans made promises to the Jews and issued threats against those attacking the Jews, their motive was one of self-interest rather than that of standing on the side of the oppressed. But even though the Jews felt somewhat let down by the attitude of Rome, they felt that even being associated with Rome was some advantage (Smallwood 1981, 4-11).

In 63 BCE Pompey formally added Syria to Rome's dominion, with Egypt being added to Rome's jurisdiction after the battle of Actium in 31 BCE. The Roman empire thus extended as far as the Euphrates river in the east. Sean Freyne explains that the consequence of Roman territorial expansion meant that Palestine became a strategic buffer zone against Rome's rivals, the Parthians, and that "Rome had to ensure at all times this small but strategically important land was firmly in its control" (1981, 50). The Jews, for their part, also realised that it was to their advantage to remain actively loyal to Rome if they were to be protected against invasions that might come from nations further east.

(c) Roman Intervention in Jewish Affairs

Pompey's annexation of Syria in 64 BCE was a precautionary measure to forestall possible unrest in the eastern part of the empire, and since it would have proved potentially difficult for Rome if Palestine had been allowed to maintain its independence, Pompey decided also on the incorporation of Palestine under Roman rule. The quarrel between the Hasmonaean brothers as to who should rule and the ensuing power struggles that developed regarding allegiance provided a convenient opportunity for Pompey to act and establish Roman control (Smallwood 1981, 16-7). He allowed specific hellenistic cities to retain their freedom, and then proceeded to divide the Jewish state into four separate territories "in which Judaism in some form was the sole dominant religion—Galilee, most of Samaritis, Judaea and eastern Idumaca. It had a foot across the Jordan only along the narrow strip of Peraea, and included no large cities except Jerusalem" (1981, 29). Hyrcanus II was restored to the office of high priest and assumed the title of ethnarch. Smallwood interprets Pompey's action of removing the Greco-Syrian population from Jewish administration and dividing up the Jewish regions as a way of crippling the Jews economically and humbling them politically (1981, 29). Although Pompey's aim was eventually to arrange for the client kingdom to be incorporated under Roman jurisdiction as a province, he initially judged that it was wiser not to begin arrangements for annexation as this would have resulted in explosive resistance on the part of the Jews. Rather, in setting up a client kingdom he allowed the Jews a semblance of freedom in allowing them to manage their own affairs, and which up to a certain extent satisfied Jewish patriotism (1981, 30). By reducing the power of Hasmoean rule, Pompey was able to forestall any "cnergetic political action hostile to Roman interests" (1981, 30).

Antipater, the Idumaean whose ambition it was to assume kingship, was far from pleased with Pompey's solution to the situation, but as he had no redress, his only course of action was to demonstrate his loyalty to the Roman leader. His opportunity to prove his loyalty presented itself when he was able to use his connections with the Nabataeans to negotiate a peace settlement between them and Rome and from which Rome benelited. According to Smallwood, pleasing Rome in this way "was the prototype of the policy which Antipater and his son Herod after him were to follow consistently" (1981, 30). The following thirty years in Rome's history was a time of power struggle amongst rival factions in Rome for positions of leadership. For those nations or city-states wanting to court favour, the important question "became one of loyalty not to Rome but to the right individual Roman" (1981, 30).

Following the death of Pompey, the pro-Pompeians, Hyrcanus and Antipater realised the precariousness of their position and sought to court alliance with Julius Caesar, who responded to these overtures of friendship. According to Josephus, Caesar commended the efforts of Antipater in the war in Egypt, confirmed Hyrcanus' role as High Priest and gave both of them Roman citizenship and exemption from taxes (*AJ* xiv. 136-7). Upon further trouble brewing at the instigation of Aristobulus, Caesar organised a settlement in Palestine in which Hyrcanus' position as high priest and ethnarch of the Jewish state was again confirmed. Josephus relates that the decree of the settlement was inscribed on a bronze tablet and written in Greek and Latin and kept at the Capitol, while a copy was sent to the Jews (*AJ* xiv. 188.91; cf. *BJ* I. 200).[24] Antipater accordingly was made procurator of Judaea (*BJ* I.199). Smallwood makes the observation that Rome's motive for giving this position to Antipater was so that in this capcity, he "was to act as resident representative of Rome, safeguarding Roman financial interests" (1981, 39). Josephus (*AJ* xiv. 185-264) relates the details of a number of other decrees which Caesar promulgated, and which were granted to the Jews, both in Palestine and in the Diaspora, as well as details of further correspondence pertaining to the favours granted to the Jews by Rome. He also adds that there were many more which he had not included, but that what he had cited was sufficient testimony to prove Rome's goodwill and thus cause enough for the Jews to respond with loyalty to Rome (*AJ* xiv. 265-7). Josephus' personal position towards Rome and towards the Jews, as it is reflected in his writings, fluctuates between support of Rome's intervention in Jewish affairs and criticism of this intervention. It is therefore somewhat difficult to judge whether he is speaking here in praise of the status quo or whether his comments contain a degree of irony.

(d) Herod's Response to Roman Authority

In spite of the settlement that Caesar had instituted in Palestine, it was not long before enmity between Hyrcanus and Antipater again erupted. When strife broke out in the north in protest against the pro-Roman stance, Antipater, seizing the opportunity and acting independently of Hyrcanus, appointed his two oldest sons Phasael and Herod as military governors of Judaea and Galilee respectively. Herod worked assiduously at securing power for himself by pledging allegiance to Sextus Caesar who was the Roman governor in Syria. In 46 BCE Sextus was murdered by the pro-Pompeians. Herod immediately retreated, but then returned at the instigation of Antipater with troop reinforcements to aid the pro-Caesarian cause (Smallwood 1981, 44-6).

Herod's rise to power in Palestine coincided with the struggle amongst the Roman generals who were vying for power in the Roman world. Josephus relates that after the defeat of Cassius at Philippi, Caesar returned to Italy, and Antony set out for Asia and was met by many embassies. Amongst the various delegations were those who brought accusations against both Phasael and Herod for virtually wresting sovereignty from

---

[24] Compare also the *Res Gestae* of Augustus. From the evidence of Suetonius (2. 101.4) and archaeological evidence pertaining to the *Res Gestae*, as well as this statement from Josephus, it would seem that it was a practice that significant decrees or statements made by Rome were inscribed on bronze tablets in both Latin and Greek and copies sent to the appropriate bodies.

Hyrcanus. But since Herod had already established himself as a friend of Antony's, and in Josephus' view bribed Antony on this occasion, Antony was able to use the situation to his advantage as both sides of the Jewish warring parties were pledging their loyalty to Rome. He granted the Jews extra privileges in Tyre, installed Phasael and Herod as tetrarchs, "and entrusted to them the government of the Jews" (*AJ* xiv. 325). Further protests and skirmishes subsequently erupted from those opposing Phasael and Herod, and as an expediency measure, the help of the Parthians was sought. The Parthians took advantage of the situation and proved to be treacherous to Phasael's and Herod's cause. When Phasael and Hyrcanus were captured by the Parthians, Herod initially sought refuge in Idumaea and eventually set sail for Rome to relay his troubles to Antony. Josephus (*AJ* xiv. 381-3; cf *BJ* I. 283.3) describes Antony's reception of Herod:

> Antony was moved to pity by the reverses of Herod ... and partly in memory of Antipater's hospitality, partly because of the money which Herod promised to give him if he became king, as he had promised once before when he was appointed tetrarch, but chiefly because of his hatred for Antigonus—for he considered him a seditious person and an enemy of the Romans—he was eager to give Herod the assistance he asked for.

Octavian was also "more than ready to co-operate in the things which Herod wished" (*AJ* xiv. 384). When Antony proposed to the Senate that it was to the advantage of the Romans in their war against the Parthians that Herod should be king, the senate voted unanimously (*BJ* I. 284). Josephus relates that

> when the senate was adjourned, Antony and Caesar went out with Herod between them, and the consuls and other magistrates leading the way, in order to sacrifice and to deposit the decree in the Capitol (*AJ* xiv. 388 cf. *BJ* I. 285).

Mary Smallwood comments that the honouring of Herod as "King of the Jews" in this fashion while somewhat incongruous, was "clear evidence of the superficiality of his Judaism and a foretaste of the way in which his rule was to be an attempted fusion between the incompatible worlds of Judaism and Hellenism" (1981, 56).

(e) The Alliance between Augustus and Herod

After the battle of Actium in which Antony was defeated by Octavian, who was later to be known as Augustus, Herod realised that his own position of power was threatened, as he had been a supporter of Antony. Having made contingency plans for his survival by arranging the death of Hyrcanus and organising the safety of his family and fortune, he went to meet Octavian. Josephus states that instead of turning to supplication or acknowledging that he had been wrong in following Antony, Herod acknowledged to Octavian his friendship and support of Antony because Antony had been his benefactor and thus deserving of his steadfast loyalty. He pledged the same degree of loyalty to Octavian. Josephus remarks that this display of loyalty "greatly attracted Caesar, who was honourable and generous so that the acts which had caused charges to be brought against Herod now served to form the basis of Caesar's goodwill toward him" (*AJ* xv. 194-5; cf. *BJ* I. 387-392). Smallwood interprets Octavian's motives for his favourable response to Herod somewhat differently. She draws attention to the fact that for over thirty years "Antipater and his sons had consistently supported whichever Roman war lord was currently in the ascendant in the East, and Octavian knew that he could count on Herod to transfer his loyalty effectively" (1981, 69). Smallwood further explains Octavian's political strategy:

> Octavian's policy was to maintain Antony's arrangements in the East, if working well: provided that a king was satisfactory, it was immaterial who had appointed him. Herod's record over the last seven years had vindicated the triumvirs' decision in 40, and it was clear that there was no practical alternative to his continued rule, if the important but turbulent Jewish frontier state was to be kept under proper control. Herod's war with Malchus had proved him competent to defend the country against external pressure, and with his personal position dependent on the retention of Roman goodwill, he could be relied on to toe the Roman line (1981, 69).

As proof of his gratitude and loyalty, Herod showered Octavian and his friends with gifts, and when Octavian arrived at Ptolemais on his way from Syria to invade Egypt, Herod "furnished his army with gifts of welcome and an abundance of provisions" (*AJ* xv. 199; cf. *BJ* I. 394-5). The level of extravagance speaks for itself, for as Josephus relates, Herod housed Octavian and his friends in a hundred and fifty apartments which "were all appointed with rich magnificence for their comfort," supplied them with all that they needed and gave Octavian a present of eight hundred talents (*AJ* xv. 200). James Newsome (1992, 284) observes that with reference to Herod, "it is not entirely coincidental that his period of greatest strength also marked the beginning of the *Pax Romana*." Roman domination in the guise of *Pax Romana* provided Herod with the opportunity of conducting the affairs of his realm with minimum interference from Rome, but at the same time of being assured of the support of Rome should he need it, and on the condition that he continued his support of Rome.

It seems that Herod's interest in Hellenism rather than Judaism became more and more apparent, for as Josephus (*AJ* xv. 267) states, "Herod went still farther in departing from the native customs, and through foreign practices he gradually corrupted the ancient way of life." Because of the competition in the provinces and cities of the

Mediterranean world for Rome's favour, Herod, as Schürer (1979, 34) states "could not fall behind" other nations. Accordingly, he arranged for athletic contests to be held every five years in honour of the new Caesar and built a large amphitheatre for that purpose. He invited famous people and people from other nations to these spectacles (*AJ* xv. 268-273). One of the areas of contention which drew hostile reactions from amongst the Jews was the inclusion of inscriptions to Caesar which adorned the theatre and an exhibition of the gold and silver trophies of the nations which he had won in war (*AJ* xv 275-6). Mary Smallwood points out that Herod's motive for including these trophies was to keep the people "aware of the overlordship of Rome, as was his duty" (1981, 85).

Herod also undertook a vast building programme. He built fortresses throughout the region, the most lavish of which was the Herodium and which was his own refuge. The city of Samaria was renamed Sebaste, and Strato's Towers became Caesarea, both in honour of Augustus. The city of Caesarea contained a "very costly palace, with civic halls" and also "a well-protected harbour" (*AJ* xv.332; cf. *BJ* I .401-414).[25] The Temple of Roma and Augustus appeared to dominate the town (Mellor 1981, 982). Josephus (*BJ*.I.414) describes the edifice:

> On an eminence facing the harbour-mouth stood Caesar's temple, remarkable for its beauty and grand proportions; it contained a colossal statue of the emperor, not inferior to the Olympian Zeus, which served for its model, and another of Rome, rivalling that of Hera at Argos

In order to assure Roman dignitaries of his loyalty, and no doubt by way of gaining status among the elite of the Roman world, he not only built cities, temples and other civic buildings in areas outside Jewish territory, but provided endowments for various projects such as parklands, shipbuilding, road building, and also set about reigniting interest and participation in the Olympic Games (*BJ* I. 422). He knew, of course, that any arrangement for the building of monuments within Jewish territory would have led to open rebellion by the people. However, Herod's plan seems to have been that of increasing his own influence within the Roman world and at the same time that of creating situations for Hellenistic influence to further permeate Jewish culture. This seems to be not just a consequence of Rome's expectations of him as a client king of Rome but also because of his predilection for Hellenistic culture.

While much of his efforts were geared to pleasing the Roman leader and Roman officials, Herod was also well aware that his position as king of the Jews was always somewhat precarious. Although he had Rome as an ally, he knew that his hold on kingship did not rest on the power of Rome alone. Various faction elements among the Jews which surfaced again and again throughout his reign as well as unrest among the

---

[25] Newsome (1992) 286-289, discusses the ambitious projects that Herod undertook.

general population, had the potential for bringing his reign to an end. In order to forestall such an eventuality, Herod appeased the Jewish people by undertaking the rebuilding of the Temple, an act which was intended to impress both the Jews as well as peoples of other nations (*BJ* I. 401).[26] Cultivating and maintaining a public image both at home and abroad was a major preoccupation for Herod, and such extravagances were geared to that end (Jacobson 1988, 386-403).

Before his death in 4 BCE, Herod had composed his will nominating Archelaus, his eldest son, heir to the throne and his other son, Antipas as tetrarch, while Philip inherited the region of Trachonitis and neighbouring districts. According to Josephus riots broke out after Herod's death particularly over the harsh punishments that Herod had exacted on those who had torn down the golden eagle from the temple as well as over other atrocities and extravagances for which Herod had been responsible (*BJ* II. 4-7). Intrigue amongst the family of Herod as to who should be the beneficiaries of the inheritance that Herod had bequeathed, resulted in deputations being sent to Rome asking for Augustus' intervention (*BJ* II. 14-92).

The response of Augustus was first of all to install Archelaus as ethnarch with the promise of making him king if he proved himself worthy and able. The ethnarchy of Archelaus comprised the whole of Idumaea and Judaea as well as Samaria. The rest of Herod's jurisdiction was divided into two tetrarchies. Antipas was given the area of Galilee and Peraea, while Philip was given the region of Trachonitis and surrounding districts (*BJ* II. 94-6). Augustus then distributed the estates and monies to various members of the family. However, deputations reaching Caesar in protest against the cruelty perpetrated by Archelaus resulted in Augustus taking direct action. He banished Archelaus and declared that his territory was to become a province of Rome and administered by a procurator with full powers which also included the administration of the death penalty (*BJ* II. 117). Josephus relates that "Philip and Herod surnamed Antipas, continued to govern their respective tetrarchies" (*BJ* II. 167). After the death of Augustus in 14 CE, and with Tiberius now as ruler, Herod Antipas and Philip retained their tetrarchies. Josephus relates that each of them founded cities: "Philip built Caesarea near the sources of the Jordan ... and Julias in lower Gaulanitis; Herod built Tiberius in Galilee and a city which also took the name of Julia, in Peraea" (*BJ* II. 168). The names of these cities were undoubtedly in honour of the Roman imperial family and a way of invoking imperial favour.

In spite of the rhetoric regarding Jewish control over their own affairs, the relationship between Augustus and Herod was not one of shared power. Rome's domination in the affairs of another nation was pervasive. The Jews were left in no doubt as to who had the real power over their destiny. Courting Rome's favour and

---

[26] In *AJ* XV 380-425, Josephus describes the Temple in great detail.

compliance to the wishes of Rome came to be regarded by the Jewish establishment as the only option if any semblance of autonomy was to be maintained.

(f) The Response of the Jews of the Diaspora to Roman Rule

The Roman administration affected not only the Jewish people residing in Palestine but also those dispersed throughout the Mediterranean world. Some had settled in other regions because of economic advantages particularly in trade, but many others had been taken as prisoners in some of the wars. The Jews of the Diaspora obviously enjoyed many of the benefits of living in an Hellenistic environment, particularly economically and in some respects culturally (Applebaum 1976, 701-727). Nevertheless as minority groups they tended to keep to themselves, vigorously maintaining their traditional Jewish customs. Mary Smallwood claims that there is much evidence in classical Roman and Greek literature which testifies to the "amusement, contempt or hatred" that was levelled at the Jew living in a gentile world (1981, 123). One of the specific customs to which the Jews felt honour bound was that of contributing to the temple tax in Jerusalem. Consequently the city of Jerusalem amassed great wealth. After relating the incident where the Roman governor Crassus violated the temple and carried off all the gold, Josephus adds:

> no one need wonder that there was so much wealth in our temple, for all the Jews throughout the habitable world, and those who worshipped God, even from Asia and Europe, had been contributing to it for a very long time. And there is no lack of witnesses to the great amount of the sums mentioned, nor have they been raised to so great a figure through boastfulness or exaggeration on our part, but there are many historians who bear us out ... (*AJ* xiv. 111).

Smallwood (1981, 126) points out that "under Roman rule the Jews in Asia were free to send their Temple tax to Jerusalem" and that this was consistent with the legislation that Julius Caesar had decreed. It was this freedom allowed to the Jews by Caesar that often provoked hostile reactions from non-Jews who were subject to the tithes and taxes of the state. Another source of contention between Jews and non-Jews living under Roman rule was the issue of conscription. Permission was given to the Jews for exemption from conscription because of their dietary laws and the fact that their religious practices did not permit them to bear arms on the Sabbath, nor to march on the Sabbath (*AJ* xiv. 226). Even though the religious practices and laws of the Jews were often ridiculed, nevertheless the Roman authorities for the most part allowed the Jews freedom in relation to their customs as long as this did not undermine Roman authority as such.

Augustus even went so far as to confirm sanctions against infringements regarding the religious freedom of the Jews. It would appear that although the Jews received preferential treatment from the highest authorities, it seems that from the number of appeals by the Jews of Asia and Cyrene they were not always so well treated by local authorities. Josephus (*AJ*. XVI. 162-165) cites the following example of Augustus' intervention on their behalf:

> "Caesar Augustus, Pontifex maximus with tribunician power, decrees as follows. Since the Jewish nation has been found well disposed to the Roman people not only at the present time but also in time past, and especially in the time of my father the emperor Caesar, as has their high priest Hyrcanus, it has been decided by me and my council under oath, with the consent of the Roman people, that the Jews may follow their own customs in accordance with the law of their fathers, just as they followed them in the time of Hyrcanus, high priest of the Most High God, and that their sacred monies shall be inviolable and may be sent up to Jerusalem and delivered to the treasurers in Jerusalem, and that they may not give bond (to appear in court) on the Sabbath or on the day of preparation for it (Sabbath Eve after the ninth hour). And if anyone is caught stealing their sacred books or their sacred monies from a synagogue or an ark (of the Law), he shall be regarded as sacrilegious, and his property shall be confiscated to the public treasury of the Romans. As for the resolution which was offered by them in my honour concerning the piety which I show to all men, and on behalf of Gaius Marcius Censorinus, I order that it and the present edict be set up in the most conspicuous (part of the temple) assigned to me by the federation (*koinon*) of Asia in Ancyra. If anyone transgresses any of the above ordinances, he shall suffer severe punishment." This was inscribed upon a pillar in the temple of Caesar.

Although Augustus appears here to be on the side of the powerless, it was in fact a display of his power, and on which as the *Res Gestae* indicates, all subject people became dependent.

It seems that after Judaea was officially constituted as a Province in 6 CE, the Jews of this region were allowed to retain their religious customs and practices that the Jews of the Diaspora under Roman rule had secured from both Caesar and Augustus. Instead of honouring the emperor with the customary oath or offering sacrifices to the emperor as befitted a deity in the manner of their Greek neighbours, it seems that they had devised a custom in keeping with their own Law, of offering sacrifices and prayers for the well-being of the emperor. These rituals took place twice daily (Smallwood 1981, 148).[27] Thackeray (1976, 399) surmises that this ritual was presumably held at the morning and evening observances in the Temple. Here then, as in the Greek context,

---

[27] Both Josephus (*Ap*. ii, 77; *BJ* . II. 197) and Philo (*Leg*. 189-329) relate the incident regarding the altercation between Gaius Caesar (Caligula) and the Jews in 40 CE, when the Jews expressed their opposition to Gaius' insistence that a statue of himself be placed in the Temple. Josephus states that the Jews offered prayers in the Temple twice daily for the emperor but refused to have the statue placed there. Philo (*Leg*. 189) likewise refers to prayers, votive offerings and sacrifices offered for Caesar.

albeit in a different mode, the authority and person of the emperor was kept firmly before the people.

Voices of Protest

The *Pax Romana* promulgated by Augustus and to which successive emperors appealed in order to win over the people, was the product of a system of Roman administrative procedures by which structures were set in place to ensure that the power of Rome did not come under threat. Hence it was the policy of Augustus and one which was largely adopted by his successors, to allow the subject nations in the eastern part of the empire to maintain their traditional and cultural practices and forms of administration on the local level provided that Rome's power and authority was not undermined. Rome's role in the appointment of client kings, magnates, governors, procurators, chief priests, officials, publicans and tax collectors, as well as the stationing of army units in various regions, was designed to ensure that both the service of Rome and loyalty to the ruler were maintained (Neusner 1982, 40). While theoretically Rome provided for the safety and security of the populace, imposition of Roman officialdom severely restricted the people's self-determination. The net result was that in the Greek cities of Asia Minor the vital political activity which had constituted the very life force of the Greek city state, was stifled. In its place there arose competitive efforts to win recognition from higher authorities through embassies to those authorities, extravagant building programmes and lavish festivals to please the authorities or to win recognition or favours from them. The funds for such ventures were more often than not, extracted from the general populace (Price 1974, 96-7).

In the regions of Palestine the people were well aware that their very survival as a nation depended on the protection of Rome, and as a consequence the desire to appease Rome took on extravagant proportions. Again as in Asia Minor, the furnishing of such extravaganza devolved upon the populace. On a day to day basis, it was not the emperor himself, but the appointed officials clinging to their spheres of power with whom the populace had to deal. Often motivated by personal ambition and greed for power and wealth, the officials could be unscrupulous in the execution of their duties and their dealings with the people. When this was combined with the authority of emperors who were administratively weak or who exhibited megalomaniac behaviour, the result spelt disaster for those caught in the system.[28]

In comparison with other sectors of the Roman empire, there is extensive evidence available from the eastern part of the Roman occupied world concerning Roman rule

---

[28] On the relationship between the political and social structure of the Greek city and Roman *imperium*, see Anthony D. Macro (1972) 658-697.

and the notion of *Pax Romana*. However, the perspective that is presented by ancient historians, and which is also to be found in edicts, letters, inscriptions and numismatic evidence is generally the view that was espoused by the upper echelon of officialdom. There is little available directly from the perspective of the general populace.[29] Nevertheless evidence can be gleaned from official sources which indicate the mood of the people from time to time.

In a detailed and comprehensive examination of the laws that were promulgated and the various decrees that emanated from Rome both in the late Republic and the early principate, Brunt (1961, 189-223) has demonstrated that these laws were set in place as a response to complaints which related such actions as extortion, malpractice, and oppressive administration that was endemic in the provinces throughout the Roman occupied world at that time. It was the practice that actions and sanctions could be brought against individuals as well as whole cities or communities. Both Suetonius (Suet. *Tib.* XXXVII. 3) and Cassius Dio (54. 7) mention the situation at Cyzicus in 20 BC when the citizens forfeited the freedom that they had earned in the war with Mithridates because of the lawlessness of some of their number and the atrocities perpetrated against Roman citizens. In spite of the impression abroad that nations under Rome's sway were enjoying the fruits of the *Pax Romana*, Macro states that there is evidence to support the claim that "there was a reservoir of ill-will among the lower classes ready to be converted into open violence which was inevitably directed against those who were seen to represent imperial power, namely, the magnates, whenever social conditions reached a level of desperation" (1972, 690).[30]

From the Jewish sources available, three categories of protest against the power of the authorities can be identified. The first was the complaint to official bodies against excessive demands or maltreatment by officials of a lower order. Josephus recounts the deputation of an embassy to Augustus who brought complaints against the excesses of Herod's administration (*BJ* II 80-92 [vi. 1, 2]). In a further incident which Philo recounts, a petition was sent to Tiberius asking his intervention in a dispute with Pilate over the placing of shields bearing the emperor's name and which had been set up in Jerusalem (*De lege* XXX viii. 209-306). The protest of complaint tended to centre on specific local issues regarding the right to exercise power.

A second category of protest was the resistance movement. This could take a number of forms, with some being more moderate than others. However, all had as

---

[29] Brunt draws attention to the fact that there is more evidence available from Jewish sources relating to conditions in the province of Judaea than from other provinces. He makes the point that "if we had similar evidence from other provinces, we might well find that *mutatis mutandis* like conditions prevailed to some extent"(1961) 214.

[30] For example the speech that Josephus attributes to Agrippa who attempts to dissuade the Jews from war with Roman authorities, there is a long litany of the benefits that all nations enjoyed because of their submission to the power of Rome (*BJ* II, 345-388). In particular see the reference to the liberty enjoyed by Greece and Asia in *BJ* II, 365-8.

their common *raison d'être* opposition to new situations, ideas and practices that were alien to national traditions and aspirations. The first of these resistance groups and perhaps the more ambivalent of any of the groups in their attitude to Rome, was that of the Pharisees, who are described by Josephus as "the most accurate interpreters of the laws" (*BJ* II 162-3). Rhoads claims that the essence of Pharisaism was "the attempt to put the whole of life under the control of the law" (1976, 34). Essentially they were a religious group rather than a political group (Schürer 1979, 394). Freyne states that the movement probably originated among temple priests who held the view that the sacredness of the temple needed to be extended to every day life situations (1980, 110-111). This was probably the reason for their preoccupation with interpreting the law according to the changing conditions of the times. According to Freyne (1980, 111), Pharisees were lay men, "middle class artisans, traders, officials and other service people, whose emergence was the direct result of the economic and social impact of Hellenism." Josephus (*AJ* XVIII, 15) states that they were "extremely influential with the townsfolk." While ostensibly they did not regard themselves as a political force, they were not, as Rhoads points out, "completely depoliticized" (1976, 38). There were occasions when some Pharisees opposed Herod and his methods and refused to take the oath to Herod or Caesar. The Pharisees were not necessarily uniform in their political views or in their interpretation of the laws. While they opposed gentile rule in principle, they nevertheless generally regarded the presence of Rome favourably.

Another resistance group was the Sadducee party. The Sadducees belonged to the wealthy aristocratic ruling class of Israel, and "were the most conservative class in Judaism" (Rhoads, 1976, 30-40). They controlled the temple religion, and because of their wealth and social standing exerted great influence in the political direction of the nation (Schürer 1979, 404-414). Rhoads (1976, 41) explains their strategy:

> By means of the applications of the Torah throughout the land and the proper worship in the temple, the Sadducees hoped to secure liberation of the nation, so that the Israelite kingdom might be free as it had once been under the rule of David. In principle this implied the exclusion of gentiles, that is, Romans, from the land. In practice, however, the Sadducees sought to bring about their eschatological vision of an independent temple-state by trying to achieve as much autonomy as possible within the Roman Empire by use of the realistic political and diplomatic means at their disposal.

Generally then they accommodated to Roman rule as it ensured their position of influence in the society and access to maintaining their wealth and power. Josephus states that the Sadducees had "the confidence of the wealthy alone but no following among the populace, while the Pharisees have the support of the masses" (*AJ* XIII, 298). However they played a significant role in the national resistance against Rome, particularly in relation to the holding of temple administration.

A third resistance group was the Essene community. Freyne points out that in relation to the political ambitions of the Sadducees, the Essenes stood at the other end of the spectrum (1980, 105). Rhoads argues that they probably originated from the Hasidaeans, "strict Jews who had remained loyal to Jewish tradition in the face of forced Hellenization by Syrian overlords in the early second century B.C.E." (1976, 43). They seemed to have lived parallel with mainstream society in that although they resided "in large numbers in every town," they developed their own ascetic life styles and customs (*BJ* II, 119-27).[31] For this reason, Rhoads (1976, 44) suggests that they probably did not make "any significant contribution to the political history of Israel." However, their very life style as counter culture would certainly not have gone unnoticed by mainstream society, and in their own way the Essenes would have challenged the extravagant life style and political aspirations of the rich and influential in Palestine.

The fourth group which Josephus mentions were the Zealots. These were fanatical freedom fighters who resorted to armed rebellion against the ruling parties, and sought to drive out Roman presence and influence from Palestine. Their ultimate goal was to re-establish Jewish control whatever the cost. Their motive was both religious and political, as Freyne (1980, 120) points out:

> The passion for liberty and the refusal to accept man as lord except God, attributed by Josephus to the Fourth Philosophy have a certain archaic ring about them, echoing the earlier Israelite religion. Freedom from slavery was the fundamental Israelite experience of the exodus from Egypt and the second command of the decalogue prohibited the acceptance of any other gods except Yahweh, which the Zealots turned into a political programme for rejecting Roman rule."

Any knowledge that has come down to the modern reader concerning the Zealots is mostly derived from the writings of Josephus. Theissen (1977, 80-81) drawing on the information from Josephus explains the political agenda of this resistance movement:

> Great stress was laid above all on the first commandment. The sole rule of God stood at the centre of the programmme of the zealots (*BJ* 2.8.1, § 118; 7.10.1, §§410, 418f.; *Antt.* 18.1.6, §23). The prohibition against making images was observed with fanatical seriousness. It was forbidden to make, look at, touch or carry images. Coins were tabu. So, too, were the Hellenistic cities, in which one would inevitably come upon the images of the gods (Hippolytus, *Adv.haer.* 9.26). The commandment to practice circumcision was also observed fanatically. Uncircumcised Jews were kidnapped and given the alternative of execution as lawbreakers or observing the law (*Adv.haer.* 9.26). On the other hand, fundamental social laws, e.g. the commandment to honour one's parents, were broken. In the Jewish war, deserters were killed and left unburied. Members of the movement who wanted to bury their relatives were

---

[31] See also Schürer (1979) 562-590.

themselves executed and left unburied (*BJ* 4.6.2, §§381ff.; cf Matt. 8.21f.). It was impossible to avoid the commandment against killing. The prohibition against slavery was disregarded: hostages were taken to force the release of imprisoned fellow-members (*Antt.* 20.9.3, §§208ff.)... They excluded the rich, treating them as if they were 'no difference between them and foreigners, as they were thought to have betrayed the freedom won by the Jews at such cost and avowedly to have chosen servitude to Rome' (*BJ* 7.8.1, §255).

According to Josephus the group marshalled their rebellion against the procurator Florus in 66 CE as a result of the many abuses and atrocities he and his troops had metered out on the people. The rebelliousness escalated into outright revolt against Rome with the Jewish War of 67-70 CE. However, while the Zealots seemed to have developed into a formal party and unified in their mission of overthrowing the ruling authorities, their organisation consisted in a number of leaders who gathered supporters mainly from the peasant classes of the society. These people, no doubt, would have been ready to support any leader who would extricate them from the poverty and the powerless situation that was their lot. Although Josephus writes that the Zealots rose to prominence at the beginning of the war in 67 CE, he also refers to the activities of a revolutionary movement instigated by Judas the Galilean in 6 CE., whom Josephus names as the leader of the "fourth of the philosophies" (*AJ* XVIII, 23-25), and identifies other revolutionary groups that were in existence prior to 67-70 CE.

Besides naming the Zealots, he also identifies the *Sicarii* who were so named because they went armed with concealed daggers, as well as the Idumaeans, the followers of John of Gischala and the followers of Simon bar Giora (*BJ* VII, 262-70). Josephus does not provide any information as to how these groups originated, but his account of their various revolutionary activities and methods suggests that revolutionary movements of one kind or another were very much in existence from the beginning of the first century CE. What is interesting about these movements was their very stark ideological differences, motives and methods for achieving their aims. At the same time, they had as their common enemy Roman authorities and Roman sympathisers.

Broadly speaking, then, these "four philosophies" of which Josephus speaks constituted the major organised "resistance" in Palestine in the first century CE. Each of the four groups strove to exert its influence in order to claim power. All were intent on setting up a system of governing control which would ensure the fulfilment of their aims.

Occasions when the people were pushed to the edge and rose in revolt could be regarded as a third form of protest. More often than not the people took their grievances to any one who would champion their cause. However, Josephus relates a number of occasions when the people acted of their own accord. One such example occurred at Pentecost in 4 CE with the arrival in Jerusalem of the officer Sabinus who had commandeered the royal treasures (*BJ* II, 39-54). On another occasion when Pilate under cover of night brought the standards of Caesar into Jerusalem, "the indication of the townspeople stirred the countryfolk who flocked in crowds" to protest against this violation of the temple (*BJ* II, 169-174). While these and other instances which Josephus relates provide evidence of the people taking a stand on issues, for the most part the crowd was not aligned.[32] However, at the same time they could be very easily swayed by one or other of the "four philosophy" groups that Josephus describes, or indeed by Roman officials themselves. All protests, at whatever level, were regarded as a means of claiming a way out of the power and control exerted over them by other people or parties.

In spite of the different political allegiances to which groups within the Jewish population adhered, and in spite of the difference in the ways and means of registering their protest against Roman domination, the one uniting factor for the Jews was the hope of freedom which was conceptualised in their expectation of a messiah who would restore to them what they regarded as their rightful inheritance of peace and prosperity. This was celebrated religiously in their stories, poetry and ritual ceremonies.

The social, economic and political reality of first century Palestine, however, was of a different order. Myers (1988, 54) identifies five main currents that contributed to the instability of the nation:

1. the waning fortunes of the native kingship;
2. direct and indirect Roman administration of the colony;
3. the power of the high priesthood and clerical aristocracy, including the Sadducean party;
4. the shifting political alignments of the Jewish renewal groups, especially the Pharisees and Essenes;
5. the various strands of popular resistance and dissent among the masses.

Another voice of protest in the first century was heard initially in the margins of the Roman empire in the regions of Galilee and Judaea, and which in time was heard throughout the Roman occupied world. The initiator of this protest was Jesus of Nazareth whose agenda was the articulation of both a social critique and a social vision. His critique was neither that of a restorationist nor a revolutionary, but rather that of a subverter of those social institutions and the ideologies that shaped them, and which had created such vast inequalities within society. His vision was one of proclaiming a radical way of creating a social reality where domination, enslavement and elitism would give way to mutuality, love, compassion and inclusiveness; where the dignity

---

[32] Horsley (1993) 99, points out that the protests of the general population were by no means always those of spontaneous rioting. He cites evidence indicating "massive popular demonstrations," particularly around the time of Jesus' public ministry.

and worth of the human person would be respected and upheld and where no person was called father except God (Mt 23:9). In essence, Jesus of Nazareth set out to preach a concept of freedom which was to challenge the notion of freedom that was promulgated by the dominant political forces prevailing in the Mediterranean world of the first century CE.

CHAPTER FOUR

THE GOSPEL OF MARK

Preamble

The communication of the message that Jesus of Nazareth proclaimed was not inscribed on stone. Initially communicated by word of mouth, the message or kerygma was gradually transcribed into textual forms. A further step in the process in the transmission of the message of Jesus, as Walter Ong (1987, 11) explains, "was to reorganise the oral kerygma so as to bring out its current relevancy."[1] The author of Mark's Gospel undertook the interpretation of the oral kerygma by producing a unified narrative which encapsulated the message of Jesus. The Gospel of Mark, therefore, represents two worlds; the one constructed by the author, that is the world of Jesus of Nazareth, and the one in which the author himself lives (Myers 1988, 40). Although these worlds stand approximately forty years apart they stand within the same socio-political era of first century Mediterranean society. The narrative world of Mark draws the reader both to the world of Jesus and to the author's own world. According to Myers (1988, 40), the narrative world constructed by the author is "an ideological product" of the world in which the author lives. However it can be argued that the narrated world constructed by the author is a theological reflection of the message of Jesus of Nazareth and the relevance of this message in the life experience of the author and of the audience for whom he was writing.[2] This theological reflection is concentrated on the social situation of the world of the author, and focuses on the religious, ideological, political and economic implications and consequences with which such a reflection is engaged. What is of historical significance regarding Mark's textual interpretation of the message of Jesus, as Myers (1988, 39) succinctly states, is that it "stands virtually alone among the literary achievements of antiquity for one reason: it is a narrative for and about the common people."[3]

---

[1] See also Bultmann's discussion on the development of the kerygma in the Hellenistic Church (1952, 63-92).

[2] Martin Hengel also emphasises this aspect (1985) 37-8.

[3] Among the numbers of recent studies pertaining to the socio-literary dimension of the Gospel of Mark, the following have particularly influenced this work: Bilezikian (1977), Borg (1994), Burridge (1992), Collins (1992), Crossan (1993), Donahue (1992), Dormeyer & Frankemölle (1984), Dormeyer (1989), Fowler (1991), Freyne (1988), Mack (1988), Malbon (1993), Powell (1993), Rhoads & Mitchie (1982), Robbins (1992), Schüssler Fiorenza (1989), Shuler (1982), Stock (1989), Theissen (1991), Tolbert (1989).

The Historical Context of Mark's Gospel

(a) The Quest for the Provenance of Mark's Gospel: Location and Date

In order to probe the meaning of Mark's "good news", scholars have turned to questions relating to the community setting and dating of the Markan text. These questions and investigations have been the subject of considerable debate amongst biblical scholars (Donahue, 1992, 820).[4] With reference to its place of origin, opinion is divided between Rome and the eastern part of the Mediterranean world. Those who have argued for the latter have also been divided in their opinions as to whether Galilee, Syria or Egypt was the original setting of this Gospel. With reference to the dating of the Gospel, the Roman destruction of the Jewish Temple in 70 CE has generally been regarded as the bench-mark, with scholarly opinion divided as to whether the Gospel was written before or after this event. The following brief overview reflecting the major arguments for the setting and dating of the Gospel indicates the divergence of opinion and perhaps the reasons for the lack of consensus at this point in time. It also suggests that what is warranted for an understanding of the historical context of the Gospel of Mark is not only a different approach to the questions related to the historical environment of Mark's Gospel, but also the need for a different set of questions.

John Donahue draws attention to the fact that before the publication of the studies on Mark's Gospel undertaken by Willi Marxsen in 1956, "there existed a rare thing in New Testament studies—a near consensus on the dating and setting of a specific gospel" (1992, 817). The traditional consensus was that the gospel of Mark was composed in Rome between 64 and 70 CE. Marxsen however, argued for a compositional setting in or near Galilee just prior to the destruction of the temple in 70 CE.[5] This view subsequently set the scene for a plethora of studies, regarding the original location and dating of the gospel. According to Donahue (1992, 835) the studies undertaken by Martin Hengel and by Gerd Theissen in particular, "will be indispensable for any further discussion of the topic," since both these scholars have discussed the evidence in depth, but in fact, have reached opposite conclusions. Both have as their starting point the evidence from what is commonly regarded as the eschatological discourse in chapter 13 of Mark's Gospel.

Although for many centuries a traditional consensus had prevailed concerning the origin of the Gospel, Hengel points out that the debate over the origin of Mark's Gospel was the subject of much controversy as early as the second century CE. He refers to sources such as Irenaeus, Papias, Clement of Alexandria, the anti-Marcionite Prologue, Origen, Jerome and Eusebius regarding the origin of Mark's Gospel, all of

---

[4] For an overview of a variety of opinions in this regard, see Schnelle (1994) 237-9.

[5] See specifically Marxsen (1968) 142-3.

which seemed to depend predominantly on variant traditions that were in circulation in the early Christian church (1985, 2-6). Hengel claims that since it is difficult to draw definitive conclusions from these sources as to the history of the origin of the Gospel, any information regarding the origin of Mark's Gospel has to be gleaned from the text itself. Hengel's thesis is that the Gospel was written for Gentile Christians "at a clear distance from Palestine," namely in Rome after the persecution of Nero and before the destruction of Jerusalem, probably 69 CE (1985, 29). To support his argument he refers to Mark 13 and interprets the text against the background of events surrounding the destruction of the temple, arguing that references are to events which precede the destruction of Jerusalem. With reference to the dating of this Gospel, Hengel (1985, 20) claims that Mark 13 contains no reference to the destruction of Jerusalem by Titus in 70 CE, and because of its importance in Jewish history it would not have been overlooked by the author of the Gospel. According to Hengel (1985, 20) the injunctions in Mark 13 are of a prophetic nature regarding the fate of Jerusalem and not a reference to events that have occurred. He thus claims that a dating prior to the destruction of Jerusalem is more likely. With reference to the place of origin, Hengel draws attention to the number of Latinisms contained within the Markan text and which, as he points out, are more numerous than in the other three Gospels. This, Hengel argues, "is unusual in comparison with other writings," and so would suggest a situation where Latin terminology had to be used in order to explain conventions and geographical regions with which the audience would not have been familiar (1985, 29). For this reason, Hengel argues that Rome would seem the logical place of origin for the Gospel of Mark.[6]

Theissen (1991, 125-65) appeals to the historical evidence gleaned from other ancient literary sources which describe the political and social events surrounding the time of the destruction of Jerusalem. He agrees with those who advocate that the temple prophecy in Mark 13 "presupposes the destruction of the temple" (1991, 259). However, he claims that this prophecy was probably circulated in textual form amongst the Christian groups suffering persecution prior to the destruction of the temple and that the author of Mark's Gospel in using this prophetic text "looks back to the destruction of the temple as an event within history, but expects within his own life time a universal, eschatological catastrophe" (1991, 259). Regarding the original location of the Markan text, Theissen firstly appeals to evidence from within the text that refers to "the socio-ecological milieu of Mark's Gospel" relating to the notion of sea and ocean as well as the specific rural terminology which is prominent within the text and which reflect eastern Mediterranean rural concepts (1991, 238). Secondly, he refers to the

---

[6] Daniel Harrington (1990) 596, also advocates a Roman setting and before 70 CE. He argues that the Christians in Rome lived under the threat of persecution and that they believed the impending revolt in Jerusalem would have its ramifications on their situation in Rome.

community traditions "stemming from early, pre-Pauline, and Pauline-influenced Hellenistic Christianity" contained in the Markan text which in his opinion, suggests a local acquaintance with the traditions (1991, 239). Thirdly, in addressing what has also generally been regarded as geographical inconsistencies in the Markan account, he cites other ancient historical writers whose works likewise contain geographical discrepancies (1991, 242-9). Theissen, while acknowledging the plausibility of Hengel's evidence and argument for a pre-70 CE dating of Mark's Gospel, and Rome as its place of origin, nevertheless draws the conclusion, based on his evidence, that Mark's Gospel was more likely to have been written "in Syria, near Palestine, shortly after the destruction of the temple" (1991, 262).

There are other configurations of these two opposite positions that have been proposed regarding the origin and dating of the Markan text. Myers, for example, argues for a pre-70 dating, but agrees with an increasing number of scholars who place the production of Mark's Gospel in or near northern Palestine.[7] He interprets the significance of the Latinisms differently from Hengel by arguing that "they indicate the expected linguistic penetration in the socio-economic and administrative spheres of the colonized culture of Palestine" (1988, 41). Myers also focuses upon the socio-political conditions in agrarian Palestine, which he argues is different from urban Hellenism. He contends that dating the Gospel is difficult but important, in that the placement of Mark before or after the Roman destruction of the Temple in 70 CE, largely determines how Mark's polemic against the Temple is to be interpreted (1988, 41). Myers claims that scholars who opt for a post-70 date "typically argue that Mark was simply trying to justify the Christian community's theological rift with the Jewish cult" and that those in support of a Roman provenance "also see an oblique endorsement of the Roman victory over the Jewish revolt that began in 66 CE" (1988, 41). In contrast, Myers holds that "a date prior to 70 and during the revolt (thus after 66 CE) is essential to the coherency of the political and economic ideology of Mark's narrative" (1988, 41). He claims that "Mark's criticism of the temple state would have been superfluous once the temple had been destroyed" (1988, 41). Myers reads the Gospel of Mark against the socio-political situation of 1st century Palestine and argues that its message confronts the social and political domination system of the time. He claims that resistance to a pre-70 dating by modern scholars is "an example of their (docetic) tendency to suppress the economic and political aspects of the text in favour of the theological" (1988, 41).

Rudolf Pesch (1968, 236-8) placed the Gospel of Mark after 70 CE. Pesch also draws his evidence for the dating of the Gospel from chapter 13 as other scholars have done. However, just as Theissen was also to argue some fifteen years later, Pesch

---

[7] Ellis (1992) 801-815, takes into account the early christian traditions regarding Rome as the place of origin. He claims that evidence from the text suggests that the Gospel was composed in Caesarea in the mid-fifties and then delivered to Rome in the mid-sixties.

regarded chapter 13 as the result of Markan redaction of a written document which was widely circulated some years prior to the events of 70 CE, and which predicted in an apocalyptic style, the destruction of Jerusalem. Hence his choice of a post-70 dating. In his commentary on Mark's Gospel (1976, 3-11) he locates the origin of the Gospel in Rome. Donahue (1973, 224) also favours a post-70 dating for the Gospel of Mark, but does not commit himself to suggesting a specific location other than proposing that the text was meant for a Jewish Christian community.

Each of these four positions have attracted supporters, with the result as Donahue observes, "[a]lmost a generation after Marxsen's work no consensus has emerged on the community and setting of the Gospel of Mark" (1992, 835). In more recent times some scholars have tended to rely on the evidence put forward by previous scholarship and have chosen to opt for one position and then have proceeded to interpret the text of the gospel on that basis. Richard Rohrbaugh, for example, acknowledges the variety of opinions regarding the place of origin, but proceeds to discuss the social location of the Markan audience on the presumption "that Mark's Gospel was in fact written in a village or small town context in either southern Syria, Transjordan, or upper Galilee at a date very close to the events of A.D. 70" (1993, 380).

There are other scholars who also acknowledge the divided opinion on the issue, but who have attached less importance to pin-pointing an exact location. Dieter Lührmann's assessment, for example, is that Mark and his audience were located somewhere in the vicinity of Palestine, perhaps in the area of Syria between the Mediterranean Sea and west as far as modern day Iraq or Iran (Lührmann 1987, 7).[8] Generally, it seems that scholars have tended to equate the setting of the audience and that of the author as being in one and the same general location.

(b) Quest for the Provenance of Mark's Gospel: Mark's Audience

Initially, Mary Ann Tolbert turns her attention not to the location but rather to the composition of the audience. In her view all that can be said at this point with some degree of certainty is that the Gospel of Mark was produced by "[a]n anonymous author writing in *koine* Greek to a Greek-speaking, predominantly Gentile audience during the second half of the first century C.E." (1989, 36). Tolbert draws attention to the fact that many scripture scholars have tended to presume that the author of Mark's Gospel wrote for a specific community much in the same way as Paul had done when addressing his letters to individual christian communities. She explains that Pauline

---

[8] Also cited in Donahue (1992) 835. For references to examples of the tendency to locate the Gospel of Mark within a broad geographical area, see Donahue (1992) 835 n.101. Also Botha (1993) 27-38; van Iersel (1998) 30-56.

scholarship has tended to focus on particular issues which Paul was addressing in his letters to each of the communities as a way of identifying Paul's theological perspective (1989, 303). However, as she correctly states, form critics would argue that "different genres imply different functions and different settings" (1989, 303). She claims that scholars have not taken into account the different genres between that of Mark's Gospel and the Pauline letters and that the genre of Mark's Gospel, in her view, is a narrative "in the realm of *popular culture and popular literature*"(1989, 60).[9] Tolbert states that her definition of "popular literature" is different from Schmidt's notion of *Kleinliteratur* as "collectively created writings out of the cultic activities of a community" (1989, 60). Dibelius claims that the gospel writings were originally intended for "the unlettered men and women of the first Christian churches" (1937, 17). He explains that it was not until the second century when "Christianity penetrated into propertied and educated circles" that a corresponding Christian literature "adapted itself to the larger world" in terms of vocabulary and thought (1936, 17). Scholars who propose that Mark wrote for a specific community have not, in Tolbert's opinion, taken the genre into sufficient consideration when citing the evidence for a particular community location.

If indeed her view is correct, it would follow that Mark's Gospel was intended for a wide readership rather than for a specific community. However, Tolbert adds that although the setting of the audience may be indeterminate, this does not mean that the Gospel was not written in a certain place (1989, 305). Unlike Myers (1988, 39-87) who argues that Mark's Gospel takes up an anti-Roman stance, Tolbert claims that there is "a strong pro-Roman apologetic tone" pervading the narrative and suggests that "on the basis of the story alone almost any city in the Mediterranean area might be its author's home" (1989, 305). Contrary to Rohrbaugh (1993, 380) and other scholars such as Howard Clark Kee (1977, 77-105) who claim that the Gospel was written in a village or small town context, Tolbert proposes that "Rome or another large city under Roman rule of the late first century as the place of origin may supply a concrete historical context to explain why a religion that relied so heavily on preaching and oral tradition might see the value of a written manuscript" (1989, 305).

It seems that scholarly enquiry regarding the Markan audience tends to presume that the geophysical and socio-cultural descriptions inherent in the text, reflect the experience or social location of the audience. Waetjen (1989, 13) for example, claims that the description of places, language, idiom and customs suggests that the Markan audience was in fact from the lower-strata of society. However by way of analogy, a novel written in Australia in the latter part of the 20th century CE and which contains descriptive elements of settlement in rural Australia in the early part of this century, does not imply that the author is particularly writing for people living in rural Australia.

---

[9] David Aune (1987) 47, also identifies the language and style of Mark's Gospel as a "popular literary style."

The same thing may be said for the Gospel of Mark. Rather than the author's construction of the content intentionally reflecting the social location of the audience, the author either from first hand information, secondary sources or oral tradition, is in fact describing the political, religious, economic and socio-cultural situation in which Jesus and his contemporaries lived. The message of Jesus that Mark constructs and communicates will therefore be interpreted by readers through the lens of the socio-cultural situation of Galilee and Judaea which the Gospel author describes.

Although the discussion still continues regarding the dating of Mark's Gospel, the consensus that has been reached from the evidence based on the Two-Source Theory debate, is that the Gospel of Mark is now generally accepted as the first of the four canonical Gospels to be written (Marxsen 1968, 113-9).[10] It is also generally agreed that the Gospels of Matthew, Luke and John were written post-70 CE, and that the Pauline letters preceded the composition of the Gospel of Mark in its final form.[11] Therefore on the information from source-criticism, it would seem that the Markan Gospel must have been written in its final form in the early to middle period of the second half of the first century. However, recent socio-rhetorical approaches to the studies of the Gospels would cast some doubt on the certainty of the chronological priority of Mark. While it appears that socio-rhetorical studies have not set out to prove the priority of any of the Gospels, it would seem that with the emphasis on identifying the compositional techniques that each of the Gospel authors employed, it may be that each author drew on a common source or sources and crafted the sayings or stories according to the specific purpose that the author had in mind. This seems to be the perspective that Mack (1990) and Robbins (1987) are taking as they explore the socio-literary context of early Christianity. Given the different views regarding the priority of the Gospels, it would seem that at the present time the argument for Mark as the earliest Gospel cannot be said to be definitive.

Donahue states that the trend among scholars for identifying the community of Mark has been that of focussing "on the external factors of the location and date of the Gospel rather than the kind of community to which such a work is directed" (1992, 838). Correctly, his point here is that even if Mark's audience could be more exactly located in time and place, this information would not lead scholars to a clearer understanding of the nature of the community to which Mark's message is addressed. In establishing the kind of audience to which the Gospel is addressed, it is important to identify factors such as the cultural, socio-political, and religious world-view, and the resultant issues in which this audience was engaged. All of these factors would have had some effect on the audience's receptivity or otherwise to a message that the author had set out to convey. As Donahue rightly points out "there is no agreed upon method

---

[10] For an overview of more recent scholarship in this regard, see Neirynck (1990) 587-595.

[11] See also Collins (1992) 3-4.

available for describing on the basis of a text, the social make-up of a given community" (1992, 838). However, it can be argued that scholars have generally focused too narrowly on a few specific elements contained within the Markan text upon which to draw their conclusions regarding the nature of the Markan audience. In coming to an understanding of the socio-historical context of Mark's Gospel and its implied audience, it is important to focus not just on specific elements within the text itself, but to also draw on evidence from a socio-literary analysis of the text which indicates the socio-political environment in which the composition of the Gospel had its origins.

The Socio-literary Context of Mark's Gospel

(a) Literary Environment

George Kennedy (1984, 32) identifies three different Greek prose styles that were in current use in the ancient world, namely Asianism, Atticism and *koine*. He explains that Asianism was "a highly, self-conscious search for striking expression in diction, sentence structure, and rhythm" (1984, 32). Atticism was "the use of Greek literary prose of the fifth and fourth centuries before Christ as models for imitation in diction and composition" (1984, 32). On the other hand, *koine* was "neither artificial nor very self-conscious and results from the use of Greek as a medium of communication throughout the near East, by persons without deep roots in Greek culture" (1984, 32). One important and obvious clue the Markan text provides regarding the kind of audience to whom the Gospel is addressed, is the language in which it was written, namely in a rather simple form of *koine* Greek. From this information it can be taken for granted that the author wished to communicate with an audience comprised of those who were able to read or at least converse in and understand *koine* Greek. As this was the language of the popular culture, it can be presumed that Mark's Gospel was intended for an audience from a wide cross-section of the populace, not just the literary elite.[12] Elements in the text also suggest that the audience would have been familiar to some extent with Roman political structures to which the text refers, and that their lives were governed or at least influenced by them in some way. There is also an emphasis on Jewish political, social and religious practices which indicate that the audience would also have had some awareness of the Jewish world-view. It may be presumed then that both the author and the audience shared something of the same socio-political context.

---

[12] See also Voelz (1984) 893-977, particularly the discussion on κοινή Greek, (931-937).

Another dimension which sheds light on the environment of Mark's Gospel is the literary milieu in which it was produced. From the evidence of the literature that was in circulation in the first century CE, Gilbert Bilezikian (1977, 17) describes this world:

> Mark lived in a sophisticated, polycultural, multilingual, erudition-conscious age, when the works of the masters of Greece and Rome along with the sacred texts of Judaism were available to scholar and layman alike. The treasures of Greek literature were cherished, studied, memorized, translated, and imitated wherever Hellenistic culture had penetrated. All forms of Roman literature originated in or were influenced by the literary genius of the Greeks. These genres included dramatic, epic, lyric, and satiric poetry. Prose forms consisted of history, biography, essay, oratory, and philosophic literature. The degree of dependence of Latin literature upon its Greek progenitor can be measured by the fact that the former had its beginnings in the translations of Homer's *Odyssey* and of the tragedies of Aeschylus, Sophocles, and Euripides by Livius Andronicus in the third century B.C.

Bilezikian points out that the books of the New Testament would have been written in what he says is termed the Silver Age of literature which began with the reign of Tiberius in 14 CE. This followed the Golden Age of literature which as Bilezikian says "politically covers the period of the Republic and the Augustan Empire," and "is traditionally considered to span the careers of Cicero, Sallust, Julius Caesar, and Livy in prose and, in poetry, of Lucretius, Vergil, Horace, and Ovid, to mention only a few of the outstanding authors of this epoch rich in literary productions" (1977, 16).

The literature of the so-called Silver Age did not reach the same classic standard as that of the Augustan era. However as Bilezikian states "the literary accomplishments of this period ... bear witness to an intense traffic of ideas, old and new, and to the intermingling of currents of cultural influence" (1977, 18). Although there seemed to be an emphasis on the rhetorical and stylistic features in the literature of this period, it nevertheless was a time of "effervescent creativity" (1977, 18). Bilezikian cites the following as examples of the variety of creative literary accomplishments of this era:

> The Stoic philosopher Seneca wrote several works on ethics and nine tragedies. His nephew Lucan, who like him died in AD. 65, wrote the *Pharsalia*, an epic poem describing the struggle between Caesar and Pompey. The *Satyricon* of Petronius, who died one year later, represents the first realistic novel in Western literature (1977, 18).

Research into the level of literacy in the ancient world demonstrates that only a relatively small percentage of the population would have been literate and that the day to day transactions and communications among the people were usually oral rather than written (Dewey 1994, 37-65). However, the non-literate amongst the population would have been exposed to conventions associated with oral communication especially through the story-tellers and those leading the community in religious ritual and teaching. It can be assumed then, that the oral and literary communication conventions of the time would have had some bearing on the choice of genre that the author of Mark's Gospel adopted in conveying his message.[13]

(b) The Genre of Mark's Gospel

Any understanding of a text depends first and foremost on the ability of the receptor, whether this be a reader or listener, to identify with the particular "genre" of the text. The notion of "genre" as Collins (1992, 2) states "includes expectations about literary form and style, content, and function." She explains that there are three broad or "basic" genre possibilities under which the Markan text can be categorised. These are gospel, history, and life or biography (1992, 2). She points out that identifying the specific genre of the Markan text is not just a matter for academic pursuit; rather any "assumptions about the literary form of Mark affect the way this work is allowed to function in the lives of readers, in the life of the church, and in society"(1992, 2). In other words one's understanding of the genre of the Markan text affects the receptor's interpretation of the text. This of course would have been as valid for readers and listeners of Mark's text in the first century as it is for those of the modern day.

However, just as the "quest for the community of Mark" has generated debate amongst scholars, so too has the "quest for the genre" of the Gospel of Mark brought forth a variety of opinion which has ranged from the argument advocating the *sui generis* nature of the gospels to claims that the gospels do in fact resemble or are modelled on biographical works of Graeco-Roman literature and therefore can be included in the same generic category. Many scholars have tended to discount the notion of "history" as a generic category for the Gospel.

The argument for the *sui generis* nature of the Gospel is based on the notion of εὐαγγέλιον as a literary form. The opening line of Mark's Gospel (ἀρχὴ τοῦ εὐαγγελίου Ἰησοῦ Χριστοῦ υἱοῦ Θεοῦ) is considered by some scholars as a designation that the Gospel represents a new literary genre, since the form and arrangement of the content of Mark's Gospel do not have parallels in ancient literature.[14] A counter argument is that εὐαγγέλιον is a superscription that refers to the content contained in the text. In other words, it represents a concept rather than a literary form. This would be analogous to the superscription of the *Res Gestae Divi*

---

[13] On the widespread influence of literary ideas in ancient society, see also Burridge (1992) 252.

[14] See Bultmann (1952) 86-88; Dormeyer's analysis of views regarding "gospel" as literary genre (1984) 1545-1634; and monograph on the literary and theological nature of *Evangelium* (1989); Tiede (1984) 1705-1729 with reference to *Gattungen* as a basis in the formation of the gospel texts.

Augusti in its reference to the content contained in that inscription.[15] In the case of the Gospel of Mark some would argue that the term εὐαγγέλιον denotes a theological concept.[16]

Richard Burridge (1992, 82-106) who provides a critique of the more recent major contributions to the debate on the gospel genre which has taken place this century, agrees with those who propose that the gospels can be included in the genre of ancient Graeco-Roman βίος literature. However he claims that many of the arguments that have been put forward for this hypothesis are of "poor quality" in that they do not provide a satisfactory or systematic methodology for judging whether or not a work belongs to the βίος genre. He argues that since "genre functions as a flexible set of expectations affecting both author and reader; the proper recognition of genre is absolutely basic to the interpretation and appreciation of written communications" (1992, 105).

Burridge, identifies a number of generic features or indicators which he claims are constitutive of βίος, and tests these against a selection of ten examples of βίος from Graeco-Roman literature. This selection ranges from early rhetorical works from the fourth century BCE to examples written sometime towards the end of the first century CE. Although he would regard βίος is a flexible genre, he nevertheless points out that "there is an overall pattern or family resemblance of generic features which identify the group as the genre of βίος" (189-90). These generic features are as follows:

1. Opening features	title
	formulae
2. Subject	analysis of verbs' subjects
	allocation of space
3. External features	mode of representation
	metre
	size and length
	structure
	scale
	literary units
	use of sources
	methods of characterisation
4. Internal features	topics/motifs
	style
	tone, mood, attitude, values
	quality of characterisation
	social setting and occasion
	authorial intention and purpose

---

[15] The Latin text reads: *Rerum gestarum divi Augusti, quibus orbem terrarum imperio populi Romani subiecit ... exemplar subiectum.* The Greek text reads: Μεθηρμηνευμέναι ὑπεγράφησαν πράξεις τε καὶ δωρεαὶ Σεβαστοῦ Θεοῦ.

[16] See Frankemölle's analysis of views regarding "gospel" as a theological concept (1972) 1635-1707.

Burridge then applies the same criteria to the synoptic gospels and draws the conclusion that "there is a high degree of correlation between the generic features of the Graeco-Roman βιοι and those of the synoptic gospels" (1992, 218). However, he concedes that the gospels "may well form their own sub-genre because of the shared content."

The notion of βίος itself is a very wide category and as Burridge acknowledges, may include "a number of different *genera proxima*" (1992, 65). By this he means that βίος can borrow elements or features from other species of genre. He explains that the *genera proxima* in relation to βίος may include moral philosophy; religious or philosophical teaching, dialogue and discourse; encomium; story and novel, interest and entertainment; political beliefs and polemic; history. (1992, 66). In summary Burridge (1992, 69) states that

> Ancient genres were flexible and existed within the whole web of literary relationships of their day. There was plenty of scope for mixing and overlap at the boundaries of the genre, with a resulting rich mix of other features within the genre itself ... Ancient βίος was a flexible genre having strong relationships with history, encomium and rhetoric, moral philosophy and concern for character.

Burridge claims that the outcome of his proposed methodological approach to the question of the genre of Christian literature is that one is more easily able to identify which texts actually belong to the βίος genre and which do not. The Gospel of Thomas, the Gospel of Truth and the Gospel of Philip, for example, all have a "different pattern of generic features from the canonical gospels" (1992, 250). According to Burridge, they do not contain the generic features which can be identified as belonging to the category of βίος , whereas according to the methodology that he employs, the synoptic texts do have the generic features of βίος. Consequently, Burridge argues, a reader has a different set of expectations when reading the synoptic gospels than when reading the Gospel of Thomas. However if it is assumed that the Gospel of Mark is the first of the "gospels", then the question remains as to what are the distinguishing factors that identify the sub-genre of the Gospel of Mark and indeed the Gospels of Matthew and Luke, from that of other βίοι such as Suetonius' lives of the Caesars. In the case of Mark's Gospel, the question also remains as to what are the specific elements which distinguish it from each of the other synoptic gospels. Collins is surely correct when she names the distinguishing features as content and function (1992, 21).

Perhaps the major point that Burridge's study demonstrates may be summarised in his own words (1992, 255-6):

> It has become clear in this study that the narrower the genre proposed for the Gospels, the harder it is to prove the case, but the more useful the hermeneutical implications; whereas the wider the genre, the easier it is to

> demonstrate that the gospels belong to it, but the less helpful the result ...
> if Philip Shuler had proved that his genre of 'encomium biography',
> actually existed, and that the gospels belong within it, we should then
> have interpreted them encomiastically ... since he managed to establish
> neither ... we are not helped in the hermeneutical quest. On the other
> hand, our solution may be easier to demonstrate, but produce less direct
> results.

However, identifying a text as βίος leaves it in the realm of categorisation. One also needs to identify the nature of βίος in order to construct the purpose and meaning of the βίος text. According to Collins (1992, 2), virtue and vice are constitutive of βίος and therefore people who read biography do so in order to find out how others have acted in life. Biography focuses on a description of the life of a person. Suetonius' life of Augustus, for example traces the life of Augustus by providing details of his actions, character and ability. The reader's attention is drawn to the subject, Augustus, in some way. Collins claims that if the Markan Gospel is placed in the category of βίος, the reader is drawn to construct meaning in terms of the life of Jesus as a model to be imitated (1992, 2). If that is the case, its function or purpose in terms of the audience or reader is then understood to be the promotion of the "ethics and piety of the individual" (1992, 2).

As Burridge (1992, 66) himself states, "a different picture could be drawn" by replacing βίος at the centre of the *proxima genera* with that of "history". While the genre of history could also enlist much of the same *proxima genera* as that of βίος, the hermeneutical perspective of history provides a different understanding of the nature and purpose of the text. Whereas biography focuses on the life of a person, history relates to the interplay of events or the "how" of these events surrounding the life of a person or persons. An example of an ancient text as "history" is Cassius Dio's account of the historical significance surrounding the events in the life and death of Augustus (Cassius Dio, 50-56).[17]

As Collins (1992, 27) points out, Mark does not write of Jesus with the prime aim of "establishing his character or essence." Nor indeed does Mark write in the vein of aretalogy or encomium, a sub-genre of βίος , whereby the specific focus would be that of praising Jesus by enumerating his benefactions on humankind.[18] Rather a reading of Mark's Gospel reveals that it is an account of the life of Jesus who acted in historical time, and which focuses on the interplay of "events" in the life of Jesus. In this regard then, Mark's Gospel is nearer history than biography. However there is also another added dimension. The Markan account is a claim that the Jesus "event" has changed reality. Collins draws attention to the eschatological dimension of the Gospel of Mark

---

[17] Although this post-dates Mark's Gospel, it nevertheless provides a good example of the difference between Suetonius' life of Augustus and Cassius Dio's historical account of Augustus.

[18] See thesis proposed by Shuler (1982) concerning the synoptic gospels as encomium, a subgroup of βίος.

and cites examples from ancient Jewish apocalyptic literature that functioned to provide a vision and a challenge for altering the course of "historical" events (1992, 27-28). Hanhart (1992, 1005) refers specifically to the function of the prophecy of Daniel which provided both vision and hope to Jewish-Christians in the face of Roman political domination:

> [T]he prophecy of Daniel 7 inspired thousands with apocalyptic hope. With the breaking in of the Rule of God, a Human One would come to liberate the Saints of the Most High and judge the nations, bringing with him a realm of freedom, justice and peace. This expectation had flared up in the first century, to be thwarted ruthlessly by the Roman legions. They wreaked far greater havoc on the population than the Syrians had ever done at the time Daniel 7 was written.

The opening lines of the Markan account indeed witness to this eschatological dimension which continues as a theme throughout the course of the text.[19] The nature of apocalyptic Jewish literature was that it contained both a strong socio-historical and theological function. The eschatological or in other words, the apocalyptic nature of the Gospel of Mark also contains both a historical and theological function.

   Collins (1992, 37) sums up the author's purpose in combining both an historical dimension and a theological dimension in the composition of the Markan text:

> Mark was written not only to avoid reductionism or to provide a controlling context for the tradition about Jesus but to place the various genres of that tradition into an historical framework. The genres of this tradition were integrated into a historical narrative of a particular type that became a host genre to those smaller forms. The result was that the various insights into "the presence of God in Jesus" were incorporated into a vision of the significance of God's activity in Jesus for history and for the world.

In taking as a starting point that the genre of the Markan text "combines realistic historical narrative with an eschatological perspective" (Collins, 1992, 34), the hermeneutical perspective is more realistically and more specifically focussed, and provides the framework out of which the Markan text can be interpreted. That is not to say that the *proxima genera* of which Burridge speaks need to be discounted. In fact a reading of the Markan text has to take into consideration not only the literary components that its author has incorporated into the text, but also the other generic features that intersect with the notion of history and apocalyptic genre.

---

[19] Kee (1977) 64-76, also makes this point in his discussion on the structure of Mark's Gospel.

The Structure of Mark's Gospel

(a) Overview of Current Proposals

The key to understanding a written communication lies not merely in the content of the text, but is also to be found in the structure or framework which gives shape to the meaning of the content. In other words the structure also generates its own discourse and as such contributes to the meaning inherent in the text. In exploring the meaning that Mark is conveying, scholars have sought to identify the framework that is particular to this Gospel. As well as revealing the meaning of the text, the structure that the author of Mark's Gospel adopts, as Kee (1977, 50) points out, also reveals something of the situation that the author is addressing.

One of the outcomes of earlier form-critical research was that there seemed to be a general consensus in support of the theory that Mark's Gospel was a compilation of traditional material which reflected the sayings and deeds of Jesus. Debate, however, centered on whether the compilation was a random collection of the material or whether there was a pattern to the arrangement of the material. Some scholars put forward the theory that the passion narrative was the starting point of Mark's Gospel and that the arrangement of the material consisted of sayings and deeds of Jesus arranged in episodes which drew the reader's attention to the passion narrative. Following Schüssler Fiorenza (1985, 151) the term "episode" is to be understood as a "brief unit of action that is integral but distinguishable from the continuous narrative."

In more recent times, there is general consensus that Mark's Gospel was composed as a whole document, the content of which was not randomly selected but carefully selected from traditional material and intentionally arranged in order that the message inherent in the text would be comprehended by the reader. However, just how the Gospel has been arranged has drawn forth a variety of suggestions. Eugene Boring (1991, 44) draws attention to the study of Heinrich Baarlink who, having analysed 27 different proposed outlines of Mark's Gospel found that the divisions ranged "from two to ten or more."

Ten years previous to Baarlink's study, Rudolf Pesch provided a comprehensive overview of the variety of opinions regarding the principle divisions that scholars have suggested. The divisions that he cites ranged from three to seven (1968, 50-53). As he points out, the variety of suggestions have naturally led to a variety of interpretations of the Markan text as a whole. Pesch (1968, 54-82) put forward yet another proposal. Taking his cue from other ancient literature in which chiastic structure was evident, Pesch applied a technique known as stichometry, whereby he counted the number of lines and divided the text accordingly from what he identified as signal markers within the text. He identified six major sections, with each section containing three sub-sections. The major divisions are as follows:

A	1:2 - 3:6
B	3:7 - 6:29
C	6:30 - 8:26
D	8:27 - 10:52
E	11:1 - 12:44
F	14:1 - 16:8

According to Pesch the divisions A, C, and E are shorter than the sections B, D and E. Each large section, that is B, D and E, contains three sub-sections, forming a pattern of a long section, a shorter section and a longer section. He argues that on this basis Mk 8:27-30 is the mid-point of the text. The divisions that he identifies within the text form natural breaks within the narrative. Pesch has not included Mk 13 into his calculations. He also includes the longer ending of the Gospel of Mark, whereas most scholars would now argue that the shorter ending is in fact more likely to be the original version.[20]

Vincent Taylor claims (1966, 67-106) that the Markan material was gleaned from the traditions about Jesus which were circulating among the first-century Christian communities, and he argues that except for the Passion and Resurrection narratives, the author of the gospel arranged the material around the theme of ministry. He identifies seven major divisions, with each containing sub-sections (1966, 107-111):

I	Introduction	1:1 - 1:13
II	The Galilean ministry	1:14 - 3:6
III	The height of the Galilean ministry	3:7 - 6:13
IV	The ministry beyond Galilee	6:14 - 29
V	Caesarea Philippi: journey to Jerusalem	8:27 - 10:52
VI	The ministry in Jerusalem	11:1 - 13:37
VII	Passion and resurrection narrative	14:1 -1 6:8

Taylor (1966, 106) claims that the Passion and Resurrection narrative is the climax to which the whole Gospel is oriented. His assessment is that Mark was not a skilled writer, arguing that "[a] more gifted writer would have arranged things differently" (1966, 112). He therefore regards Mark's purpose as that of "preserving, more or less intact, didactic complexes already familiar to his first readers" (1966, 112). According to Taylor (1966, 113) this is obvious from the selection of material that the author had gathered:

> His selection of material is influenced by his interest in exorcisms, crowds, and miraculous events, in the Gentile Mission of his day, in

---

[20] See Achtemeier (1975) 31-40 who also discusses the structure advocated by Pesch.

mission of Jesus. Many of these interests he shared with the Church of his day.

Howard Clark Kee (1977, 63), argues that Taylor's outline does not take into consideration the thematic shifts in Mark, but instead concentrates on the change of locale. Kee (1977, 64) claims that "Mark no more lends itself to analysis by means of a detailed outline developed by simple addition of components than does a major contrapunctal work of music." He suggests that what is required in analysing Mark is to recognise from the outset the multiple themes that are sounded throughout the gospel (Kee 1977,64). In his view, the text has to be viewed as a whole. He acknowledges that the text contains a beginning, middle and end, but claims that the major themes of Mark are set out in the opening verses 1:1-23, and that "[o]nce announced, these themes will run like a great fugue throughout the gospel" (Kee 1977, 74-75). He states that by dividing the Gospel into sections "the richness of literary and conceptual skill by which Mark has constructed his gospel" is missed (Kee 1977, 76). In particular Kee draws attention to the apocalyptic theme as a significant indicator that "the Gospel of Mark addressed the critical needs of his community in his own time" (Kee 1977, 76).

Udo Schnelle (1994, 242) also proposes that Mark's Gospel contains a beginning, middle and an end, but claims that these sections focus on the theme of the theological understanding of the death of Jesus, and that it is this understanding that is central to Mark's purpose. Schnelle identifies the specific focus of each section as follows:

I	The works of Jesus in Galilee	1:1 - 8:26
II	Jesus' path to the passion	8:27 - 10:52
III	Jesus in Jerusalem	11:1 - 16:8

Schnelle (1994, 243) claims that Galilee is the place of the eschatological revelation of God, while Jerusalem is the place where Jesus faces on-going enmity. The significance of the middle section, according to Schnelle, is that it contains the three passion and death predictions.

Eugene Boring (1991, 46) subscribes to the notion that Mark's structure is bipartite, "corresponding to his christological emphases, with "the" division between parts one and two coming somewhere between 8:22 and 10:52." Both Mk 8: 22 and Mk 10:52 are episodes in which Jesus cures men who were blind. Thus Boring suggests that the middle division "both separates and joins these two sections by representing the transition from blindness to sight" (1991, 46). While Boring identifies corresponding themes or characteristics from each section, he does not place them in any specific sequential order. However, he does state that each characteristic from one section is a reversal of that characteristic in the other section, for example "success/rejection", "unhealed blindness/healed blindness". Boring claims that except for the Galilee/Jerusalem correspondence which he regards as a "geographical-biographical" characteristic, the other characteristics "have to do not with the location or chronology of Jesus' ministry, but with its christological character" (1977, 46).

Rhetorical criticism in New Testament scholarship in more recent times has influenced approaches to the study of form and structure of Mark's gospel. Augustine Stock (1989, 25) draws attention to the work of Standaert who, having studied the literary form and structure of ancient writings, concluded that the Gospel of Mark followed the conventional patterns of writing current in the first century CE. Standaert identified a five-part concentric structure in Mark's Gospel. Stock (1989, 25) quotes Standaert's explanation:

> Mark's entire Gospel is constructed according to a concentric schema: prologue and epilogue correspond, while the three parts of the body of the narrative are centered upon the middle part (6:14-10:52). This middle part is itself divided into three parts, organised according to the concentric principle: the multiplication of the loaves and the section on following Christ frame the central passage, 8:27-9:1. This central passage gathers together all the principle themes, not only of the framing sections but of the entire gospel, and the arrangement of this passage is also concentric— it consists of five sections centered around the great exhortation of 8:34-9:1.[21]

Bas M.F. van Iersel developed Standaert's theory further by adding "a topographical framework which gives the work an overall concentric structure" (Stock, 1989, 26). Van Iersel identified five major sections (Stock 1989, 26):[22]

I	Wilderness	1:2 - 13
II	Galilee	1:14 - 8:26
III	The Way	8:27 - 10:52
IV	Jerusalem	11:1 - 15:42
V	The Tomb	15:42 - 16:8

Stock (1989, 26) explains the connectedness inherent in this schema:

> The wilderness and the tomb are linked together by continuity, and Galilee and Jerusalem by contrast." These four parts surround the center part, the way, which stands forth as the center and the key of the entire gospel.

Within this structure there are also four markers or "hinge" pieces namely, 1:14-15; 8:22-26; 10:45-52; 15:40-41 which both divide each of the topographical sections and at the same time link them together (1989, 28).

---

[21] Stock cites this explanation from Standaert (1978). *L'Evangile de Marc, composition et genre Littéraire.* Zevenkerken-Brugge, 174-175.

[22] Van Iersel (1995) 75-97, distinguishes between concentric structures based on macro-divisions and those he identifies as micro-divisions. He claims that readers/hearers would more easily recognise the repetition of key elements if the divisions were not too large. Also van Iersel (1998) 68-86.

Scott (1985, 17-26) also argues that the plan of Mark's Gospel is chiastically determined. He identifies three main parts, each of which is divided into two subsections. A brief prologue and epilogue frame these three major sections. While his schema has merit, the weakness is that he does not include the eschatological discourse and its prelude Mk 12:41-13:37. His reasoning is that this section is a supplement as it does not correspond to the chiastic pattern that he claims is inherent in the text. He also suggests that the prologue to the gospel begins at 1:9, and so it appears that he discounts the previous verses, perhaps because they do not fit into the schema. A point that is interesting is that he argues that the confirmation of Jesus as God's son at 9:7 is the mid-point of the middle section of the chiasmus, and thus is central to the message of the Gospel. This is pre-empted in the first section of the text, namely 1:11 where Jesus is revealed as God's son and finally affirmed in the third part of the chiasmus 15:9 where the centurion announces that Jesus was the son of God.

Both Myers (1988, 109-121) and Tolbert (1989, 108-121) propose a bipartite framework. Tolbert, as did Taylor, proposes that the reference to geographical locations is a significant factor. She claims that there are two geographical locations that divide one major division from the other: "the action in the first ten chapters of the Gospel takes place in and around Galilee, while all of the action in the last six chapters takes place in and around Jerusalem" (1989, 114). These two divisions have individual introductions, namely 1:14-15 and 11:1-11. She explains what she regards as the significance of these introductions:

> the audience, in good epic or ancient novelistic style, is informed be-
> forehand "what the work is about." In Mark 1:14-15, the narrator
> declares the location and role of Jesus and then allows Jesus, speaking
> for the first time in his own voice, to give a programmatic summary of his
> message ... In Mark 11:1-11, the narrator indicates the location, "they
> drew near to (ἐγγίζουσιν) Jerusalem," but the role of Jesus is
> proclaimed by the crowd ...

In the first division, Tolbert identifies four sections. In the second division there are three sections. Each section is encompassed by "episodic *inclusios* " (1989, 120). For example the fourth section 8:22-10:52 begins with the episode of the healing of the blind man 8:22-26, and closes with the healing of the blind Bartimaeus who follows Jesus 10:46-52. Tolbert demonstrates that some of these sections contain chiastic patterns. For the most part she generally identifies chiasmus in the text in much broader terms than what Scott has proposed.

Contrary to Taylor's view, Myers claims that Mark's Gospel exhibits literary sophistication and as such "defies any definitive structural model" (1989, 109). He explains the reason for the difficulty in identifying a neat structure to Mark's Gospel:

> On the one hand, Mark's literary techniques, such as repetition or concentric composition, encourage the quest for overall structural symmetry in the story. On the other hand, any neat pattern that may emerge is inevitably upset by the way in which Mark weaves together his different narrative strands (1989, 109).

Having said that, Myers claims that "a rough symmetry between the two halves or "books" of Mark is discernible" (1989,111). He divides the gospel according to corresponding narrative themes:

Narrative Theme	Book I	Book II
A) Prologue/call to discipleship	1:1 - 20	8:27 - 9:13
B) Campaign of direct action	1:21 - 3:35	11:1 - 13:3
C) Construction of new order	4:35 - 8:10	8:22 - 26; 9:14 - 10:52
D) Extended sermon	4:1 - 34	13:4 - 37
E) "Passion" tradition	6:14 - 29	14:1 -1 5:38
F) Symbolic epilogue	8:11 - 21	15:39 - 16:8

Myers explains that the structure which he advocates is also "cross-hatched with many substructures." However, he states that the function of the key themes in each section or "book" is to recapitulate the corresponding theme in the other section. At the centre, or to what Myers (1989, 116) refers as the "narrative fulcrum," are the challenges put to the reader : "Do you not understand?" (8:21) and "Who do you say that I am?" (8:29). Myers (1989, 116-117) explains that at this point there is "a crisis of reading, which prepares us for Jesus' second call to discipleship (8:34ff) ... The call to the cross is thus established as the ideological center of the narrative, the 'fulcrum' upon which the whole story balances."

Caetano Minette de Tillesse (1992, 905-933) also identifies a bipartite structure in the Gospel of Mark (Mk 1:14-8:26 and 8:27-16:8). He divides these sections into sub-sections and argues that parallelisms can be identified in each of the sub-sections, for example, Mk 2:1-12 can be paralleled with Mk 11:1-12:44. Both sections, he points out, begin with a pericope concerning the controversy with the authorities over the ἐξουσία of Jesus, and in turn are followed by five "controversy" stories (1992, 920). Minette de Tillesse argues that the parallelism between 6:6b-8:26 and 8:27-10:52 is a clear indication of the persecution of the Church at the time when the Gospel was composed.

These theories of the structure of the Markan text seem somewhat at odds with the simple style of *koine* Greek of the text. However as already indicated in the discussion of the *Res Gestae*, structural elements rather than punctuation guided the ancient reader's understanding of a text. The genius of the author of Mark's Gospel is that he wrote in a style that was easily understood by a wide cross-section of the population, not just the literary elite.

(b) The theme of ἐξουσία in the Structure of the Markan Text.

The examples that have been discussed in the previous section are indicative of the variety of opinion regarding the structure of Mark's Gospel. The samples included for the discussion, however have not been randomly selected. Each has some bearing on a proposal for another structure evident in the text and which as it will be demonstrated, suggests a way of identifying a central concern in the Markan narrative, namely that of freedom.

Perhaps Fowler (1991, 152) is correct when he draws attention to the fact that architectural patterns, particularly on the lines that the modern critic discovers in an ancient text are "more typical of the discourse of the visual-literate modern critic than of the oral-aural ancient reader or listener." Thus frameworks such as those that have been discussed here, may probably have been lost on the Gospel author's more immediate readers or listeners of first century Mediterranean culture. This does not mean that chiastic structure is not evident in the text. As already pointed out with reference to the *Res Gestae,* symmetry was a framework out of which ancient peoples were able to construct their world. In the literary arena of the ancient world, it was very often the juxtaposition of ideas and concepts which were more easily comprehended and from which people derived meaning, rather than a division of the text according to a mathematical formula.

Rather than focus on a division of the gospel based on stichometric evidence or even on a geographical or ideological basis, a different picture emerges if the focus is brought to bear on two significant concepts within the Markan text and their placement within the text. These two key concepts, namely that of Jesus as Χριστός and as υἱὸς Θεοῦ, are also to be found in the early Christian community's confession of faith. The Pauline writings bear testimony that these were basic understandings of Christian belief. A few examples from Paul's letters to communities in Asia Minor, Greece and Rome will suffice to illustrate that these understandings of the nature of Jesus were widespread beliefs amongst the Christian communities throughout the eastern part of the Roman empire as well as in Rome itself:

Rom 1:3b-4a   It was about his Son: on the human level he was a descendant of David, but on the level of the spirit—the Holy Spirit—he was proclaimed son of God by an act power that raised him from the dead. It is about Jesus of Christ our Lord.

1 Cor 2:2	I resolved that while I was with you I would not claim to know anything but Jesus Christ—Christ nailed to the cross.
Rom 5:15b	For if the wrongdoing of that one man brought death upon so many, its effect is vastly exceeded by the grace of God and the gift that came to so many by the grace of the one man, Jesus Christ.
Gal 2: 16	yet we know that no one is ever justified by doing what the law requires, but only by faith in Christ Jesus.
Gal 3:22	But Scripture has declared the whole world to be prisoners in subject to sin, so that faith in Jesus Christ should be the ground on which the promised blessing is given to those who believe.
1Thess 1:9-10	everyone is spreading the story of our visit to you; how you turned from idols to be servants of the true and living God, and to wait expectantly for his Son from heaven, whom he raised from the dead, Jesus our deliverer from the retribution to come.
Gal 4:4	but when the appointed time came, God sent his Son, born of a woman, born under the law, to buy freedom for those who were under the law, in order that we might attain the status of sons.

In the Markan text, these concepts of Jesus as Χριστός and as υἱὸς Θεοῦ occur at strategic points, namely: at the beginning Mk 1:1; 1:11 and also at the end of the Gospel, Mk 14:62; 15:39.[23] These concepts occur again in the pericopes Mk 8:27-30 and 9:2-13, both of which are juxtaposed on each side of the pericope Mk 8:31-9:1. A chiastic pattern that is evident in the structure of the text is outlined on the following page:

---

[23] See also Rhoads and Michie (1982) 48-9. They claim that "a two-step progression" is a stylistic feature in the Marcan text occurring "in phrases, sentences, pairs of sentences, and the structure of episodes," and argue that it is also a feature of the overall framework of the story.

A	Narrator announces Jesus as the Christ	The beginning of the gospel of Jesus Christ [the son of God]. 1:1
B	Jesus is announced as God's son	And a voice came from heaven: "You are my beloved Son, with you I am well pleased." 1:11
A	Disciple acknowledges Jesus as Christ	Peter answered: "You are the Christ." 8:29
C	Jesus announces his free choice of action. The challenge to do likewise is put to the disciples and the crowds and by inference, to the reader	And he began to teach them that the Son of man must suffer many things, and be rejected by the elders and the chief priests and the scribes, and be killed, and after three days rise again. And he said this plainly. And Peter took him, and began to rebuke him. But turning and seeing his disciples, he rebuked Peter, and said, "Get behind me, Satan! For you are not on the side of God, but of men." And he called to him the multitude with his disciples, and said to them, "If anyone would come after me, let him deny himself and take up his cross and follow me. For whoever would save his life will lose it; and whoever loses his life for my sake and the gospel's will save it. For what does it profit a man, to gain the whole world and forfeit his life? Or what can a man give in return for his life? For whoever is ashamed of me and of my words in this adulterous and sinful generation, of him will the Son of man also be ashamed, when he comes in the glory of the father with his holy angels." And he said to them, "Truly, I say to you, there are some standing here who will not taste death before they see that the kingdom of God (τὴν βασιλείαν τοῦ θεοῦ) has come with power." 8:31- 9:1
B'	Jesus is confirmed as as God's Son	"This is my beloved Son; listen to him." 9:7
A'	Jesus claims that he is the Christ	Again the High priest asked him, "Are you the Christ, the Son of the Blessed ?" And Jesus said, "I am." 14:61-2
B'	Centurion professes Jesus as Son of God	And when the centurion, who stood there facing him, saw that he thus breathed his last, he said, "Truly this man was the Son of God." 15:39

The mid-section of the text, Mk 8:31-9:1 is highly significant for an understanding of Mark's Gospel. The concepts of Jesus as Χριστός and as υἱὸς Θεοῦ are organising principles around which the author has developed key themes in the text, and which are encapsulated in Mk 8: 31-9:1. Viewed from the perspective of a chiastic structure, the concept of freedom appears as a central focus in the Gospel of Mark. Incorporated into the structure of Mark's Gospel is a variety of literary forms such as parables, sayings, pronouncement stories, miracle stories, and summary statements. Rather than a random collection, this material has been arranged carefully and with intention in the structuring of the gospel text giving coherence to the major themes that the author is wishing to emphasise.

The Significance of ἐξουσία in the Structure of Mark's Gospel

(a) The Location of ἐξουσία in the Markan Text

The choice that Jesus makes to act that is evident in Mk 8:31-9:1, is taken up as a major theme in the Gospel of Mark. This theme is carried through the Gospel narrative by means of the key word ἐξουσία. As already explained in the third chapter of this thesis, the term ἐξουσία conveys the meaning of "being free to act." Joanna Dewey (1980, 32) explains that a word may be considered as a key term in a text when it is used throughout the text "as the leitmotif or theme of a passage or longer section of narrative." Examples she cites are "to fast" in Mark 2:18-20 or "bread" in Mark 6-8. She further explains that "[s]uch key words help to give thematic unity to a narrative, without demarking any structural pattern" (1980 32). Van Iersel (1995, 90) identifies the word ἐξουσία as an example of a key word in what he regards as the thematic unity of Mk 1:14-4:1.

The word ἐξουσία occurs nine times in the Gospel of Mark.[24] On three occasions it relates to the establishment of the ἐξουσία of Jesus (Mk 1:22; 1:27; 2:10), and on two occasions to the establishment of the ἐξουσία of the disciples (Mk 3:16; 6:7). With reference to the proposed chiastic structure of the text, the ἐξουσία of Jesus and the disciples occurs in the first half of the gospel text. The other four occurrences of the term ἐξουσία occurs in the second half of the text, in which the ἐξουσία of Jesus is challenged by the authorities (Mk 11:28, 29, 33) and where the ἐξουσία of the

---

[24] The verb κατεξουσιάζω occurs in the Gospel of Mark at 10:42 (κατεξουσιάζουσιν). According to Foerster (1964) 575, "its primary sense is that 'they exercise power over them'. There is no earthly government without force ... it is likely that the word implies the tendency˙ towards compulsion or oppression which is immanent in all earthly power, and not merely political." This word will be discussed in the context of the subject matter in chapter six.

disciples is put to the test by Jesus in parable form (Mk 13:34). The location of the ἐξουσία pericopes and its juxtaposition with those texts that refer to Jesus as Χριστός and υἱὸς Θεοῦ within the chiastic structure of the Markan text, is depicted as follows:

A	Narrator announces Jesus as the Christ		The beginning of the Gospel of Jesus Christ [the son of God] 1:1
	B	Jesus is announced as Son of God	And a voice came from heaven: "You are my beloved son, with you I was well pleased." 1:11
		X The ἐξουσία of Jesus	1:22; 1:27; 2:10
		Y The ἐξουσία of the disciples	3:15; 6:7
A	Disciple acknowledges Jesus as the Christ		Peter answered: "The Christ of God." 8:29
	C	Jesus exercises his freedom of choice. The challenge to do likewise is put to the disciples and the crowds and by inference to the reader.	8:31-9:1
B '	Jesus is confirmed as God's Son		"This is my beloved Son; listen to him." 9:7
		X ' the ἐξουσία of Jesus is challenged	11:28-29, 33
		Y ' the ἐξουσία of the disciples is challenged	13:34
	A '	Jesus claims that he is the Christ	Again the High priest asked him, are you the Christ, the son of the Blessed ?" And Jesus said, "I am." 14:61-2
B '	Centurion professes Jesus as Son of God		And when the centurion, who stood facing him, saw that he thus breathed his last, he said, "Truly this man was the Son of God. 15:39.

(b) Conclusion

It would seem that the subject of Christian freedom was an issue that the author of Mark's Gospel wanted to convey to his audience. He chose to do this not by presenting his audience with a philosophical dissertation or a political treatise. Rather he selected material from the tradition and provided a "narrative" through which he could demonstrate how the concept of freedom was exemplified in the life of Jesus and in the response of the disciples. In selecting ἐξουσία as a key term in his "narrative", the author of Mark's gospel wanted to draw the attention of his audience to the concept of the *praxis* of Christian freedom. The specific ways in which the author demonstrated the various dimensions of the freedom that Jesus proclaimed in word and deed is the subject of the following chapters.

CHAPTER FIVE

The ἐξουσία of Jesus and the Disciples

The Context of the ἐξουσία of Jesus

The term ἐξουσία as it relates to Jesus in the first half of the text, occurs three times in the first two chapters of Mark's gospel, namely 1:22; 1:27 and 2:10. In each case the narrator relates a particular incident in order to illustrate to the reader the specific dimension of the ἐξουσία of Jesus as it occurs in these texts. To further illustrate how the ἐξουσία of Jesus is established, the narrator in the Gospel provides a report of a number of other incidents that support this fact. The rhetorical framework in which the ἐξουσία of Jesus is established, extends from Mk 1:16-3:6. This framework or major rhetorical unit contains minor rhetorical units, each of which provides a different dimension regarding the ἐξουσία of Jesus.

Structurally the major rhetorical unit may be divided into two sections. The first section contains the three incidents in which the narrator explicitly mentions the ἐξουσία of Jesus and in which this concept is central to each of the incidents. The second section further illustrates the *praxis* of ἐξουσία as it pertains to Jesus. Each section is prefaced with a "Call" narrative. The first, Mk 1:16-18, is the call of Simon and his brother Andrew, and James and John. The second, Mk 2:13-14, is the call of Levi, a tax-collector. The first section begins with the two incidents in which the ἐξουσία of Jesus is established for the reader. This is followed by four incidents in which Jesus' ministry of healing is emphasised, and concludes with the encounter in which Jesus challenges the Scribes' disapproval of his actions. The second section recounts four episodes in which controversy develops over Jesus' contravention of prescribed religious convention, and which ultimately culminates in a plot by the authorities to suppress Jesus' activities. Some scholars have claimed that there is evidence of concentric structure and parallelism between 1:16-2:12 and 2:13-3:6, particularly in relation to the four healing episodes and the four controversy incidents.[1] However the case for specific and direct parallelism or concentric structure is difficult to prove conclusively. In more general terms, it can be said that the theme of the first section which identifies the positive reaction to the ἐξουσία of Jesus from those who

---

[1] Tolbert (1989) 140, argues that there are both generalized as well as specialized comparisons in the two sections. Also Robinson (1994) 64.

come to him for healing, is contrasted in the second section with the negative reaction of those who represent the establishment.

It can be argued therefore, that the author has consciously designed the structure of Mk 1:16-3:6 for rhetorical effect, in that the first section is further developed in the second section. The following outline emphasises the bipartite structure of this segment and the major divisions of the Markan text as well as the theme of each episodic event: [2]

1. Call of disciples   1:16-20
   ἐξουσία of Jesus is stated by the narrator   1:21-22
   Healing/exorcism in the synagogue: ἐξουσία
   is acknowledged by the crowd   1:23-28
   Healing of Simon's mother-in-law and others   1:29-34
   Jesus goes to a lonely place to pray   1:35-39
   Healing of man with leprosy   1:40-45
   Healing of paralytic and challenge to Jesus'
   claim of ἐξουσία   2:1-12

2. Call of Levi   2:13-14
   Controversy: eating with sinners   2:15-17
   Controversy: over fasting   2:18-22
   Controversy: over the sabbath   2:23-28
   Controversy: doing good on the sabbath   3:1-5
   Pharisees plot with Herodians   3:6

The ἐξουσία of Jesus is thus established at the beginning of Jesus' mission, and as such, it underscores the character of his mission. In fact, as Freyne (1988, 45) states, it was the ἐξουσία of Jesus that was "the fundamental question that the Galilean ministry raised." By including each of the episodic events, the rhetorical effect is to provide a different perspective or "proof" of the ἐξουσία of Jesus. Each episodic event is in the form of a story, a rhetorical device that Mark uses here by which to engage the reader's attention, interest and imagination. However each episode has its own distinctive form. While Jesus is the centre of interest in each episode, the responses or reactions of the other characters serve to emphasise the notion of the ἐξουσία of Jesus throughout this section of the Markan text.

---

[2] Tolbert has suggested much the same structure. However she emphasises different connected elements than what is being discussed here. Another structural outline that has been proposed is a three-step progression (Robbins 1992) 25-34.

The ἐξουσία of Jesus: Mk 1: 21-22

(a) Comparison of Synoptic Texts

The freedom with which Jesus taught and the reaction of the people to the ἐξουσία of Jesus is recounted by each of the synoptic writers, which indicates that this notion was part of the received tradition regarding Jesus and the message that he proclaimed.

Mk 1:21-22
And they went into Capernaum; and immediately on the sabbath he entered the synagogue and taught.
22And they were astonished at his teaching, for he taught them as one who had ἐξουσία, and not as the scribes.

Mk 1:21-22
καὶ εἰσπορεύονται εἰς Καφαρναούμ· καὶ εὐθὺς τοῖς σάββασιν εἰσελθὼν εἰς τὴν συναγωγὴν ἐδίδασκεν.
²² καὶ ἐξεπλήσσοντο ἐπὶ τῇ διδαχῇ αὐτοῦ· ἦν γὰρ διδάσκων αὐτοὺς ὡς ἐξουσίαν ἔχων καὶ οὐχ ὡς οἱ γραμματεῖς.

Mt 7:28-29
And when Jesus finished these sayings, the crowds were astonished at his teaching,
29for he taught them as one who had ἐξουσία, and not as their scribes.

Mt 7:28-29
καὶ ἐγένετο ὅτε ἐτέλεσεν ὁ Ἰησοῦς τοὺς λόγους τούτους, ἐξεπλήσσοντο οἱ ὄχλοι ἐπὶ τῇ διδαχῇ αὐτοῦ·
²⁹ ἦν γὰρ διδάσκων αὐτοὺς ὡς ἐξουσίαν ἔχων καὶ οὐχ ὡς οἱ γραμματεῖς αὐτῶν.

Lk 4:31-32
And he went down into Capernaum, a city of Galilee. And he was teaching them on the sabbath
32and they were astonished at his teaching, for his word was with ἐξουσία.

Lk 4:31-32
καὶ κατῆλθεν εἰς Καφαρναοὺμ πόλιν τῆς Γαλιλαίας. καὶ ἦν διδάσκων αὐτοὺς ἐν τοῖς σάββασιν·
³² καὶ ἐξεπλήσσοντο ἐπὶ τῇ διδαχῇ αὐτοῦ, ὅτι ἐν ἐξουσίᾳ ἦν ὁ λόγος αὐτοῦ.

An analysis of the structure of this episode indicates a basic similarity across the three versions. It is obvious from these three texts that not only is the ἐξουσία of Jesus significant, but also the reaction of the crowd is equally important. Both ideas are included in all three gospels. The Lukan version follows the Markan version in the composition of place, namely in Capernaum. Both refer to Jesus' teaching occurring on the Sabbath. However, contrary to Mark, Luke does not mention the synagogue. In Matthew's Gospel, this story is situated in quite a different setting and in quite different circumstances. After the lengthy sermon on the mountain, the reader is told that the people are astonished at Jesus' teaching. However, Matthew follows Mark in drawing a comparison between the teaching of Jesus and that of the scribes. Luke does not include this aspect. What seems to be the message common to all three gospels is that Jesus' teaching was highly significant for the people, or at least very different from what they had come to expect from a teacher. It would seem then, that the three versions drew on a common tradition. The story in a condensed form would have been as follows:

> When Jesus began teaching early in his public ministry, he drew crowds around him and the people reacted with astonishment to his teaching, because he taught with ἐξουσία.

It is not readily apparent whether Matthew and Luke followed Mark, which could be argued from a two-source theory perspective, or whether each drew on a traditional story. What is apparent, is that each gospel writer has taken the story and expanded it or shaped it for a specific rhetorical effect. The inclusion or omission of specific details indicates the particular purpose or intention that the author wished to convey. Matthew links the episode to a specific body of teaching which the author has recorded. Luke's major interest is that of emphasising the wonderment of the crowd at the ἐξουσία of Jesus.

As the following table indicates, the Markan text contains more elements in this story than that contained in either the Matthean or Lukan versions. Only Mark names the location of this action as occurring in the synagogue:

Matthew	*Luke*	*Mark*
—	Capernaum	Capernaum
—	Galilee —	
—	Sabbaths	Sabbaths
—	—	synagogue
crowds	they	they
astonishment	astonishment	astonishment
teaching	teaching	teaching
ἐξουσία	ἐξουσία	ἐξουσία
scribes	—	scribes

The comparative diagram therefore reveals that in respect to the Markan text, the synagogue is an aspect which Mark has considered to be relevant in relating his version of the story. Another aspect of difference is that he has not seen the need as Luke has done, in naming Galilee as the region in which Capernaum is located. Although Mark refers to Galilee in 1:14 and in 1:16 as the place where Jesus begins his mission of "proclaiming the good news of God" 1:14, his interest in 1:21 seems to be that of locating the synagogue in a specific village or town.[3]

(b) The Markan Text: 1:21-22

The author of Mark's Gospel constructs a scenario in which Jesus' teaching is contrasted with that of the scribes, and immediately the conflict between Jesus and the scribes is established. For the most part scholars seem to treat verses Mk 1:21-22 and Mk 1:23-28 as the one incident. Although they are connected, the author is conveying two distinct dimensions regarding the ἐξουσία of Jesus. Therefore, it is necessary to consider each of these texts separately. Mk 1:21-22 is in reality, a summary statement of the freedom with which Jesus taught. The following incidents that are reported in Mk 1:23-3:5, serve to explain the many dimensions of the freedom with which Jesus spoke and acted.

The narrator reports that Jesus goes into Capernaum and immediately (εὐθύς) on the sabbaths (τοῖς σάββασιν) he entered the synagogue and taught. As Myers (1988, 141) states: "In one sentence Mark moves Jesus from the symbolic margins to the heart of the provincial Jewish social order: synagogue (sacred place), on a Sabbath (sacred time)." In naming Capernaum as the place where Jesus begins teaching, the author alerts the reader that the teaching of Jesus is to take on a different dimension from John's mission of preaching which was undertaken in areas withdrawn from activities of daily life. At the beginning of Jesus' ministry, Mark associates Jesus' teaching activity with the synagogue, and his teaching is initially targeted to agrarian communities in the villages and towns. The synagogue is the focal place of such communities, and the sabbath is their focal time.

The Greek word εὐθύς (*immediately*) in this context, is a word that Mark uses many times throughout the entire gospel text. Mary Anne Tolbert (1989, 135) and others have suggested that the term used by Mark on so many occasions is indicative of the urgency of the mission of Jesus. However, according to Pöhlmann (1991, 78) εὐθύς is an important compositional element in the narrative which indicates a temporal or logical result. He claims that it does not have the connotation of unexpectedness or suddenness. Nor would it imply a notion of urgency. Pöhlmann's view would seem to fit with the Markan text, since the author is telling his reader or auditor that Jesus, after gathering his disciples, acts with intention in going into the synagogue at Capernaum.

---

[3] Strange (1992) 42, states that Capernaum would be a large village or town and its location on a metropolitan strip along a major highway "implies traffic, commerce, the flow of ideas and information, including gossip."

The intentionality of Jesus' actions is an important aspect which Mark emphasises throughout the gospel text.

Evidence from the New Testament texts suggests that the synagogue was a gathering point for Jewish communities, particularly in the rural regions. They served as "meeting houses ... town halls, legal buildings, repositories for lost items, collection rooms and schools" (Frankemölle 1993, 295). Schrage (1971, 823) explains that the offering of gifts and the sacrificial worship, which would have been conducted by the priests in the temple, were replaced in the synagogues "by a ministry of the word influenced by prophetic traditions." However the major function of the synagogue was the study of the Torah, and so it was a place for instruction, and in particular it was a place for prayer. The synagogue was essentially a lay institution in which Pharisaism dominated (Schrage 1971, 823). It is significant, therefore, that Mark relates the beginning of Jesus' mission of teaching, not out on the mountain as Matthew does, but in the very heart of village life.

The other feature that is important in this opening sentence, and one that is often overlooked, is that Jesus goes to the synagogue on the sabbath, τοῖς σάββασιν. In Taylor's view successive sabbaths are not meant because as he argues, the plural is usual when feasts are mentioned. He gives the examples of Mk 6:21 (τὰ γενέσια), Mk 14:1 (τὰ ἄζυμα) and John 10:22 (τα ἐνκαίνια), all of which refer to celebratory feasts (1966, 172). However, the reference in 6:21 is to the birthday celebrations of Herod, hence the plural form (Balz 1990, 242). The reference in Mk 14:1 is to the feast of Unleavened Bread which was celebrated over seven days. In John 10:22, reference here is to the feast of Dedication which was celebrated over eight days (Balz 1990, 376). All of these feasts are in the plural. Therefore it can be assumed that the plural form τοῖς σάββασιν is intended as being connected with a feast cycle. In fact, the author of the Gospel most probably could have been alluding to the Feast of Weeks. Karel Hanhart (1992, 1015) explains the connection:

> Around the beginning of the Common Era the plural τὰ σάββατα (cf 1,21; 2, 23f; 3,2.4) was a Greek translation of the series of seven Sabbaths followed by the Feast of Weeks (Pentecost) of the Spring harvest, celebrated according to the ancient priestly calendar.

Hanhart (1992, 1015) argues that the sabbath controversies "do not concern the Sabbath in general" but that Mark, in writing for Christians after the events of 70 CE has "reversed the liturgical order in his gospel: from Pentecost to Passover." While this is an interesting interpretation, the theory stands or falls on whether one argues for a pre-70 or a post-70 dating of the gospel. John Castelot and Aelred Cody (1990, 1278) state that for the Jews, the "feast of weeks ... marked the end of the grain harvesting season, 50 days after the beginning of the barley harvest." The beginning of the barley harvest, in fact was the feast of Unleavened Bread. Castelot and Cody (1990, 1278) explain that there was "a sort of organic unity between the feast of Weeks and the earlier feast of Unleavened Bread, and through the latter, with the Passover."

Whether historically Jesus began his mission during the cycle of Sabbaths, and Mark thereby is drawing out the theological significance of this, or whether Mark is constructing his narrative so that it resonates with the experience of those involved in liturgical celebrations in early Christianity, is perhaps difficult to know. However, the use of the plural (τὰ σάββατα) in the context of the gospel text itself, seems to mean that the narrative is stressing that teaching in the synagogue was a practice that Jesus had carried out on other occasions.[4] The same connotation occurs where it is stated explicitly in Lk 4:15 that Jesus went into the synagogue "as was his custom." Mark is here emphasising that the observance of the sabbath was an important aspect of Jewish tradition that Jesus upheld.[5] Emphasis here on the sabbaths at this point is intended to foreshadow the controversy over the sabbath observances that is later on reported in Mk 2:23-3:5.

Unlike the parallel text in Matthew's Gospel where the essence of Jesus' teaching is recorded prior to the people's reaction of astonishment, exactly what Jesus teaches on this occasion is not recorded by the narrator of the Markan text. Instead, Mark's emphasis is on the fact that Jesus' teaching is different from what his audience had been accustomed (Waetjen 1989, 80). A clue as to the radical nature of Jesus' teaching comes from the narrator's emphasis on the response from the people who are "astonished" at his teaching, because it is different from how they were taught by the scribes. The English translation of the word ἐξουσία is usually rendered in English as "authority." This is not the concept that the author of the Gospel is conveying in this context. The meaning that Mark is conveying here demonstrates that ἐξουσία in this instance is implying that Jesus is teaching with great freedom. A first century reader of Mark's Gospel would have realised the full significance of this statement in that the teaching role in Jewish society was the prerogative of the scribe. Those who had any connections with the Jews, whether living in Palestine or in the Diaspora, would have been familiar with the role of the Jewish scribes, since they carried out a number of functions within society, as Günther Baumbach (1990, 260) explains:

> The scribes were exegetes of scripture who established its instructions in a binding way for the present; teachers, who sought to equip the greatest possible number of pupils with the methods of interpretation; and jurists who as trial judges, administered the law in practical situations. They

---

[4] Robinson (1994) 73; Stock (1989) 72 also makes this point.
[5] The Jews defence of their freedom to uphold the observance of the sabbath was a political sticking-point with non-Jews. However, the Jews right to maintain this observance was sanctioned by the Roman emperors themselves. See Lohse (1971) 17-18, who cites references from Greek and Latin authors relating to the Sabbath practices of the Jews. Also Freyne (1980) 69-78.

> exerted their greatest influence through their teaching activity in the synagogue. ... Because knowledge of the Torah distinguished the scribes, birth and descent did not form the basis for entrance into their respected position; but rather intensive study at the feet of a famous teacher, which consisted essentially of learning by memory the rabbi's teachings.

As Saldarini (1988, 10) points out, "[t]he scribes are the point of reference for Jewish religious teaching." In Mk 1:2-23 the implication is that they are ordinarily the teachers with whom the people are familiar. Here, the contrast between Jesus and the scribes is introduced into the narrative and sets the stage for the eventual conflict that emerges between Jesus and the establishment, and in which the scribes are key players.

In Mark's Gospel scribes are mentioned on 21 occasions in both Galilee and Jerusalem

Scribes	1:22; 2:6; 3: 22; 9:11; 9:14; 12:28, 12:32; 12:35; 12:38
Scribes and Pharisees	2:16; 7:1; 7:5
Scribes, Chief priests and elders	8:31; 11:27; 14:43; 14:53; 5:1
Scribes and Chief priests	10:33; 11:18; 14:1; 15:31

Thus from the Gospel of Mark, a clear picture is given as to who were the scribes' associates. In Jewish society, scribes generally worked for the king and for the Temple in the capacity of what would be described in modern terms as bureaucrats and minor officials. Their social class position, according to Lenski's categories of social class, would have been that of the "retainer" group.[6] From this perspective they would have had the potential for influencing the decisions of those higher up on the social scale, as well as influencing the social conscience of those in social classes below them.

In describing the various "philosophies" within society, Josephus does not include the scribes. According to Saldarini (1988, 206) the scribes were not "a coherent social group with a single identity and goal." Rather they were a professional group within the society (Lohse 1976, 115). Just when the scribes emerged in Israel has not been exactly determined. Lohse (1976, 115) explains that traditionally the task of communicating and teaching the word of God was the prerogative of the priest, while the role of scribe was normally given to someone who was able to practice the art of writing and who served as a royal official. Ezra who established postexilic Judaism and who had the approval of the Persian king, was able to assume both roles, the office of priesthood by virtue of his origins, and the office of scribe because he "had obligated the Jerusalem community to keep the Law" (Lohse 1976, 115).

---

[6] Lenski's description of the function of the "'retainer" class is consistent with the function of the scribes within the Jewish society to which other ancient sources bear witness.

Lohse (1976, 116) explains that the scribal profession would have developed "in the encounter and conflict with Hellenism," and the pervasiveness of Greek education throughout the Mediterranean world would have had some influence on the methods of teaching and learning:

> ... they began to copy the methods of the Greeks and apply them to the study and expounding of their own scriptures. Thus "they" learned from the Greeks how to conduct a didactic conversation of questions and counter-questions such that the teacher and learner would simultaneously derive answers to the problems at hand. Just as the Greeks appealed to the authority of the teachers and preserved the lineage of their names in the philosophical schools, the Jewish scribes also began reciting the list of names deserving honor, those supposedly associated with Ezra and the men of the Great Synagogue.

As a group, the scribes allowed themselves to be bound by the tradition, and in doing so, their best interests as moral guardians of the law were served and their position in society was secured. It would seem that in recounting this episode of Mark 1:21-23, the author is emphasising that the crowd's reaction of astonishment was because Jesus exercised his freedom and taught differently from the traditional teaching of the scribes. The Scribes would have felt threatened, not just because Jesus taught differently but because he aroused the interest and amazement of the crowd.

Acknowledgement of the ἐξουσία of Jesus: Mk 1:23-28

Comparison of Synoptic Texts

The first instance in the Gospel of Mark that demonstrates the ἐξουσία of Jesus, is his encounter in the synagogue with the man possessed by an unclean spirit. This story is not included in the Matthean text. Instead, Matthew places the people's expression of astonishment at Jesus' teaching, as their reaction to the content of the teaching in what has been called the "Sermon on the Mount" (7:28-29). The Lukan version, however, follows the Markan account very closely. The Markan text is set out on the following page:

Mk 1:23-28

And immediately there was in their synagogue a man with an unclean spirit; 24and he cried out, "What have you to do with us, Jesus of Nazareth? Have you come to destroy us? I know who you are, the Holy One of God." 25But Jesus rebuked him, saying, "Be silent, and come out of him!" 26And the unclean spirit, convulsing him and crying with a loud voice, came out of him. 27And they were all amazed, so that they questioned among themselves, saying, "What is this? A new teaching! With ἐξουσία he commands even the unclean spirits, and they obey him." 28And at once his fame spread everywhere throughout the surrounding region of Galilee.

Mk 1:23-28

καὶ εὐθὺς ἦν ἐν τῇ συναγωγῇ αὐτῶν ἄνθρωπος ἐν πνεύματι ἀκαθάρτῳ καὶ ἀνέκραξεν 24 λέγων, Τί ἡμῖν καὶ σοί, Ἰησοῦ Ναζαρηνέ; ἦλθες ἀπολέσαι ἡμᾶς; οἶδά σε τίς εἶ, ὁ ἅγιος τοῦ θεοῦ. 25 καὶ ἐπετίμησεν αὐτῷ ὁ Ἰησοῦς λέγων, Φιμώθητι καὶ ἔξελθε ἐξ αὐτοῦ. 26 καὶ σπαράξαν αὐτὸν τὸ πνεῦμα τὸ ἀκάθαρτον καὶ φωνῆσαν φωνῇ μεγάλῃ ἐξῆλθεν ἐξ αὐτοῦ. 27 καὶ ἐθαμβήθησαν ἅπαντες ὥστε συζητεῖν πρὸς ἑαυτοὺς λέγοντας, Τί ἐστιν τοῦτο; διδαχὴ καινὴ κατ' ἐξουσίαν· καὶ τοῖς πνεύμασι τοῖς ἀκαθάρτοις ἐπιτάσσει, 28 καὶ ὑπακούουσιν τὴν περίχωρον τῆς Γαλιλαίας.

Luke refers to the possessed man as "having the spirit of an unclean demon." Mark refers to the man as having "an unclean spirit." The response from the bystanders to the action of Jesus in each account is given a different nuance. In the Gospel of Luke the command of Jesus to the demon: "Be silent, and come out of him!" is met with the astonished question from the bystanders: "What is this word?" This is followed by an explanation for their astonishment: "For with ἐξουσία and power he commands the unclean spirits, and they come out." In Mark's account the response from the bystanders to the expulsion of the unclean spirit is: "What is this? A new teaching!" The reason for their wonderment is expressed in the words: "With ἐξουσία he commands even the unclean spirits and they obey him."

From these two accounts, the story in its original form would have contained the following information:

> Once when Jesus was teaching in the synagogue a man who was possessed confronted Jesus demanding what he was doing. Jesus, in reply expelled the demon from the man. The bystanders were amazed at the power that Jesus displayed and commented accordingly on the ἐξουσία that he had demonstrated.

Again the rhetorical effect of each of these accounts is to be found in the inclusion of specific details which each Gospel author incorporates into the text, and which then serves the particular perspective highlighted in the text. However the differences are slight:

Luke	*Mark*
spirit of an unclean demon	an unclean spirit
the synagogue	their synagogue
What is this word?	What is this? A new teaching!

(b) The Markan Text: 1:23-28

This story begins with the narrator's reference to the man with the unclean spirit, by emphasising "their" synagogue. It is not immediately clear to whom the narrator is referring as the "other." If it follows from the previous sentence it is in juxtaposition with the word "scribes" and so the reference to "their" in Mk 1:23 would refer to the scribes. It could refer generally speaking to the people of Capernaum who would claim "ownership" of the synagogue as their place. In either case it seems that the narrator is distancing it from either himself or from the main character, Jesus. The events that follow suggest that Jesus does not claim this synagogue as his place because of the "uncleanness" that dwells within its walls.

The inaugural action of Jesus' public ministry begins with the conflict between the holy and the unholy. This first public action of Jesus, according to Myers (1988, 143), "begins to specify the political geography of the apocalyptic action begun in the wilderness." In Mk 1:12, the narrator has already introduced the reader to the conflict between Jesus and Satan, the prince of demons, so the reader is already aware that Jesus has overcome the power of evil. In the ancient world the wilderness represented the "symbolic" place where demons were thought to reside. It was in the wilderness that Jesus encountered the temptations proffered by Satan. In Mk 1:23-28, the narrator takes the reader into the town and into the synagogue. Here, the demon in the form of an unclean spirit has also found a place in the midst of people gathered together where the interpretation of the Law was normally promulgated. Collins (1992, 47) explains that in the history of religions, evil spirits are thought of in two ways: "external" where evil spirits attack from the outside, and "internal" which is tantamount to "possession." In the scene in the wilderness Jesus is attacked from "outside," whereas in the synagogue, the attack is "within" its very walls.

Jesus' presence in the synagogue is in fact invading the symbolic space of the unclean spirit. Mark's choice of the term "unclean spirit" conveys a sense of the pervasiveness of this power. Jesus confronts the unclean spirit in this symbolic space, and immediately commands the unclean spirit to be silent. In other words, the unclean spirit is deprived of its voice to proclaim its message. The unclean spirit recognises Jesus as the "Holy One." The allusion here is to Daniel 4:3, 23 where the Holy One appears in order to "hew down the tree, lop off the branches, strip away its foliage and scatter the fruit." Alexander Di Lella (1990, 413) claims that the reference in Daniel "seems to be borrowed from Ezek 31, where the great tree of Lebanon, symbolising the king of Egypt, is also "cut down" (31:12) "because it became lofty in stature, raising its crest among the clouds and because it became proud in heart at its height" ... the biblical writers had in mind the insolent pride that would raise humans above God." [7] The apocalyptic imagery in Mk 1:23-28 is that the unclean spirit identifies Jesus as the "Holy One" who is to dismantle the monolithic institution of "uncleanness." Jesus is immediately portrayed by the narrator as standing within the true tradition of Israel. The synagogue is representative of the symbolic space where the confrontation between Jesus and the unclean spirit takes place. However, it is not the synagogue in itself which is the focus of Jesus' critique, but rather the socially constructed institution which the synagogue embodies as the focal point of the community's life. The scene here in Mark 1:25 with its reference to "unclean spirit" suggests that what is at stake is the basic institutional understanding of what constitutes "cleanness" and "uncleanness."

The rhetorical function of the use of apocalyptic language in describing Jesus' encounter with the powers of darkness is to establish the point of reference. In noting the apocalyptic elements in the text, Waetjen (1989, 81) poses the question as to whether there is an inference of a possible link between demon-possession and the institution of the synagogue as an oppressive force within the society of the time. He draws attention to the apocalyptic language in 1 Enoch 6-7 which interprets the myth of Gen 6:1-4 and which is illustrative of oppressive social institutions

> 1 Enoch 6-7 and 15 identify the nephilim of Gen. 6:4, born out of sexual union with "the sons of God" and the "daughters of human beings," as giants that transcend the flesh-and-blood realities of human existence. That is, they are institutions. "They take no food," the apocalypse declares, "but nevertheless hunger and thirst and cause offences. They consume all the acquisitions of human beings; and when human beings can no longer sustain them, they turn against them and devour humankind" (1 Enoch 7:3-4).

Waetjen (1989, 81) then spells out how this image exemplifies the situation of social institutions in the ancient world:

> In agrarian society, systemic structures such as kingship and its exchange system of retribution, the temple and its priesthood, which legitimated them, were dominant realities that deprived the greater majority of the people of much, if not most, of their livelihood through taxes, rents and tithes. Metaphorically viewed as giants they were too powerful to be conquered or overthrown. They breathed evil breath, unclean spirits, into society, which, although invisible, manifested itself in the loss of specifically those qualities which were considered to belong to being

---

[7] Di Lella (1990) 406-420, has revised Hartman's article on the book of Daniel.

created in God's image and likeness: autonomy, glory, honor, freedom, and dignity (Ps 8: 4-6) ...

Waetjen (1989, 82) sees here a direct connection between that of the apocalyptic myth in 1 Enoch 6-7 and 15 and that of Mark's account of the encounter between Jesus and the unclean spirits:

> it is difficult to avoid the conclusion that the synagogue as a socio-religious institution is insinuated to be one of those giants, a subversive reality which in its own way fosters necessity, bondage, destruction of individual sovereignty, and living death. Having established itself in society, like so many other institutions, it is resistant to the teaching of a new moral order which the rule of God inaugurates in which human beings will begin to recover the essential attributes of being divinely human. Jesus begins his work of restoration, as well as teaching, in the synagogue in order to liberate a fellow Jew from its oppression and dispossession.

In this episode in the synagogue, Mark is here stating that the mission of Jesus as that of announcing the reign of God is in contrast to that of the reign of the Evil One. The expulsion of demons is a recurring theme throughout the Markan text, namely, Mk 1:25; 3:12; 4:39; 8:30,32,33; 9:25; 10:13; 10:48. These demons take many forms and are found in different situations.

The response from the crowd to Jesus' confrontation with the unclean spirit is amazement at this "new" teaching. Obviously the Greek term καινός (*new*) is an important emphasis here. It conveys the sense of quality rather than the sense of time (νέος). Therefore, the inference here is that there is a different quality of teaching that Jesus is presenting. The action of Jesus in preventing the unclean spirit from taking control, is a teaching point for the crowd gathered at this scene. As Giesen (1991, 43) explains, Jesus "demonstrates that he stands entirely on the side of God who according to the OT (Ps 18:6=2 Sam 22:16; Ps. 104:7 etc) and Qumran literature (1 QapGen 20:28; 1QM 14:9-11 etc) alone has the right to overcome the godless powers."

While this story appears in essence as a healing/exorcism, it also contains elements of an apophthegm or "pronouncement."[8] According to Tannehill (1984, 1794) an apophthegm may be defined as

> a complete narrative scene which is meaningful in itself, and the climactic utterance is significant apart from events which may have been caused by it. The relative independence of an apophthegm is usually indicated by a shift in some characters or by a shift in time and place, marking the scene as an occasion separate from other occasions.

---

[8] "Pronouncement story" is now the more commmon term for what Bultmann called "apothegms" or to what Dibelius called "paradigms."

Tannehill (1984, 1795) explains that an apophthegm consists of two parts, namely, "the response of the primary character and the occasion which stimulates that response." The particular typology under which an apophthegm may be classed is based on an analysis of the interaction of these two parts. Tannehill (1981, 1) states that pronouncement stories are generally brief, but can be longer with descriptive detail added. Basically a pronouncement story is determined where "the description and dialogue lead on to a climactic utterance which summarizes the respondents response to the situation. The utterance must be the dominant element in the story as a whole" (Tannehill 1981, 2).[9] In the case of Mk 1:23-28, the utterance of pronouncement does not come from Jesus as the main character. Rather it is the action of Jesus in his encounter with the unclean spirit which leads to the climactic utterance of the people gathered at this scene and whose response in fact "pronounces" the ἐξουσία of Jesus. The response from the crowd serves two rhetorical functions in that it conveys the message regarding the ἐξουσία of Jesus, and at the same time draws the reader who has also "witnessed" the action of Jesus, to respond in this way as well.

The Claim to ἐξουσία: Mk 2:1-12

The third occasion in which the ἐξουσία of Jesus is emphasised in Mark's Gospel occurs in the episode of the healing of the paralytic. It is a healing/miracle story which includes a controversy story. This time instead of the narrator or the crowd drawing attention to the ἐξουσία of Jesus, it is Jesus himself who makes the statement. This episode is included in all three Gospel accounts.

Mk 2:1-12
And when he returned to Capernaum after some days, it was reported that he was at home.

2And many were gathered together, so that there was no longer room for them, not even about the door; and he was preaching the word to them.

3And they came, bringing to him a paralytic carried by four men.

4And when they could not get near him because of the crowd, they removed the roof above him; and when they had made an opening, they let down the pallet on which the paralytic lay.

5And when Jesus saw their faith, he said

Mk 2:1-12
καὶ εἰσελθὼν πάλιν εἰς Καφαρναοὺμ δι᾽ ἡμερῶν ἠκούσθη ὅτι ἐν οἴκῳ ἐστίν.

² καὶ συνήχθησαν πολλοὶ ὥστε μηκέτι χωρεῖν μηδὲ τὰ πρὸς τὴν θύραν, καὶ ἐλάλει αὐτοῖς τὸν λόγον.

³ καὶ ἔρχονται φέροντες πρὸς αὐτὸν παραλυτικὸν αἰρόμενον ὑπὸ τεσσάρων.

⁴ καὶ μὴ δυνάμενοι προσενέγκαι αὐτῷ διὰ τὸν ὄχλον ἀπεστέγασαν τὴν στέγην ὅπου ἦν, καὶ ἐξορύξαντες χαλῶσι τὸν

---

[9] The name "pronouncement story" was coined by Vincent Taylor. It corresponds with Rudolf Bultmann's definition of an "apophthegm," but is unlike Dibelius' definition of a "paradigm." It also has some affiliation with the *chreia* form (Tannehill 1981, 1).

to the paralytic, "My son, your sins are forgiven."
6Now some of the scribes were sitting there, questioning in their hearts,
7"Why does this man speak thus? It is blasphemy! Who can forgive sins but God alone!"
8And immediately Jesus, perceiving in his spirit that they thus questioned within themselves, said to them, "Why do you question thus in your hearts?
9Which is easier, to say to the paralytic, 'Your sins are forgiven,' or to say, 'Rise, take up your pallet and walk?.'
10But that you may know that the Son of man has ἐξουσία on earth to forgive sins" – he said to the paralytic –
11"I say to you, rise, take up your pallet and go home."
12And he rose, and immediately took up the pallet and went out before them all; so that they were all amazed and glorified God, saying, "We never saw anything like this!"

κράβαττον ὅπου ὁ παραλυτικὸς κατέκειτο.
⁵καὶ ἰδὼν ὁ Ἰησοῦς τὴν πίστιν αὐτῶν λέγει τῷ παραλυτικῷ, Τέκνον, ἀφίενταί σου αἱ ἁμαρτίαι.
⁶ἦσαν δέ τινες τῶν γραμματέων ἐκεῖ καθήμενοι καὶ διαλογιζόμενοι ἐν ταῖς καρδίαις ὑτῶν,
⁷Τί οὗτος οὕτως λαλεῖ; βλασφημεῖ τίς δύναται ἀφιέναι ἁμαρτίας εἰ μὴ εἷς ὁ θεός;
⁸καὶ εὐθὺς ἐπιγνοὺς ὁ Ἰησοῦς τῷ πνεύματι αὐτοῦ ὅτι οὕτως διαλογίζονται ἐν ἑαυτοῖς λέγει αὐτοῖς, Τί ταῦτα διαλογίζεσθε ἐν ταῖς καρδίαις ὑμῶν;
⁹τί ἐστιν εὐκοπώτερον, εἰπεῖν τῷ παραλυτικῷ, Ἀφίενταί σου αἱ ἁμαρτίαι, ἢ εἰπεῖν, Ἔγειρε καὶ ἆρον τὸν κράβαττόν σου καὶ περιπάτει;
¹⁰ἵνα δὲ εἰδῆτε ὅτι ἐξουσίαν ἔχει ὁ υἱὸς τοῦ ἀνθρώπου ἀφιέναι ἁμαρτίας ἐπὶ τῆς γῆς --- λέγει τῷ παραλυτικῷ,
¹¹ Σοὶ λέγω, ἔγειρε ἆρον τὸν κράβαττόν σου καὶ ὕπαγε εἰς τὸν οἶκόν σου.
¹² καὶ ἠγέθη καὶ εὐθὺς ἄρας τὸν κράβαττον ἐξῆλθεν ἔμπροσθεν πάντων, ὥστε ἐξίστασθαι πάντας καὶ δοξάζειν τὸν θεὸν λέγοντας ὅτι Οὕτως οὐδέποτε εἴδομεν.

(a) Comparison of Synoptic Texts

The importance of this story in the memory of the early Christian community is evident in that all three synoptic authors have incorporated it into their respective narratives. There is a reliance on a common source, with each author slightly varying the details contained within the story. According to Taylor (1966, 192), the section, Mk 5b-10a, "has a strong resemblance in form and construction to the Pronouncement-stories in 16f., 18-20, 23-6, iii. 1-6." Taylor (1966, 192) compares the form of this story with that of the account in Mt 9:1-8, "in which, with the miracle in the background, the foreground is occupied by the question of the forgiveness of sins." The Lukan version of this story which closely follows the Markan account in detail, also includes the "pronouncement" (Lk 5.20-24a).

In the synoptic versions of this story, the narrative outline is virtually the same:[10]

A   Introduction Mt 9:2a ‖ Lk 5:18-19 ‖ Mk 2:3-4
        Healing Mt 9:2b ‖ Lk 5:20 ‖ Mk 2:5
B   Controversy 9:3-6a ‖ Lk 5: 21-24a ‖ Mk 2:6-10a
A'   Healing Mt 9:6b-7 ‖ Lk 5:24b-25 ‖ Mk 2:10b-12a
        Conclusion Mt 9:8 ‖ Lk 5:26 ‖ 2:12b

The Matthaean account is the briefest, in that unlike the Markan and Lukan versions, it does not mention the difficulty the people had in getting the man to Jesus. However, apart from this, the details in all three accounts are similar, if not identical, as the following schema indicates:

Matthew	*Luke*	*Mark*
they (9:2)	men (5:18)	four men (2:3)
paralytic (9:2)	man ...paralysed (5:18)	paralytic (2:3)
—	difficulty with crowd (5:19)	difficulty with crowd (2:4)
—	brought man through roof (5:19)	brought man through roof (2:4)
son (9:2)	man (5:20)	son (2:5)
sins forgiven (9:2)	sins forgiven (5:20)	sins forgiven (2:5)
scribes (9:3)	scribes/ Pharisees (5:21)	scribes (2:6)
questioning to themselves (9:3)	questioning (5:21)	questioning in their hearts (2:6)
man is blaspheming (9:3)	speaks blasphemies (5:21)	it is blasphemy (2:7)
knowing their thoughts (9:4)	perceived their questioning (5:22)	perceiving in his spirit that they questioned (2:8)
Son of Man has authority on earth to forgive sins (9:6)	Son of Man has authority on earth to forgive sins (5:24)	Son of Man has authority on earth to forgive sins (2:10)
rise ... go home (9:6)	rise ... go home (5:24)	rise ... go home (2:11)
he rose and went home (9:7)	he rose before them and went home glorifying God (5:25)	he rose and went out before them all (2:12)

---

[10] Joanna Dewey (1980) 66, proposes a similar structure for the Markan pericope, but allocates 2:1-2 as the introduction and 2:3-6 as the first healing.

crowds afraid; glorified God who had given such authority to men. (9:8)	amazement seized them all; and they glorified God and were filled with awe saying, "We have seen strange things today" (5:26)	they were all amazed and glorified God saying, "We never saw anything like this." (2:12)

(b) The Markan Text: 2:1-12

This story is the first of the "controversy" stories in Mark's Gospel. In the context of the rhetorical unit Mk 1:21-3:6, it is the third statement regarding the ἐξουσία of Jesus.

The story begins with "four" men bringing a paralysed man to Jesus. It is obvious that the four acknowledge the ἐξουσία of Jesus, otherwise they would not have gone to all the trouble to place the man before him. The inclusion of this detail in Mark's Gospel has a rhetorical function in that the symbolic action of bringing the paralysed man into the midst of the crowd, into the very heart of the community, means that this man who, because of his handicap would normally be regarded as an "outsider," that is a sinner, has now becomes an "insider." According to Peter Fiedler (1990, 66) the word ἁμαρτία (*sin*) "signifies primarily a failure to achieve a standard (whether culpable or unintentional) in the broadest sense, both as deed and the nature of deed." In this scene in the gospel, the words of Jesus to the man "your sins are forgiven" confirm that the man's "standard" is that of an "insider." The words are also deliberatively provocative in that Jesus is calling into question the scribes' assumed sole prerogative of interpreting the Mosaic covenant, particularly where that interpretation has led to structural injustice and violence in the form of ostracising those suffering misfortune, sickness or poverty.

The reference in this episode, to the many people crowded around the door recalls the mention of the numbers of people gathered around the door in Mk 1:33. Throughout the narrative, the crowd (ὄχλος) plays a significant role as witnesses to the events that occur. The term (ὄχλος) is used in the Markan narrative some thirty-eight times and refers generally to the mass of the poor and dispossessed (Myers 1988, 156). The reaction of the crowd, particularly with reference to the vacillating mood of the crowd, heightens the dramatic impact of the story.

Tolbert (1989, 139-40) draws attention to the fact that it is in this scene that the scribes are first introduced into the Gospel narrative. Their first response to Jesus is to accuse him of blasphemy in their hearts (2:6). It is the charge of blasphemy that the high priest and the Jewish leaders will later level at Jesus to condemn him to death (14:63-64). It is important to note the irony of the situation in 2:1-12. Here, the scribes accuse Jesus of blasphemy because he dares to pronounce a man's sins as forgiven, whereas they have assumed that their "authority" is from God by virtue of their acquired status within the society. Their presumption is that this "status" gives them the right to act as adjudicators as to who are guilty of sin and who are not guilty. Here, Jesus is not only asserting his freedom to act on the man's behalf, but is also challenging the controlling power that the scribes hold within the social system. The "intertextual" allusion to the Son of Man (Mk 2:10) is to be found in Daniel 7, where the Son of Man confronts the dominions of oppressive power. Thus it is obvious that the author is further emphasising Jesus' understanding of his mission as that of exposing oppressive practices that were endemic within the society.

Stories of Healing

(a) The Healing of Simon's Mother-in-Law: Mk 1:29-31

It may be said that the ἐξουσία texts frame the two healing stories, both of which state how the freedom with which Jesus acted was transferred to those who came to him in faith. The first of such stories is that of the healing of Simon's mother-in-law. Myers (1988, 144) explains that the account of the healing of Simon's mother-in-law establishes the paradigm for subsequent stories of healing in the Markan text :

> 1. The subject is brought to Jesus' attention (often with the mediation of friends/relatives as here)
> 2. Jesus encounters the subject (sometimes with dialogue first)
> 3. Jesus responds (with touch as here or with word)
> 4. Healing is reported (often with instructions given)

The four disciples are those whom Jesus called in 1:16-20. Mention of these disciples by name suggests that the story claims to be an eye-witness account of the situation, and as credible witnesses they can verify that the power of Jesus to act is not only the expulsion of the demons, but his action also effects healing and transformation. Simon's house represents another symbolic space where the action of God takes place at the personal level. Lührmann (1987, 52) states that proof of the woman's healing was that she got up and served (διηκόνει) the meal, while Waetjen (1989, 83) adds that in serving the meal it is apparent that she considered that the Sabbath rest was no longer binding.

As Beyer (1964, 83) points out, the concept of service in Judaism was built on the commandment of Lev 19:18: "Thou shalt love thy neighbour as thyself." This included full readiness and service for and commitment to one's neighbour. However, in later

Judaism three factors obscured this. A sharp distinction came to be made between the righteousness and the unrighteousness in the antithesis of the pharisees, and this dissolved the unconditional command of love and service. The service became less and less understood as a sacrifice for others, and more and more as a work of merit before God. Finally there arose in Judaism the idea not to accord service, especially service at table to the unworthy (Beyer 1964, 83). In serving Jesus and the disciples, the woman is affirming their worthiness. The woman's response is in contrast to the reaction of the Pharisees in Mk 2:15-16, where Jesus is deemed to be "unworthy" because of his practice of eating with "tax collectors and sinners."

Rhetorically, this story of service (διακονία) is reminiscent of the account of Jesus in the wilderness (Mk 1:13) where the angels ministered to Jesus (οἱ ἄγγελοι διηκόνουν αὐτῷ). This concept is taken up again in 10:45 where Jesus, in reply to the request of James and John for the first places at either side of him, states that in fact "the Son of Man did not come to be served but to serve" (ὁ υἱὸς τοῦ ἀνθρώπου οὐκ ἦλθεν διακονηθῆναι ἀλλὰ διακονῆσαι). The issue in Mk 10:45 is not who should serve and who should be served. Rather, Jesus here is stating what his mission is all about, that of serving. It is not about appointing people to places of honour. In these instances where Jesus is both served and has come to serve, the author of the Gospel is emphasising that the way of Jesus demands a radical change in relationships, where service of one another is not based on status or the promise of reward, but on free mutual regard between persons.

(b) Healing of the Crowds: Mk 1:32-39

The incident concerning the healing of Simon's mother-in-law is followed by a summary statement by the narrator that many people who were in need of healing were brought to Jesus and he healed them. Taylor (1966, 181) draws attention to the periphrastic construction ἦν... ἐπισυνηγμένη which he claims "vividly describes the growing crowds" and which denotes not merely a "gathering around" Jesus, but conveys a stronger sense of flocking around or congregating around him. As Myers (1988, 144) states, the narrative world of Mark reflects the social reality of the author's world, in which illness and disability "were an inseparable part of the cycle of poverty." The "crowds" sought liberation from illness and physical disability as a way of lifting them out of this state of impoverishment. Mark portrays the healing ministry of Jesus "as an essential part of his struggle to bring concrete liberation to the oppressed and marginalised of Palestine" (1988, 144). Jesus did not set out to recruit the dispossessed as followers (Horsley, 1993, 228). It was common for people with factional interests to recruit the dispossessed to serve as mercenaries. They were thus bound to their leader. Augustus, for example, boasts that at the age of nineteen, and of his own accord and at his own expense, he "raised an army" (*RG* 1.1) in order to avenge his father's death and to seize power. The intention of Jesus in his interaction with the so-called outcasts and dispossessed, and in his ministering to them, was not to bind them to himself as followers, but to restore them "to regular interaction in their own communities" (1993, 228).

(c) Healing of the Man with Leprosy: Mk 1:40-45

This incidence in which Jesus cures a man of leprosy in fact does not initially follow the pattern that Myers has noted as being the usual format of healing stories. In this instance the man with leprosy is not brought to Jesus by someone else, but of his own accord presents himself before Jesus with the statement that: "If you will, you can make me clean." This man is both affirming the healing power of Jesus and at the same time subverting the notion that it is only the priests of the temple who can declare someone clean. Myers (1988, 152) explains that this episode "serves to subvert the very purity regulations that at first glance it appears to respect." He draws attention to the "extensive regulations regarding leprosy" that were set down in Lev 13:2-14:57. In essence it was considered that "(1) the disease was communicable, (2) a priest must preside over ritual cleansing" (1985, 152). Both principles are challenged at this point in the Gospel. Myers argues that the emphasis here is not so much on the cure but on the cleansing aspect. He cites C.H. Cave, who following J. Weiss, argued that the term καθαρίζω meant "to declare clean." Carl Kazmierski (1992, 45) points out that to "concentrate on the cure-miracle aspect is to miss ... the central concern of this part of the story, namely, not whether Jesus can declare the leper clean, but will he do it?" (1992, 45). The question is, as Kazmierski proposes, "is Jesus willing to break the official boundaries within which human intercourse is permitted within the official interpretation of the Tradition, and to accept the leper into community ...?" (1992, 45). Jesus shows he is willing by responding to the leper's request. He assumes the priestly role of the ritual cleansing by declaring the man as clean. In touching the leper, instead of Jesus contracting the disease, the leper is cleansed.

There is a variety of opinion concerning the ending of this story. Taylor states that Jesus' instructions to the man to present himself to the priest and offer sacrifice, is in keeping with Jesus' respect for the Mosaic law. While some scholars agree with Taylor's view, others argue that it and the injunction to keep silent about his cure is part of Mark's rhetoric of emphasising the theme of the messianic secret which Wrede and others following him have argued is a constant throughout the Markan text. However, Mark relates that the man disregards this injunction and proclaims what has happened.

According to Taylor the man "disobeyed" Jesus. Kazmierski (1992, 49) argues that this is not the case. He claims that the leper does respond to Jesus' injunction to show himself to the priests as would be required by law, and that the man subsequently responded as did others who were healed, by speaking out publicly. As a consequence, it was not Jesus but the leper himself, who could no longer go about openly in the towns and villages. Elliott (1971, 153) states that "many commentators on Mark have noticed the ambiguity in the verse within the context of the pericope of the healing of the leper. The ambiguity concerns the identity of the subject of ἤρξατο. Is it Jesus or the leper?" He notes that a number of scholars hold that the subject is the leper and that "the ὁ δέ construction introduces a contrast with the preceding command" (1971, 154). Elliott proposes another view claiming that Jesus is the subject of ἤρξατο and that Mk 1:45 is not in contrast to the preceding verse, but in fact is a new statement in which Jesus is the one who begins talking freely. Elliott believes that if the leper is the subject, then it would be out of character with Markan usage in which only the Baptist, Jesus and the apostles "preach the word." He argues that Mk 1:45 is a summary statement which is not connected to the story of the leper, and that the story of the leper reaches its climax in the usual way with a command to silence (1971, 155). However, it seems that Elliott has not considered the statement in Mark 1:32-33 where many people arrived at the door seeking healing from Jesus. This obviously suggests that the news is being spread far and wide by those who have experienced or witnessed the healing actions of Jesus. Daniel Harrington (1990, 601) likewise subscribes to the view that the subject is Jesus and not the leper, and that Mk 1:45 is a summary statement. He claims that this solves two difficulties with the text in that the healed man's alleged disobedience is resolved and the connection with the "messianic secret" is also resolved.

In contrast to Taylor's perspective, Ched Myers (1988, 153) argues that if the story of the leper was to record a mere healing story, then "the episode would be entirely uncontroversial." He claims that the man would have already been to the priests who for some reason have rejected him, and that the instructions that Jesus gives is to challenge the whole ideological system as a protest or "testimony" against the control which the priests exerted over the society. While this view may be consistent with the socio-political reading of Mark's Gospel from which Myers interprets this episode, it does seem to be reading too much into this particular text.[11]

The man's so-called "disobedience" to Jesus' directives is rhetorically significant here. In the story, Jesus' instructions to the man to show himself to the priests serves to remind the reader of the particularities of the law regarding diseases and their cures. However, the man's action of coming to Jesus in the first place and requesting that

---

[11] Kasmierski (1992) 48, also disagrees with Myers' interpretation here.

Jesus declare him as clean, indicates that the man had chosen to by-pass the requirements of this law. In not presenting himself to the "authorities" after Jesus had declared him as clean, the man is in fact exercising his freedom of action in this regard. Had he followed Jesus' directives and gone to the priests he would be acknowledging the power of the "authorities" to declare him clean. This was something he chose not to do in the first place, because he believed that Jesus could declare him as clean. It is important to note that nowhere else in the Markan text, does Jesus order or suggest that the healed person present himself or herself to the "authorities." In fact, the man's action here is consistent with the actions of other people healed by Jesus in that each response was particular to the situation and to the individual.

Myers' explanation of miracles as "symbolic acts" is an important consideration here. He points out that in each of the miracle stories, Mark "locates the agency of 'power' in the subjects of Jesus' actions" (1988, 147). Those he heals "are all made whole on account of *their* initiative and action, or 'faith.' Conversely in the presence of unbelief, the power of both Jesus (6.5) and his disciples (9.18f) to heal and exorcise is radically proscribed" (1988, 147). He argues that Jesus' symbolic acts were powerful not because they challenged the laws of nature, but because they challenged the very structures of social existence.

Myers (1988, 146) explains his use of the term "symbolic action":

> By "symbolic action" I do not mean action that was merely metaphorical, devoid of concrete historical character. Quite the contrary: I mean action whose fundamental significance, indeed *power*, lies relative to the symbolic order in which they occurred.

Myers provides a number of examples to illustrate his meaning. However, it may be necessary here only to cite one example, that of Martin Luther King whose actions, Myers (1988, 147) claims, were symbolic:

> Their significance cannot be interpreted apart from factors of socio-symbolic "space" (segregation in the southern U.S.A.) and "codes" (discriminatory law and tradition).

In the case of the miracles of Jesus, Myers (1988, 147) explains that

> the historical character of these actions was not diminished for their being "symbolic," nor were they any less "miraculous" for being nonsupernatural. Their "divine power" lay not in a manipulation of nature but in confrontation with the dominant order of oppression and in witness to different possibilities.

The declaration by Jesus that the man is cleansed of his leprosy, and the man's rejection of the cleansing ritual are indicative of the "symbolic action" that Mark is recounting in this episode. In being declared clean by Jesus the man is able to take charge of his life by rejecting the control of the priests over his fitness or worthiness to belong to the society. Jesus' action not only effects the man's healing but also effects his freedom. The man chooses not to have the priests confirm this, but to confirm it himself by spreading the news far and wide. In this encounter the emphasis is that both Jesus and the man with leprosy acted with freedom.

Stories of Controversy

(a) Eating with Sinners: Mk 2:15-17

The call of Levi (2:13-14) introduces the four controversy episodes in the second section of the rhetorical unit regarding the establishment of the ἐξουσία of Jesus. At the same time it also functions as a literary device by bridging the story of the paralytic, regarded by the scribal authorities as a "sinner," and the story of the first controversy where the Pharisees object to Jesus receiving hospitality from a toll-collector whom they regard as a "sinner." Donahue (1971, 49) points out that the Greek term τελώνης is incorrectly but generally translated as "publican" or "tax collector." In his view "toll collector" is the more appropriate translation. Tax collectors were generally "Roman officials or Jews in direct employ of the Romans," whereas "indirect taxes, the tolls and other imposts, were farmed out to individual lessees" (1971, 49). Donahue explains that the "farming of taxes brought with it all the evils of dishonesty and exorbitant tariffs inherent in such a system" (1971, 49). Hence they were generally regarded as "sinners."

Horsley (1993, 218-219) claims that there are three categories of meaning to which the term "sinner" is generally referred in the Gospel tradition. The first refers to those who were hostile to Jesus, that is, the priestly aristocracy who ruled Jewish society for the Romans. Reference in the Gospel of Mark is the statement in Mk 14:41: "The Son of man is to be betrayed into the hands of sinners." The second meaning refers to people generally who "could and would in some way transgress the provisions of the Torah" (Horsley 1993, 219). The third category, which Horsley states is that of associating the term "sinners" with tax collectors or toll collectors, that is the outcasts of society. In Horsley's view it is the second category to which reference is made in Mk 2:16. He argues that there is no evidence that "sinners" were the despised and the outcasts of society (1993, 223). However, there is enough contextual evidence that suggests that it is the third category to which reference is made here. In the case of the healing of the man with leprosy, for example, the man was considered ritually "unclean" and consequently a "sinner" (Mk 1:40-44). The distorted idea of sin as a cause for a person contracting a disease or of suffering a calamity is attested in the story of the man born blind (Jn 9:1-41). In Mk 2:16, the narrator of the Gospel is recounting the conversation in which the Pharisees use the term "sinners." It is the distorted idea of who were sinners and what constituted sin which Jesus was addressing in his action of eating with the despised and outcasts of society.

In this section of the Markan narrative, (Mk 2:15-17), the author introduces the Pharisees, another group within the society with whom Jesus takes issue. In each of the controversy stories Mark depicts this group as the opponents of Jesus. Initially they are named as "the scribes of the pharisees" which as Myers (1988, 158) says is intended to link them with the scribes as opponents of Jesus. Myers notes that "Mark later introduces the Herodians (3:6) and chief priests and elders (8:31)" in the same way. He claims that the author is using a narrative device which "expresses Mark's conviction that all sectors of the ruling class are ultimately aligned in their opposition to the kingdom" (1988, 158).

The response to the Pharisees' question regarding why Jesus chose to eat with sinners is met with Jesus' answer that he is not out to consort with those who consider themselves righteous and thus an "insider," but that his mission is to those whom the so-called "righteous" have judged as unworthy. It is at this point that the disciples are also criticised by the Pharisees, since they too are with Jesus as recipients of the hospitality of "sinners."

(b) Regulations on Fasting: Mk 2:18-22

In the second controversy episode Jesus and his disciples are asked why they are not adhering to the fasting regulations as do both John's disciples and the Pharisees and their disciples. Again the question is a literary device in order that in the context of the dialogue within the narrative, a statement is made whereby Jesus critiques the Pharisees' way of interpreting the social reality and which became burdensome for ordinary people. As already mentioned, the Pharisees' interpretation of the law tended to cover everyday life situations, not just those pertaining to the Temple and its precincts. For example, as Zmijewski (1991, 465) explains, the law required fasting only on the day of Atonement (Lev 16:29-34; 23:27-32; Num 29:7). However voluntary fasting was promoted by the Pharisees and was often undertaken by individuals and groups as a religious practice. Fasting, along with prayer, was regarded as being synonymous with one's righteousness. The Pharisees were regarded as "righteous" because they adhered to the Law. John's disciples were regarded as "righteous" because of their ascetic life style. The people in this episode of Mark's

Gospel, note their habit of fasting. Jesus, whom the people also regarded as "righteous" because of his teaching and actions, did not appear to fast. In relating the people's questioning, the narrator is also calling on the reader to judge Jesus' action of not complying with the practices of fasting. In this episode, the author is demonstrating that Jesus challenges the suppositions of equating holiness with religious practices. For Mark, holiness is being in communion with God (Mk 1:35) and in communion with others. The "others" are particularly the poor and the outcasts, the "sinners," for whom such religious practices as fasting had little meaning when access to food for them was always limited. For these people, "fasting" was a way of life.

Jesus' reference to the metaphor of the bridegroom is often interpreted as a reference to the impending death of Jesus. Mann (1986, 234) for example, claims that the emphasis is on mourning and not on fasting. However as Waetjen (1989, 91) rightly points out, the metaphor is used here by way of comparison rather than a foreshadowing of the Passion. The point is, that although Jesus does not discount the value of fasting altogether, life is meant to be lived in the present reality in engagement with others, not lived for gaining reputations for being "righteous" and attempting to accrue status in society.

With reference to the metaphors of the new patch on the old garment and the new wine in old wineskins, both Taylor (1966, 213) and Mann (1986, 235) put the question as to whether "the contrast between the new and the old" was meant as a criticism of John's disciples or of the Pharisees. According to Mann (1986, 236), the reference is to John's disciples because "the messianic kingdom having been proclaimed, there could be no room for the *new* community and the Baptist's community existing in uncomfortable parallel." Taylor (1966) does not provide a point of view on this matter. However, a closer analysis of these metaphors reveals that the metaphors are intended here as criticisms of both the Pharisees and also the disciples of John, who were most likely Essenes, for adapting to present life situations with outmoded or inappropriate religious practices (cf. Tolbert, 1989). Waetjen's comment on these metaphors is worth noting:

> The new... cannot be maintained by making adjustments and adaptations. In the face of the new, the continuities of the patterns of habituation and institutional structures perpetuate existing injustices and incur the loss of an open and vibrant future and with it human creativity and self-determination. Not reformation but revolutionary transformation is being asked for here (1989, 92).

It would seem then that the readiness on the part of the Pharisees to graft the practices relating to Roman ideology on to that of Judaism, is critiqued by Jesus as being not just incompatible but ruinous. In the same way the Essenes' way of endeavouring to be the new Israel within the context of a decadent Hellenised Roman culture is also pointless.

What Jesus proposes is the establishment of a new social order, the "reign of God," which Jesus images as a wedding feast. Its realisation would require transformation rather than restoration or reformation. In this metaphor of the bridegroom's friends not fasting while the bridegroom is with them, it is not Jesus, but God who is the bridegroom.[12] The guests are all those who are included in the celebration of the "reign of God." It is only when God is absent that there is reason to fast. This metaphor is the first of a number of images of the βασιλεία of God that Mark will introduce into the narrative.[13]

(c) Sabbath Observance: Mk 2:23-28

Controversy over the Sabbath observance is the subject matter of both the third and the fourth story in this section of Mark's Gospel. Again the story is used by Mark as a teaching point regarding this issue. In the first of these two episodes objection comes from the Pharisees that the disciples of Jesus are violating the sabbath because they are plucking wheat as they pass through the fields. Jesus responds by referring to the story of David and his men, who when fleeing from the murderous intentions of Saul, were given the bread of the presence to eat. According to the Law, only the priests were able to eat this bread. Mann (1986, 239) claims that the mention of David's action was to emphasise that the special circumstances in which David and his followers found themselves warranted the breaking of the law and thus it is implied that the disciples' action was also a special circumstance and so did not contravene the law.

However, the real point of the Markan episode is that the Gospel author is emphasising the level of pedantic absolutism to which the laws of the sabbath have been reduced. Even though they are pedantic, they are nevertheless oppressive regulations. An interesting observation that Waetjen (1989, 93) makes is that it is not Jesus, but the disciples who are accused of breaking the law. This suggests that the narrator is indicating that the disciples are identifying with the freedom of action that Jesus has demonstrated. Jesus does not excuse their action on the grounds that the disciples are hungry. Instead he alludes to a story in the Jewish tradition where David judged it appropriate that he and his companions ate the bread reserved for the priests because the circumstances warranted that they do so. The Markan version is an adaptation of 1 Samuel 21:1-6. Jesus is stating that David's action was one of freedom of response. Had David not acted in this way, he and his companions would have

---

[12] Fowler (1991) 179, insists that the metaphor of the bridegroom refers to Jesus.

[13] The Greek term βασιλεία τοῦ θεοῦ is mostly translated as "kingdom of God." The Greek word is retained here to distinguish it from the concept of the functional meaning or a geographical dimension of kingdom. For a discussion of the term see Luz (1990) 201-205.

perished. Borg (1984, 153) states that in the Jewish tradition "David and his career were the subject of continuous reflection." Had David not acted as he did, then he would have perished and the course of Jewish history would have changed. Borg (1984, 154) states that Jesus is referring to the urgency of the mission in which he and the disciples were involved. They did not have time for pedantic regulations regarding the Sabbath. This is not to say that Jesus repudiated the practice of sabbath observance as a ritualised expression of Jewish devotion. Jesus' pronouncement here, is that the circumstances of the people should be the yardstick which dictates what is the appropriate observance of the Sabbath, rather than the Sabbath being the yardstick for people's behaviour. The point that Jesus makes is that the laws pertaining to the sabbath are not inviolable.

(d) Healing on the Sabbath: Mk 3:1-5

Just as the healing of the paralytic was a combined healing/controversy story, so too is the cure of the man with the withered hand a combined healing/controversy story. It also follows on from the statement referring to the Sabbath in Mk 2:27-28 in the previous controversy story. Jesus not only freely preaches his views regarding the pedantic teachings of the Pharisees, but when the occasion presents itself, Jesus also freely acts as he does in this case.

The location of this final story is again situated in the synagogue on the Sabbath, as was the case when Jesus began his first act of teaching in the synagogue where the crowd were enthralled by his display of ἐξουσία. Here, the words of Jesus are translated into a display of action. The point of the story is not to prove that the circumstances of the man warrants contravention of the Sabbath regulations as Thomas Budesheim (1971, 191) advocates. The question that Jesus poses: "Which is lawful on the Sabbath, to do good or to do evil, to save life or to kill?" (Mk 3:4) is not rhetorical. Borg (1984, 157-158) claims that the question alludes to the situation where it was permitted to wage war on the sabbath if indeed Israel was under attack. However, generally their observance of the Sabbath prevented them from being involved in other nations' wars. The question Jesus puts to his adversaries demands that they consider what their normal response is to such situations. In curing the man's hand, Jesus is in fact responding to a situation which is life-giving to the man. The episode ends with a "pronouncement story" that places the Sabbath observance in proper perspective. Just as life-threatening situations are a valid reason for taking action on the Sabbath, so too are life-giving situations valid reasons for taking appropriate action on the Sabbath. In this story the author is here emphasising that the action of Jesus is a proof of his commitment to expose the oppression of people for which the hard-line adherence to the sabbath law was responsible.

The Rhetorical Significance of Mk 1: 21-3:5

In the opening verses of the Gospel of Mark, 1:1-12, the author portrays Jesus in eschatological terms as the spirit-filled Son of God who embarks on a campaign of claiming victory over the demons and to proclaim freedom to those who have been oppressed. There is a familiar tone in these chapters with that of the opening verses of the *Res Gestae*, where Octavian, claiming sonship and acting on behalf of freedom, claims victory over the factional powers that had left Rome in turmoil. Here the similarity between the actions of Octavian and that of Jesus ends. The contrast is that Mark portrays Jesus as one who opposes the forces of domination, not by military might and violence, but by challenging in word and in action, the very ideology on which the powers of domination are based. The episodes recounted by Mark are not intended to be reminiscences of single isolated events in the life of Jesus or accounts of his "deeds," but signs of the ἐξουσία of Jesus.

In line with the true prophets of Israel (Mk 1:2), the last of whom is John the Baptist, Jesus begins his critique against those institutions of Judaism which have perpetuated domination and oppression. Jerome Murphy-O'Connor (1990, 372) points out that at some stage within the ministry of John the Baptist and Jesus " there came a change." He draws attention to the fact that "Jesus' life-style, ministry, and message as depicted in the gospels differ radically from those of John" (1990, 372). Murphy-O'Connor is correct when he states that Jesus saw something more than John (1990, 372 n.54). John challenged those whose actions contravened the Mosaic Law, for example his opposition to Herod's unlawful marriage to Herodias. John's focus is on the law of God and repentance. The focus that Jesus adopts is on the people of God and God's mercy.

From the very beginning of the Markan narrative Jesus is acknowledged as someone who offered a new reality. John (Mk 1:7-8), the Voice from Heaven (Mk 1:11), the crowds (Mk 1:27-28), and those who were healed all bear testimony to this (Mk 1:1:32). Even the unclean spirits (Mk 1:24) acknowledge this. As Neyrey (1986, 109) points out, to Jesus' critics he was a threat because they observe him "crossing all the boundary lines regarding people, things, places and times." This is not to say that Jesus disparages the notion of purity as such. In fact his action of expelling unclean spirits bears witness to his commitment to rid the existing social order of impurity. He challenges the notion of what is clean and unclean in the purity system and commits himself to its transformation. Neyrey (1986, 118) has clearly outlined the principles on which the differences were based between the "old" to which the Pharisees adhered and the "new" that Jesus advocated:

	Pharisees	*Jesus and Followers*
core value	God's holiness (Lev. 11:44)	God's mercy (Exod. 33:19)
symbolised in	creation-as-ordering	election and grace
structural implications	strong purity system, with particularistic tendency	weaker purity system, with inclusive tendency
strategy	defence	mission, hospitality
legitimation in Scripture	Pentateuch	pre-Mosaic as well as prophetic criticisms

Walter Wink (1991, 278) states that the Jesus movement broke with the purity rules of the time "not because they found it inconvenient, or an infringement on their freedom to act. Rather, because rules of ritual purity are what keep the various people and parts of society in their 'proper' place." He outlines the implications of dismantling ritual purity rules:

> Without purity regulations, there would be a crisis of distinctions in which everyone, and everything, was the same: women equal to men, outsiders equal to insiders, the sacred no different from the profane. There would be no holy place or holy priests or holy people. Gentile would be no different from the Jew. "Clean" people would sit at table with "unclean"; no-one would be better in God's sight. Socially imposed shame about the body keeps people submissive to societal authority by weakening in them the immediacy of their own organic sense of what is right.

According to Neyrey (1986, 121), the emphasis in Mark's Gospel on Jesus crossing the boundaries of the established purity rules, is a functional statement that inclusiveness is to be the hallmark of the Markan community.

The Consequence of the ἐξουσία of Jesus

The rhetorical unit, Mk 1:21-3:5, ends with the Pharisees setting off to plot with the Herodians on how to destroy Jesus (Mk 3:6). Throughout the healing and controversy episodes, Mark shows that the opposition to Jesus is mounting. In Mk 2:6 the scribes appear on the scene, while in Mk 2:16 the scribes of the Pharisees are named as opponents. In Mk 2:24 the Pharisees are introduced into the narrative. Later, in 3:6 not only are the Jewish "authorities" depicted as opponents of Jesus, but also those who are connected with Herod, Rome's appointed leader, are enlisted by the Pharisees and so become opponents of Jesus. In subsequent chapters the chief priests, elders, and Sadducees are all introduced into the narrative as opponents of Jesus. Jack Dean Kingsbury (1990, 45) argues that "Mark's overriding goal in portraying these groups is to stress, not the distinctiveness of each, but the solidarity with one another." However, Kingsbury's claim that it is not Mark's intention to focus on the differences among these groups misses another important point that Mark is emphasising. In naming each of these groups, Mark is both reminding readers familiar with the differences or informing those readers for whom these differences would have been unfamiliar, that eventually these different groups all agreed on one thing, namely the execution of Jesus. Although the Markan narrative generally depicts these groups in opposition, a point is also made that there are individuals from these groups who do in fact respond positively to Jesus. In the light of the discussion so far regarding the concept of ἐξουσία, Elizabeth Struthers Malbon's (1989, 276) comment on the opposition to Jesus is an important one:

> Being a foe of the Marcan Jesus is a matter of how one chooses to relate
> to him, not a matter of one's social or religious status and role. And the
> same is true of being a friend of Jesus.

The healing and the teaching that take place in the fourth controversy story does not draw the same reports of affirmation and acclaim at the ἐξουσία of Jesus as other healing and teaching episodes have done. Instead, Mark introduces the growing opposition to the stance that Jesus is adopting. According to Waetjen (1989, 94-95) "the Pharisees show an unyielding determination to preserve their world and the power and privilege they possess as its guardians." However it is the negative reaction of the Pharisees and their plotting with the Herodians as to how to kill Jesus, that is in fact evidence that the ἐξουσία of Jesus has been well and truly noted, not only by the crowds and the disciples, but also by the very opponents of Jesus. They have to resort to extreme measures to extinguish his freedom to teach and to act.

The Context of the ἐξουσία of the Disciples

There are two instances in the Gospel of Mark where the ἐξουσία of the disciples is explicitly stated, namely Mk 3:13-19 and Mk 6:6b-13. The structure of the text is developed in such a way that the reader becomes aware that it is because of the disciples' response to the invitation to follow Jesus (Mk 1:16-20) and "to be with him" (Mk 3:14) that they share in the ἐξουσία of Jesus. The rhetorical framework in which these two incidences are couched extends from Mk 3:7-Mk 6:30. This section also contains minor rhetorical units which spell out the ramifications of commitment to the call to act in freedom.

Structurally, the major rhetorical unit can be divided into the following sections. The first section which extends from Mk 3:7-3:35, contains the first reference to the ἐξουσία of the disciples. This is followed by a segment containing four parables (Mk 4:20-32) and concludes with a statement by the narrator that Jesus taught the disciples in parables and with explanations (Mk 4:33). The second reference to the ἐξουσία of the disciples which is prefaced by a segment containing four miracle stories (Mk 4:35-5:43) and an introduction by the narrator (Mk 6:1), occurs in the section Mk 6:2-6:30. Although one cannot argue for evidence of parallel structure within this rhetorical unit, there are themes in the episodes recounted in Mk 3:7-3:35 which arc taken up again in different episodes in Mk 6:2-6:30 so that a pattern emerges which demonstrates the author's careful construction of this part of the narrative. A schematic outline of this major rhetorical unit can be depicted as follows:

3:7	Narrator's explanation: Jesus withdraws with his disciples
3:8-12	Crowds follow Jesus: You are the son of God
3:13-19	Call of disciples: ἐξουσία to drive out demons
3:20-30	Controversy: Jesus accused of being in league with Beelzebub—of doing evil
3:31-35	The relations of Jesus arrive
4:1-20	Parable of the sower
4:21-25	Parable of the lamp
4:26-29	Parable of the growing seed
4:30-32	Parable of the mustard seed
4:33-35	Narrator's explanation: Jesus spoke in many parables; explains everything to disciples
4:35-41	Jesus calms the storm
5:1-20	Healing of demon-possessed man
5:21-43	Raising of dead girl to life
5:25-34	Healing of woman with infirmity

6:1	Narrator's explanation: Jesus accompanied by disciples
6.2-6:	Jesus not accepted in his own town
6:6b-13	Disciples go out to preach/heal and expel demons
6:14	Herod hears about the disciples
6:15-16	Who Jesus is
6:17-29	Recall of John the Baptist's execution.
6:30	Narrator's explanation: disciples report all that they had said and done

Within this section of the Gospel narrative, repetitive themes are evident in the text as well as the progression of the involvement of the disciples in the enterprise of expelling demons and preaching the good news of the βασιλεία. Broadly speaking, this progression can be shown by the following diagram:

A   Jesus withdraws with his disciples (Mk 3:7)

    B   Call of disciples to go with ἐξουσία and to preach and expel demons (Mk 3:13-19)

        C   Jesus explains everything to his disciples (Mk 4:33-35)

A   Jesus accompanied by his disciples (6:1)

    B   Disciples sent out and with ἐξουσία to preach and expel demons (6:6b-13)

        C   Disciples report to Jesus everything that they had said and done (Mk 6:30)

The ἐξουσία of the Disciples: Mk 3:13-19

(a) Comparison of Synoptic Texts

The ἐξουσία of the disciples is also recorded in all three of the synoptic Gospels. The Markan account is as follows:

Mk 3:13-14	Mk 3:13-14
And he went up on the mountain, and called to him those whom he desired; and they came to him. 14And he appointed twelve, to be with him, and to be sent out to preach 15and have ἐξουσία to cast out demons.	καὶ ἀναβαίνει εἰς τὸ ὄρος καὶ προσκαλεῖται οὓς ἤθελεν αὐτος, καὶ ἀπῆλθον πρὸς αὐτόν. 14 καὶ ἐποίησεν δώδεκα [οὓς καὶ ἀποστόλους ὠνόμασεν] ἵνα ὦσιν μετ᾽ αὐτοῦ καὶ ἵνα ἀποστέλλῃ αὐτοὺς κηρύσσειν 15 καὶ ἔχειν ἐξουσίαν ἐκβαλλειν τὰ δαιμόνια

Each of the synoptic gospels also include the naming of the twelve companions who were chosen to be with Jesus, although Luke does not include the naming with the missioning of the disciples as does Mark and Matthew (Mk 3:13, [16-19]; Mt 10:1, [2-4]; Lk 9:1-2, [6:12-16]). Only Mark specifies the mountain as the site where the missioning of the disciples took place. The Matthean version does not contain this detail. However, both Mark and Matthew at this point indicate the reason for calling these men. The author of the Markan text states that they are to be with him and to be sent out to preach and have ἐξουσία over the demons Mk 3:14-15. In the Matthean text, the narrator states that Jesus gave them ἐξουσία over unclean spirits, to cast them out, and to heal every disease and every infirmity. Luke also records that the twelve were given ἐξουσία over all the demons and to cure diseases, and that they were sent out to preach and to heal.

The fact that the ἐξουσία of the disciples is mentioned by all three synoptic authors indicates its importance in the early Christian tradition. The on-going mission of proclaiming the βασιλεία in the Mediterranean world of the first century CE depended on the degree of commitment from those who were prepared to follow the "Way" of Jesus. Senior (1984), 31) points out that discipleship in Mark's gospel "has become a major focal point for contemporary interpretations of the Gospel.[14]

The Markan Text: 3: 13-19

The location of the naming of the twelve is the mountain. Both Waetjen (1989, 96) and Myers (1988, 163) point out that the author's intention in situating the scene on the mountain is to convey to the reader an image of the mountain of Sinai from where Moses inaugurated the community of Israel. Taken from a socio-political perspective, Waetjen (1989, 96-97) claims that in the story world of Mark, Jesus is seen here as

---

[14] For example, Best (1981); Tannehill (1977); Stock (1982).

inaugurating a new Israel in which those named to be with him can be likened to the patriarchs, but that in contrast to the patriarchs, the disciples "are not linked to one another by family ties or blood relationships." Stock's view (1989, 123) is that the author is emphasising both a theological dimension: "it is the place of God's nearness and of prayer (6:46; cf. 9:2)," and a typological dimension: "it is the place of revelation, Ex 19:3 ff." These interpretations serve as examples to indicate the author's skill in effectively employing, for rhetorical effect, these evocative images from the Hebrew scriptures in order to underline the theological character of his narrative.

Freyne (1982, 7) proposes an important perspective regarding the Markan depiction of the role of the disciples in the mission of Jesus. Having noted that "Mark's presentation of the ministry and person of Jesus draws heavily on apocalyptic images and ideas," he asks the question as to "whether the same cluster of ideas and images might not have inspired his distinctive portrayal of the disciples also." While he does not argue that there is a direct relationship between the disciples in the gospel of Mark and that of the *maskilim* in the Book of Daniel, nor does he place the works in the same literary genre, he nevertheless explores the idea that the presentation of the "elect" in the Markan text has something in common with the presentation of the "elect" in the Book of Daniel (1982, 7-8). Freyne identifies a number of similarities and differences in the text, with reference to the disciples and the *maskilim*. One important feature that he notes is that "they both share the same mythic pattern of a divine struggle between the forces of good and evil, and of the role of the elect in that struggle" (1982, 19). A dissimilarity, for which Freyne (1982, 19) argues, is that the disciples in Mark do not experience "the external political circumstances of the community's life, as in Dan., but rather in the human perversity and failure that does not recognise the true nature of God's final kingdom." However, a close reading of the text reveals that in being "with Jesus" the disciples are drawn more and more into confronting the political powers and institutions of oppression, the outcome of "human perversity" which quests after individualistic temporal power at whatever cost, and repudiates the all-inclusive promise of the $\beta\alpha\sigma\iota\lambda\varepsilon\acute{\iota}\alpha$. From this perspective, it would seem that Freyne is correct in his assessment that the author of Mark's Gospel "has given literary expression to the group's self-understanding by means of a model drawn from the literary world of the Jewish apocalyptic" (1982, 21).

A trend in some recent New Testament scholarship is that of exploring the notion of parallelism between the lifestyle of the Cynic philosopher and his followers in the ancient Mediterranean world and the life-style and mission of Jesus and his disciples.[15] A number of these studies have been based on a socio-literary approach to the study of the Gospel. In such studies, discussion has centred on the elements of literary forms

---

[15] For example Mack (1988); Robbins (1992); Crossan (1993).

attributed to Cynic rhetoric such as, "wordplay, wit, inversion, and the unexpected" (Robbins 1993, x), and for which there is evidence in the Gospel narratives. Other studies have tended to focus more on the description of social elements in the text, giving rise to the claim that the social milieu of ancient itinerant preachers known as Cynics is evident in the text. The injunction of Jesus to the disciples as they set out on mission, to take nothing for their journey except a staff; no bread, no bag, no money in their belts; but to wear sandals and not put on two tunics (Mk 6:8-9; cf. Mt 10:8b-10, Lk 9:3) has often been interpreted by some scholars as evidence of a Cynic lifestyle adopted by Jesus and his disciples. Crossan (1993, 421), for example, refers to Jesus as a peasant Jewish Cynic, since his focus was on farm and peasant life which was unlike the typical Greco-Roman Cynic whose sphere of interest was concentrated on the marketplace and on the city dweller. Sean Freyne (1988, 249), while not going so far as to say that the life-style and mission of Jesus was modelled on that of that of the Cynics, nevertheless regards the itinerant nature of Jesus' activity as being similar to the Cynic model.[16]

Richard Horsley (1993, 230) rejects this notion of Jesus and his disciples as Cynics. He also notes the difference between the focus of the Greco-Roman Cynic and the focus of Jesus, but draws attention to the fact that the Cynics "were called to become individual virtuosi and paradigms of virtue for other individuals who might emulate their example" (1993, 230). He claims that "Jesus' disciples, by contrast, were commissioned as catalysts of a broad popular movement" (1993, 230). Horsley (1993, 230-231) also identifies other significant differences:

> whereas the Cynics not only were not a social group but had no community base, the preachers and healers, as instructed in the mission discourse(s), while not a social group themselves, nevertheless worked in community bases. Cynic philosophers were indeed apparently vagabond beggars. Jesus' disciples, however, were instructed to preach and to heal in villages and towns ... Indeed, Jesus' disciples were not simply supported by local households but, as catalysts of a larger movement, focussed their activities on the revitalization of local community life as well.

Marcus Borg (1994, 116) also disagrees with the argument that Jesus lived the lifestyle of the Cynic. His claim is that

> Jesus was not simply concerned with the individual's freedom from the prison of convention, but with a comprehensive vision of life that embraced the social order.

---

[16] Botha (1993) 44-46, also sees some similarities between the Cynic life-style and that of Jesus.

Both Horsley and Borg are correct. Evidence in the Markan text suggests that Jesus and his followers were engaged in the very fabric of social life. The attainment of freedom that the Cynic and his followers advocated was to be achieved through a critique of convention from a stance of withdrawal from the culture. The message of freedom that Jesus proclaimed, and to which the disciples were drawn, was one that led to transformation of the social order through active involvement in social affairs.

The naming of the twelve at this point in the narrative is rhetorically significant. The reader's attention is now drawn to the involvement of the disciples whose presence in the narrative becomes more visible as the events unfold throughout the remainder of the Mark's Gospel.

The ἐξουσία of Jesus in Word and Deed: Mk 3:22-3:35

(a) Controversy with the Scribes from Jerusalem: Mk 3:22-30

The first instance in the Gospel where the disciples witness open hostility against Jesus and his activities is the incident in Mk 3:22-30, where a group of scribes accuse Jesus of consorting with Beelzebul, the prince of demons. The narrator states that Jesus' accusers had travelled from Jerusalem. This scene can be contrasted with that in Mk 3: 7-8 where people come from distant regions because they had heard "all that he did." The accusations of the Scribes that Jesus is in league with Beelzebub is diametrically opposite to the acknowledgment of the unclean spirits that Jesus is "the Son of God" (Mk 3:11). Myers (1988, 165) notes that it is at this point in the story that "the apocalyptic combat myth deepens significantly." It was not just the local scribes with whom Jesus was in conflict. His teaching and actions now also came into conflict with the more influential representatives of scribal authority residing in Jerusalem.

(b) The Relatives of Jesus: Mk 3:20-21, 31-35

The incident recounting the confrontation between Jesus and the scribes from Jerusalem (Mk 3:22-30), is contained within the story where the family of Jesus arrive seeking him out (Mk 3:20-21, 31-35). This is a compositional device, known as an inter-calation, which the author of Mark's Gospel employs on a number of occasions throughout the text.[17] As Fowler (1991, 143) explains, the intercalation or "sandwich"

---

[17] Fowler (1991) 143, identifies seven instances of intercalations in the Markan text, viz. 3:20-21, 22-30, 31-35; 5:21-24, 25-34, 35-43; 6:7-13, 14-29, 30-34; 11:12-14, 15-19, 20-25; 14:1-2, 3-9, 10-11; 14:53-54, 55-65, 66-72; 15:5-15, 16-20, 21-32. See also Rhoads & Michie (1982) 35-62.

arrangement in Mark's Gospel is a "paradigmatic large-scale framing device ... wherein one episode is split in two and another episode tucked between the split of halves." Key to the interpretation of Mk 3:20-35 is an understanding of the function of intercalation. According to Fowler (1991, 143-4) intercalation may be explained as follows:

> The intercalations exhibit a hermeneutical function for duality. The intercalated episodes are sharply opposed to each other, but at the same time they frequently contain so many verbal echoes of each other that the reader can scarcely fail to take up the implicit invitation to read the framed episode in the light of the frame episode and vice versa. The frame episode and the framed episode are thus placed on a par with each other, with neither having priority, either logically or chronologically. Intercalation is a sleight of hand, a crafty manipulation of the discourse level that creates the illusion that two episodes are taking place simultaneously ... Thus the commentary offered by the intercalation is the implicit direction from the narrator to read this episode specifically in the light of that one, and that one in light of this one.

In the first section of the "frame" (Mk 3:20-21) the narrator explains that initially the family of Jesus believes that his activities have gone too far. Consequently they try to take charge of him. Some scholars interpret this text rather literally and argue that the relations of Jesus believed that he was demented. Other scholars argue that the family believed he was transgressing the law, and that no one in their right mind would do so. While this seems to be the case, what is important here is that the family would have realised the danger to which Jesus was exposing himself because of his conflict with the established authorities, particularly with those who came from Jerusalem. Mann (1986, 252) also suggests that the activities of Jesus would have drawn unfavourable attention from the Roman authorities. Garnsey and Woolf (1990, 155) point out that in times of crisis in ancient peasant society, people's first recourse was to kinsmen, neighbour and fellow villagers. Social interaction was based on reciprocity among family groups or through ties of friendship, or even whole villages acting together to protect its members (1990, 156).[18] In contrast to reciprocity, was the power of client patronage which tended to undermine notions of solidarity amongst kinspeople and villagers. Although reciprocity was the norm amongst members of village societies in crisis situations, this could break down. Garnsey and Woolf (1990, 157) claim that "the strength of village solidarity in any given time will have varied and that while some peasants will have been able to rely on substantial help from their fellow villagers in times of crisis, others elsewhere will have fallen foul of a more opportunistic ethic." In this particular incident, the family of Jesus is acting as a united front in what they must have regarded as a crisis situation.

---

[18] See also Halvor Moxnes' explanation of reciprocity categories, viz. generalised, balanced and negative. He explains that close kinship tends towards general reciprocity where exchanges would be altruistic (1988) 34-35.

After recounting the controversy between Jesus and the scribes from Jerusalem (Mk 3:22-30), the narrator states that Jesus receives a message from his mother and brethren "asking him to come out to them" (Mk 3:31). Most commentators have interpreted Jesus' response as either a statement of his rejection of his family in favour of those who do the will of God, or as a statement that anyone who does the will of God is his "family" and in which of course his natural family is included. Crossan (1973, 113) takes a different view claiming that the author of Mark's Gospel redacted the tradition to emphasise the opposition between Jesus and his family. He argues that this condemnation "reflects the polemic of the Markan community against the Jerusalem mother-church."

However, in the light of the comments on family association that Garnsey and Woolf (1990) have made, it would seem that Jesus is challenging the socially determined principle of family solidarity out of which his family members acted to shield him from pursuing the dangerous project to which he was committed. The village folk would have been under no illusion that their lot in life was to stay in their place and abide by the laws and regulations promulgated by higher authorities without too much open questioning. Becoming embroiled with the powerful scribes from Jerusalem would have been considered a foolish action. His family want him to modify his stance. Jesus' response to the messengers is couched in the form of a "pronouncement story" whereby the narrator both summarises and emphasises the principle on which Jesus acts. His response is not a rejection of his family *per se* as Crossan argues, nor is it a statement here regarding the rejection of the notion of patriarchy as Horsley (1993, 237) claims. Rather, Jesus is stating that he is not going to compromise by accepting a protected situation in which reciprocity is based primarily on fear of attack and suppression rather than on freedom to act.

Parables of the βασιλεία: Mk 4:1-32

In order to illustrate the point with regard to freedom in the βασιλεία, the author introduces four parables each of which draws on images that would have resonated with the experience of people living in an agrarian society. The first two parables describe the different reactions regarding commitment to the realisation of the βασιλεία. The parable of the sower illustrates the various responses that people will make. Some find it impossible and reject it, others waver and give up, some try for a while but when difficulties emerge they too give up, while yet others are prepared to be committed. Through the parable of the lamp the hearers are reminded that the notion of the βασιλεία is to be proclaimed not concealed. In the third and fourth parables, the βασιλεία is likened to seeds sown in the earth which eventually reach full harvest, and a mustard seed which although seemingly small in its origins eventually reaches full stature. The images of the potential in the small seed, the patient waiting during its growth and the production of a full harvest or attainment of maturity would not have been lost on either those who wanted to take more immediate and/or violent means of achieving freedom from the powers that held them enslaved, or on those who had given up hope.

The four parables are followed with a summary statement from the narrator (Mk 4:33-35) that Jesus taught by means of many parables and explained his teaching to his disciples. It would seem that the point the author is emphasising here is that the disciples needed this sort of encouragement from Jesus as they came face to face with some of the realities, such as the scribes' attack on Jesus, that would challenge the commitment they had made.

Miracle Stories: Mk 4: 35-5:43

(a) Jesus calms the Storm: Mk 4:35-41

In Mark's Gospel, teaching and its *praxis* are inseparable, and hence in this section of the narrative, the four parables are followed by four stories of action. As with the above discussion on the parable stories, the discussion here will focus only on the aspects of the miracle stories that pertain to the concept of freedom. The first of these stories in that of Jesus calming the storm. Modern scholars have termed this type of miracle story as a "nature miracle" to distinguish it from the "healing miracle" (Crossan, 1993, 320). This story serves the author's purpose of focussing both on the actions of Jesus and the actions of the disciples. In the first instance it indicates the freedom with which Jesus acted. The narrator describes the scene in which Jesus and his disciples while crossing the lake, are caught in a fierce storm. Jesus, who is asleep in the boat is roused by the disciples who are fearing for their safety. Jesus rebukes the wind and commands the sea to be calm. A major point of the story is the reaction of the disciples to the freedom of Jesus, in that this freedom is also capable of confronting the natural elements. The result is that the disciples now begin to really fear, as they realise that the ἐξουσία that Jesus exercised is integrally linked with the power (δύναμις) that Jesus possesses. In commenting on this text, Waetjen (1989, 113) suggests that although the disciples had witnessed the actions of Jesus as he confronted the forces of chaos within society, the disciples were afraid "to grasp the scope of the reordering of power" in which they were asked to participate as followers of Jesus. According to Waetjen (1989, 113), the christological question "Who is this, for even the wind and the sea obey him?" serves to explain that the disciples do not fully understand the identity of Jesus, and also makes them question their own identity as disciples since it is becoming apparent to them that being disciples of Jesus does not have fixed boundaries.

Rhetorically, the function of this story within the Markan narrative is to serve as a bridge between the teaching of Jesus in Mk 4.1-34 where Jesus explains everything to the disciples, and the reality of the chaos that both Jesus and the disciples are to face as they move into the land of the Gerasenes to preach the "good news" to people dwelling in an area that was on the frontiers of the Roman empire. It was one thing to drive out the demonic spirits in Galilee, an area that they knew well. Confronting the demonic forces in unfamiliar territory, particularly where there was a strong Roman presence, was another matter.

(b) Jesus Confronts the Demons: Mk 5:1-13

The second miracle story relates the incident at Gerasa where a man possessed by an unclean spirit had been forced to make his home among the tombs. It is the unclean spirits who dwell in all their force within the man who confront Jesus. Here, Jesus displays the same freedom of action as in the previous story. Instead of the natural elements, Jesus faces a greater force, that of evil dwelling in the human which is capable of taking many forms. When Jesus demands that the unclean spirit disclose his identity, the unclean spirit replies that his name is "Legion." The word that the author uses here is λεγιών, a loan word from the Latin (*legio*). Hans Hübner (1991, 345) points out that it "designated the largest Roman unit of troops."[19] The word occurs four times in the New Testament. It occurs once in Matthew's Gospel (Mt 26:53) where the twelve legions of angels are mentioned figuratively in the context of a military battle with the powers of evil (Hübner 1991, 345). The other three occasions refer to the story of the demonic man at Gerasa. The word is used twice in the Markan account of the story (5:9,15) and once in the Lukan version (8:30). Hübner's comment is worth noting:

> The name is explicitly based on the great number of the demons that dwell in the demoniac (cf. the two thousand pigs in Mark 5:13). In addition the name indicates the violent, organised power of the world of the demons. Hatred and fear toward the Roman occupation is evident.

The narrator also relates that those who witnessed Jesus' encounter with the demonic powers were afraid and begged Jesus to leave the district. The author seems to be

---

[19] A legion consisted of 5,600 men Hübner (1991) 345.

making a deliberate reference in metaphorical terms to the power of the Roman forces. The placement of this story in Gerasa indicates that the author intended to portray Jesus' mission as extending beyond the confines of the Jewish regions of Nazareth and Capernaum to the Hellenistic regions of the Decapolis. Myers (1988, 190) explains that the Decapolis was "the loose confederation of territories that represented the eastern front of the Roman empire." Myers (1988, 191-192) also regards this story as one in which the imagery is meant to bring to mind the Roman military occupation of Palestine:

> Having been confronted by the Jewish ruling class in the scribally controlled synagogue, Jesus here meets the "other half" of the colonial condominium: the demon now represents Roman military power. In the symbolic act of exorcism, the legion "begged him (*parekalei auton*) earnestly not to send them out of the country" (5:10)! Nor is it surprising that there would be worried opposition to such an "expulsion" from the residents of the Decapolis, given the concrete experience of the Roman scorched-earth campaign of reconquest. Thus in direct contrast to the legion's petition, the locals "begged him" (*parekalein auton*) to leave their district.

An interesting point that is added here is the response of the man who has been released from these demons. Jesus does not tell him to show himself to the priest. However, the man begs (παρεκάλει αὐτόν) to go "with Jesus." Jesus' reply is for the man to return home and to spread the news there. Tolbert (1989, 167-168) claims that Jesus' refusal to have the man join him is because "being with Jesus is not a requirement for preaching." Myers (1988, 192) interprets the refusal as a statement that it was not yet the appropriate time "for the ecumenical community." Both interpretations seem to miss the connection with the liberation of the man and the social situation in which he now finds himself. The story presents an occasion for naming and exposing yet another socially constructed institution, that of the patron-client relationship in which a person is bound to another because one has received a favour from another person considered to be of higher status. According to Ramsay MacMullen (1986, 519), favours given to another of lesser status was known in the ancient Mediterranean world as *beneficia*, which he explains is "the currency by which the person who had much to give gained adherents and their services in turn." Garnsey and Woolf (1990, 154) also point out that "survival chances of the poor in antiquity ... depended to a significant degree on the quality of their relationships with more fortunate members of their own society. From time to time they were thrown back on their social and economic superiors for the satisfaction of vital needs, whether security against violence (of barbarians, bandits or tax collectors), or food, clothing and shelter." As already mentioned, this type of situation caused people to be caught in a cycle of dependence. Of course this state of affairs was not particular to societies in the ancient world. It would seem that in spite of the propaganda of so-called "progress" in the modern era, this cycle of dependence is endemic throughout the world. On a macro-scale, not only are there certain forms of government structures responsible for maintaining the cycle of dependence, other modern institutions such as the media and multinational corporations also keep sections of the society dependent on their power.

In the Markan narrative, Jesus' response assures the man that he is free to live his life without being "bonded" to Jesus. This outward display of the rejection of the institution of "patronage," a system which is indicative of the prized value of *dignitas* would have challenged this basic fabric of social networking that was considered integral to social order in the Greco-Roman world of the ancient Mediterranean region. The "good news" that Jesus was preaching was a dismantling of the traditional and accepted notion of patronage. It is no surprise that the people were yet again "amazed." It is tempting to wonder if in fact the author is implying that the many forms of abuse and oppression which the institution of patron-client relationship spawned and which was endemic throughout the Mediterranean world, was not figuratively likened to a "Legion" of unclean spirits.

(c) Jesus Heals the Women: Mk 5:21-43

The two episodes in which Jesus confronts the cosmic powers of destruction both in the natural order and in the human social order, is followed by two "miracle" stories of encounters between Jesus and people who seek his help. Again the story of one encounter, that of the woman who had suffered from a haemorrhage for twelve years, (Mk 5:25-34) is framed by another story, that of the daughter of Jairus (Mk 5:21-24; 35-43). Robbins (1987, 502) suggests that the literary device of intercalation in this instance has two functions. Firstly it "creates a time lapse which accentuates the actual death of Jairus' daughter." Secondly, "it presents the reversal of a woman's death-ridden life in anticipation of the raising of a young girl from death to life."

In Mk 5:25-34, the narrator relates that the woman with the haemorrhage heard of Jesus' arrival and, shielded in the anonymity of the crowd, decided that if she could but touch the hem of his garment she would be healed of her infirmity. When Jesus felt the "power" gone from him, he enquired as to who had touched him. Even though the disciples felt it was impossible to tell because of the crowd, Jesus persisted in his questioning until at last the woman came forward. In this encounter Jesus praises her and confirms that it was her faith that had healed her. It is the woman's faith in the ἐξουσία of Jesus which in fact restores her to health.

Robbins (1987, 510) states that "the story gives no prominence to the woman's final actions as "public events": She fell down before *him* and told *him* the whole truth." While it is not stated explicitly, surely it is implied in the text that not only is the woman's final action a public one, but indeed the actions of all the characters named in the story are "public events." In relation to the theme of ἐξουσία, there are two important points to be considered here. Firstly, the woman moves from a state of fear as an ostracised person and crosses the boundary of fear to freedom, and so gains wholeness. Again the purity rules were such that she was made to feel shame as an unclean woman (Lev 15:25-30). She would also have felt shame in being summoned into the midst of the crowd, because it would have been seen as a public admission that she was considered by society as an "unclean" woman.[20] Secondly, the purity regulations demanded that she too was bound to present herself to the priests, with a purification offering and a whole offering as expiation for her infirmity before she was allowed back into the society (Lev 15:28-30). The woman, however, crosses the threshold of fear to freedom, by daring to have faith in her action of touching the hem of Jesus' garment, and in eventually having the courage to stand out publicly.

The flip side of the story is also the freedom with which Jesus acted in this scene. According to the law, any man who was touched by an unclean woman would also have been regarded as unclean. In such a crowd, an unclean woman touching his garment would easily have gone unnoticed. It seems here, that the disciples' protests of the impossibility of detecting who had touched Jesus, masks their reluctance to draw attention to the situation. For them, it would have been easier for everyone to suppress the fact that Jesus had been touched by an unclean woman. In that way no one would have been shamed. Like his family, they also want to "protect" Jesus. However, the woman's freedom draws Jesus to also act with freedom. In bringing public attention to the fact that the woman had touched him, Jesus is prepared to stand with the woman. He also crosses the social boundaries in order to challenge laws which denied people their dignity. In this story then, the author contrasts the freedom of the woman and the freedom of Jesus with the disciples' reluctance to become involved in the situation.

The story that frames this episode Mk 5:25-34, is that of the synagogue president, Jairus by name, who asks Jesus to heal his sick daughter. Up to this point in the narrative Jesus is at odds with the Scribes and Pharisees because of their obdurateness with regard to the interpretation of the laws of Israel. In this instance it is the president of the synagogue, a Scribe who seeks Jesus and asks him to heal his daughter. Jesus' response to this request is immediate. As the story is told, Jesus is interrupted by the

---

[20] Maria Selvidge (1984) 619-623, provides a brief but excellent discussion on restrictive purity regulations in Jewish antiquity.

events related in Mk 5:25-34. Consequently, the young girl dies before he is able to reach her. However, in spite of the seeming hopelessness of the situation, Jesus raises the girl to life, much to the amazement of all present.

Again in relation to the theme of ἐξουσία in this episode, the author is drawing attention to the characters in the scene. First, there is the mention of the synagogue president who, from evidence in the text so far of Jesus' dispute with the scribes, would seem to the reader to have been unlikely to acknowledge the power of Jesus. At this juncture the author of the Markan text is emphasising a major point. It is the laws that bind others and the propensity for humans to enslave other human beings which is the focus of Jesus' critique, not people who have a change of heart. The active criticism that Jesus levels at institutions of governance is not that of an anarchist. Rather, the action that Jesus undertakes is geared to exposing oppressive and manipulative political, religious or economic social institutions, and those people who support them. The story emphasises that Jesus' response is immediate to those people who have a change of heart, no matter what their social standing may have been.

The second part of the story is in fact a teaching point about discipleship. Allowing no one except Peter, James and John, and the parents of the girl to accompany him, Jesus goes into the president's house and raises the girl to life. The symbolism in the words and actions of Jesus that the young girl only appears to be dead but is in fact asleep, is an important consideration within the context of the narrative. It conveys to the disciples and to the reader that Jairus' apparent lack of faith is in fact really "alive." This and the other three "miracle" stories that the author incorporates into his narrative at this point is to emphasise that the "power" Jesus exerts in each of these situations is to affirm not to condemn, to bring life not to destroy life. In fact, if the disciples were committed to being "with him" then they too would have to face the challenge of confronting the seemingly impossible situations for the sake of the βασιλεία.

Ched Myers (1988, 200) is correct when he states that Jairus and the woman with the haemorrhage "are portrayed as archetypical opposites in terms of economic status and honor." However Myers' contention that "the primary level of signification ... lies in the fact that Jesus accepts priority of the ("highly inappropriate") importunity of this woman over the ("correct") request of the synagogue leader" seems to be out of character with Jesus' mission to include all in the βασιλεία. Who is able to say which person's faith is the greater? The woman who has been conditioned to abide by the law for all these years, but now finds the freedom to make a decision about the quality of her life? Or the president, who in spite of his scrupulous dedication to the interpretation of the law, now finds within himself the freedom to ask for Jesus' help? In the structuring of these two particular stories in an intercalation framework, the intention of the author is not to lead the reader to stand as judge and jury over whose action is more worthy or less worthy. Rather the purpose is to confront the reader with the notion that inclusiveness in the βασιλεία is open to all who seek it in faith.

(d) Jesus is Rejected in his Home Village: Mk 6:1-6

The narrator's explanation at this point in the narrative, serves both as a closure to the parable and miracle stories, and as an introduction to the second reference regarding the ἐξουσία of the disciples. The disciples' response to both the teaching and example that Jesus has demonstrated is made clear to the reader. They go "with him" into his home village, where it would be expected because of village solidarity and because of his renowned wisdom and deeds, he would be hailed as a hero. Instead, Jesus is rejected by his fellow villagers. Most scholars have generally interpreted the rejection of Jesus as the people's dismissal of a hometown person who did not seem extraordinary as a child and young man growing up in their midst, and so are unwilling to pay him due honour when he returns. Others regard the story as a literary device in the narrative in which the true identity of Jesus is hidden from the characters in the story, but is gradually being revealed to the reader (Stock 1989, 175-178; Kingsbury 1989, 40-41).

However, it would seem that this story is emphasising that a much more contentious issue is at stake. As the narrator explains, it is the fact that Jesus' fame has become widely known that causes the people everywhere to begin to wonder who he is and from where he came. The response of the village folk to Jesus is now somewhat different from that recounted in the previous texts concerning his kinsfolk who want to protect him. It would seem that at this point, Jesus' presence in his home town causes the people to fear reprisal from higher authorities because of their association with him [21] As a result, the people fear crossing the boundaries that keep them oppressed. Instead, they prefer to submit themselves to the enslavement to which they have become accustomed rather than risk faith in the freedom that Jesus offers.

Confirmation of the ἐξουσία of the Disciples: Mk 6:6b-30

The explicit mention of the ἐξουσία of the disciples is again brought to the reader's attention in the final sub-section (Mk 6:6b-30) of the major rhetorical unit regarding the ἐξουσία of the disciples. In the context of calling the disciples together, the disciples

---

[21] It would not have been uncommon for a number of people in a village to be taken into custody, or for a whole village to be destroyed if one of their number was judged to be instigating social unrest. Josephus recounts many instances where this occurred.

are commissioned to go with ἐξουσία to drive out unclean spirits:

Mk 6:7	Mk 6:7
And he called to him the twelve, and began to send them out two by two, and gave them ἐξουσία over the unclean spirits.	καὶ προσκαλεῖται τοὺς δώδεκα καὶ ἤρξατο αὐτοὺς ἀποστέλλειν δύο δύο καὶ ἐδίδου αὐτοῖς ἐξουσίαν τῶν πνευμάτων τῶν ἀκαθάρτων

(a) Comparison of Synoptic Texts

It is only Mark (3:15; 6:7) and Luke (9:1; 10:19) who mention the ἐξουσία of the disciples on two occasions. In the Matthean account it is mentioned but once (Mt 10:1). However, in each of the second references in Mark and Luke and the one occasion in Matthew, the ἐξουσία of the disciples is linked to the instructions given to them by Jesus as they prepare for their journeys.

Although the Matthean account has already been discussed in connection with the two earlier versions in Mark and Luke, a comparison of the second references in Mark and Luke indicates the similarity in detail between that of Mark and Matthew, as well as some differences, and also the additions that Luke has incorporated into his account. Both the Markan account and the Matthean account are substantially the same. Minor variation are contained in Mark where mention is made that the disciples were sent out in pairs. The addition in Matthew is that the mission was also to heal every disease and every infirmity. Mark omits this aspect here, and instead focuses on the expulsion of demons. The Lukan account is substantially different. Instead of the twelve disciples being called, Jesus appoints seventy disciples for the mission, sending them out two by two into every place that Jesus himself intended to visit. It is when the seventy return that mention is made of the disciples rejoicing in the ἐξουσία they had been given in carrying out the task of subjecting the demons.

An aspect that all three have in common is the detailed instructions that the disciples were given in preparation for their mission. Both the Matthean and Lukan accounts contain more detail than the Markan account. What has been included in or omitted from the original story has been shaped and retold by each Gospel author to suit the particular purpose the author had in mind. In spite of these variations in the texts with reference to the ἐξουσία of the disciples, the underlying point is common to all three, namely that the disciples experienced the same freedom with which to cast out demons, to preach and to heal that Jesus himself possessed.

(b) The Markan Text: 6:7-13

In reiterating the ἐξουσία of the disciples, the author again employs the literary technique of intercalation. In this instance the story of the missioning of the disciples frames two stories relating to Herod. The first concerns Herod's fears regarding the identity of Jesus and his disciples, while the second story relates Herod's execution of John the Baptist, which as the narrator explains, is the reason for his fears concerning the news of Jesus' activities. The author has skilfully structured this section for rhetorical effect. Each of these stories is complete in itself but they are connected by the use of time frames. Thus, it is while the disciples go out on mission that the narrator breaks off to relate how people generally, and Herod in particular, regard Jesus. Then it is by means of a "flashback," a story that recalls an event which has already taken place that the focus is drawn to the kind of character Herod is and the reason for his fears. At the end of this story the narrator again takes up the story of the disciples as they return from their mission.

In the opening verses of this section of the narrative, the Twelve are called together again and are given instructions as they prepare to commit themselves to the mission of Jesus. This time the narrator is more explicit in relating the directions Jesus gives to them. Obviously, the mission of the disciples is directed further than the local area, because they are instructed as to what to take for the journey and to accept the hospitality in the place where they go. Crossan (1993, 422), in taking the view that Jesus and his disciples adopted a "Jewish-Cynic" lifestyle", claims that Jesus' strategy for giving these explicit instructions was in order to set before the disciples the notion of "the combination of *free healing and common eating*, a religious and economic egalitarianism that negated alike and at once the hierarchical and patronal normalcies of Jewish religion and Roman power." According to Crossan, the instructions given to the disciples regarding their journey supports his view that the lifestyle of the disciples was to be modelled on that of the Cynic. In arguing that the Cynic lifestyle was different to what Jesus had in mind for his disciples, Horsley (1993, 231) explains that unlike the Cynic philosophers who seemed to be vagabond beggars, the disciples of Jesus "were to preach and heal in villages and towns ... as well as to stay in local houses, eating what those households provided." The emphasis on a simple life-style and the acceptance of hospitality that was provided would not have been lost on a first century audience, who would have been well acquainted with the expectations of the Romans regarding hospitality (*hospitium*) as they moved in and out of the region. Associations no doubt would have been made with stories that circulated regarding the lavish hospitality provided for governors and emissaries of Rome on their journeys through the regions of Palestine, as well as for the military forces stationed there. As has already been mentioned, one such circulated story which Josephus records is the extravagant hospitality that Herod the Great provided for Octavian and his entourage when they passed through the region of Ptolemais on their way from Syria to Egypt (*AJ* xv. 199; cf. *BJ* I. 394-5). These "itinerants" all received the display of welcome at the expense of the tax payers.[22] Herod Antipas inherited his father's penchant for extravagant living funded largely by the tax payers.

The narrative now moves to the first part of the "framed" story regarding Herod's consternation about Jesus and his activities (Mk 6:14-16). In the light of the stories that circulated regarding Herod's extravagances, the juxtaposition of this story with that of the disciples as they set off on mission as "itinerants" is no doubt implicitly intended to focus on a comparison of the life style of the followers of Jesus and the life style of those who wielded the political power. It is through the narrator that the reader is informed as to the current opinion regarding Jesus. It was because Jesus was considered to be a prophet that caused Herod much concern. Whether the author is indicating that people held superstitious beliefs that Jesus was one of the prophets of Israel who had returned, or whether it is a way of depicting people's perceptions of the kind of prophetic role that Jesus seemed to be projecting, it is difficult to know. Nevertheless Herod classed Jesus in the same category as John. According to Josephus (*Ant.* xviii. 119), Herod feared John because he felt that a sedition might arise because of John's popularity with the people, and that it was Herod's fear that drove him to get rid of John once and for all. The Markan author presents a different version. The story that the narrator relates in Mark's Gospel is that John had challenged Herod's decision to marry Herodias, his brother's wife. It was for this reason and at Herodias' instigation that John was put into prison. Herodias continued to hold a grudge against John and seizing her opportunity when Herod promised Herodias' daughter anything she wanted, suggested to the daughter that she ask for the head of John the Baptist. The narrator relates that Herod was distressed at this request but because he was committed to his promise he complied with the wishes of the young girl. Josephus (*AJ* xviii. 117-118) provides a different version of John's death:

> When others joined the crowds around him [i.e. John], because they were aroused to the highest degree by his sermons, Herod became alarmed. Eloquence that had so great an effect on mankind might lead to some form of sedition, for it looked as if they would be guided by John in everything that they did. Herod decided that it would be much better to strike first and be rid of him before his work led to an uprising, than to wait for an upheaval, get involved in a difficult situation and see his mistake.

---

[22] Mitchell (1976)127-128, provides an excellent summary on the *hospitium* to which a legate and his quaestor, other Roman officials and the military were "entitled." Exploitation of hospitality was widespread in the Roman occupied world.

Josephus continues his report saying that John was brought in chains to Machaerus and put to death.

According to Louis Feldman (1981, 88 n.*c*), the difference between the two versions is that Josephus was emphasising the political reason, whereas Mark was emphasising the moral reason. However, Mark's emphasis on the moral aspect leads the reader also to consider the political consequences. Herod's political ambitions influenced his moral decisions and his level of immorality dictated the kind of political action he was prepared to take. The poignancy with which the story of John is told in Mark's Gospel brings into sharp focus the lengths to which Herod would go to ensure that his power remained unrivalled.

The story of John's death has a significant rhetorical function in the Gospel narrative as a whole. The statements referring to the people's assessment of Jesus as a prophet, a favoured one of God as was John the Baptist, is contrasted with the portrayal of Herod as the person who used his power to kill. Mark's inclusion of the story means that wherever the story is read or heard, Herod's deed will be remembered and condemned for the evil that it was. The rhetorical function within the context of the mission of the disciples is also significant. The narrator concludes the story about John's death by stating that John's disciples, on hearing the news came and took his body away and laid it in a tomb. The finality of John's death is made obvious in this statement, yet paradoxically the story of John as told in Mark's Gospel remains alive in the Christian tradition as a testimony against the power of evil.

Having concluded the story about John, the narrator again takes up the story of the disciples' mission as they return to report to Jesus all they had seen and accomplished. The juxtaposition of this statement with the story of John's execution indicates the point of signification regarding the ἐξουσία of the disciples. Although the disciples knew of Herod's disposition towards those whom he thought might undermine his position and and were well aware of the possible action he would take, they nevertheless were committed in their mission to cast out demons.

The Rhetorical Significance of the ἐξουσία of the Disciples

Scholars have tended to interpret the relationship between Jesus and his disciples as that of teacher-pupil or charismatic leader-follower.[23] Others have argued that Mark's depiction of the disciples as increasingly not understanding the message of Jesus, in fact places them in the same category as the other opponents of Jesus included in the

---

[23] For example, Robbins (1992); Hengel (1981).

narrative.[24] It must be acknowledged that the initial invitation Jesus extended to the disciples was, "Come, follow me" (Mk 1:17) and also that the narrator states that Jesus "taught" the disciples (Mk 8:31, 9:31). It must also be acknowledged that the disciples are depicted as not always understanding and that in the end they acted out of fear and failed to stand "with Jesus." However, the focus on the ἐξουσία of the disciples suggests that Mark's purpose in this instance was to emphasise what he understood to be the message of Jesus regarding the concept of discipleship. Mark's depiction of Jesus can be interpreted that Jesus possessed the qualities of a charismatic leader or a teacher. It can also be said that the crowds regarded Jesus as a charismatic figure and followed him (Mk 1:3), and that they too were "taught" by Jesus (Mk 4:2). Therefore the notion of charismatic leader-follower or teacher-pupil roles does not seem to define the specific relationship between Jesus and his disciples. The clue to this relationship is in the phrases that Jesus appointed twelve "that they might be with him" (ἵνα ὦσιν μετ᾽ αὐτοῦ, Mk 3:14a), and that he might send them forth to preach and also to have ἐξουσία to expel the demons (καὶ ἔχειν ἐξουσίαν ἐκβάλλειν τὰ δαιμόνια Mk 3:14b-15). As his companions they too were to proclaim the gospel and with ἐξουσία to drive out the demons. In Mk 6:7-13 the narrator states that the disciples do just that. They set off on their mission without Jesus and later rejoin him (Mk 6:30) relating what they had done and taught. The picture that the narrator conveys is that the disciples were caught up in the mission of Jesus with energy for the enterprise. They did indeed learn from him in what he said and what he did, and they were inspired by this. It would seem that Jesus recognised the seed of this energy when he initially called the four who were working as fishermen by the lake. The four parables that Jesus told and his specific explanation of them to the disciples seem to suggest this.

In relation to the ἐξουσία of the disciples, the message of Mark is that the concept of discipleship which Jesus espoused, is not based on a hierarchical model as was that of the Scribes and Pharisees of the ancient Jewish world, nor indeed on the teacher-pupil model in the Greco-Roman world. Generally speaking, the *praxis* of discipleship in both of these cases was based on an imitation of the expert or the master as role model. Mark's understanding of the concept of discipleship that Jesus espoused, was a radical transformation of the *praxis* of discipleship where inclusiveness in the mission of Jesus was the norm, and from where the initiative of response in encountering theological, religious, political, and social issues which confronted Christians in a Jewish-Hellenistic environment, was to be encouraged.

---

[24] For example, Kelber (1972); Kingsbury (1989).

CHAPTER SIX

The Challenge to ἐξουσία.

The Context of the Challenge

Having established the ἐξουσία of Jesus and the disciples in the first half of the Gospel narrative (Mk 1:1-8:30), the narrator, in the second half, then relates how the ἐξουσία of both Jesus and the disciples was tested to the ultimate degree (Mk 9:2-16:8). Again the word ἐξουσία is a key term in this section of the narrative, where it is found in two episodes that the narrator records. The first is in reference to Jesus in Mk 11:1, 27-33 where Jesus comes into direct confrontation with the "authorities" in Jerusalem. The second is in reference to the disciples by way of a parable that Jesus relates (Mk 11:33-34).

As Freyne (1988, 136) states "the political powers impinged rather lightly on the public career of Jesus in Galilee; it was in Jerusalem that the great encounter with secular power occurred." In this second part of Mark's Gospel, the focus of the critique that Jesus levels at institutions of domination is extended to that of the temple, the centre of government administration in first century Palestine, and the very heart of the nation's political power. The rhetorical unit in which the author places Jesus' critique of the temple begins with the episode where he enters Jerusalem (Mk 11:1-10), and ends with what is termed as the eschatological discourse (Mk 13:3-32). The narrator projects the obvious determination with which Jesus levels his criticism at the ruling powers through a series of episodes that emphasises Jesus' polemic against the temple authorities and for which they challenge his right to do so.

Confrontation over the ἐξουσία of Jesus: Mk 11: 22-33

(a) Comparison of Synoptic Texts

The narrator situates the scene of the confrontation between Jesus and the "authorities" in the temple precincts and as Kingsbury (1989, 76) points out "the setting itself heightens the intensity of the conflict." Whether this story reflected an actual event in the life of the historical Jesus is of course rather difficult to prove. However from accumulated evidence in the Christian tradition, the fact that Jesus was in conflict with the authorities is sure. A story which reflects this conflict has been included in each of the synoptic gospels in almost identical detail, Mk 11:27-33 ‖ Mt 21:23-27 ‖ Lk 20:1-8.

Mk 11:27-33

²⁷And they came again to Jerusalem. And as he was walking in the temple, the chief priests and the scribes and the elders came to him,

²⁸and they said to him, "By what ἐξουσία are you doing these things, or who gave you this ἐξουσία to do them?"

²⁹Jesus said to them, "I will ask you a question; answer me, and I will tell you by what ἐξουσία I do these things.

³⁰Was the baptism of John from heaven or from men? Answer me."

³¹And they argued with one another, "If we say 'From heaven', he will say, 'Why then did you not believe him?'

³²But shall we say 'From men'?" —they were afraid of the people, for all held that John was a real prophet.

³³So they answered Jesus, "We do not know." And Jesus said to them, "Neither will I tell you by what ἐξουσία I do these things."

Mk 11:27-33

καὶ ἔρχονται πάλιν εἰς Ἱεροσόλυμα. καὶ ἐν τῷ ἱερῷ περιπατοῦντος αὐτοῦ ἔρχονται πρὸς αὐτὸν οἱ ἀρχιερεῖς καὶ οἱ γραμματεῖς καὶ οἱ πρεσβύτεροι ²⁸καὶ ἔλεγον αὐτῷ, Ἐν ποίᾳ ἐξουσίᾳ ταῦτα ποιεῖς; ἢ τίς σοι ἔδωκεν τὴν ἐξουσίαν ταύτην ἵνα ταῦτα ποιῇς; ²⁹ὁ δὲ Ἰησοῦς εἶπεν αὐτοῖς, Ἐπερωτήσω ὑμᾶς ἕνα λόγον, καὶ ἀποκρίθητέ μοι καὶ ἐρῶ ὑμῖν ἐν ποίᾳ ἐξουσίᾳ ταῦτα ποιῶ· ³⁰τὸ βάπτισμα τὸ Ἰωάννου ἐξ οὐρανοῦ ἦν ἢ ἐξ ἀνθρώπων; ἀποκρίθητέ μοι. ³¹καὶ διελογίζοντο πρὸς ἑαυτοὺς λέγοντες, Ἐὰν εἴπωμεν, Ἐξ οὐρανοῦ, ἐρεῖ, Διὰ τί [οὖν] οὐκ ἐπιστεύσατε αὐτῷ; ³²ἀλλὰ εἴπωμεν, Ἐξ ἀνθρώπων; —— ἐφοβοῦντο τὸν ὄχλον· ἅπαντες γὰρ εἶχον τὸν Ἰωάννην ὄντως ὅτι προφήτης ἦν. ³³καὶ ἀποκριθέντες τῷ Ἰησοῦ λέγουσιν, Οὐκ οἴδαμεν. καὶ ὁ Ἰησοῦς λέγει αὐτοῖς, Οὐδὲ ἐγὼ λέγω ὑμῖν ἐν ποίᾳ ἐξουσίᾳ ταῦτα ποιῶ.

In each of the synoptic accounts of this scene, the setting for the confrontation is the temple (ἐν τῷ ἱερῷ). The opponents of Jesus are the authorities in Jerusalem (οἱ ἀρχιερεῖς καὶ οἱ γραμματεῖς καὶ οἱ πρεσβύτεροι). In both Mark and Luke the opponents are named as the chief priests, scribes and elders. Matthew does not include the scribes. The chief priests and elders are mentioned in all three instances. According to Rohde (1993, 148) the elders were members of the Sanhedrin or Council and "were members of the lay nobility as opposed to the high-priestly nobility." Rohde also points out that there were "elders" in the Jewish synagogue communities. The Pharisees are not mentioned in any of the synoptic versions of this story, which would suggest that on this occasion Jesus is being confronted by the officials of government. In each gospel account of this episode there is the same confrontational dialogue between these officials and Jesus; the same question from the officials, a counter-question from Jesus, discussion amongst the officials, their reply and Jesus' response.

The inclusion of the story in all three gospels suggests that each of the authors regarded this story as pivotal for conveying to the reader the hostility that Jesus encountered from the highest authorities, and Jesus' readiness and determination to expose a system of government that was essentially corrupt. A comparative table of the sequence of events in this story is outlined as follows:

Matthew	*Luke*	*Mark*
entered the temple/	teaching in the temple	walking in the temple
chief priests/ elders of the people (21:23a)	chief priests/ scribes/ elders (20:1)	chief priests/ scribes/ elders (11:27)
came up/ said (21:23a)	said to him (20:2a)	came to him and said (11:28a)
"By what ἐξουσία are you doing these things?, and who gave you this ἐξουσία?" (21:23b)	"Tell us by what ἐξουσία you do these things, or who is it who gave you this ἐξουσία." (20:2b)	"By what ἐξουσία are you doing these things, or who gave you this ἐξουσία?" (11:28b)
Jesus answered them, "I will also ask you a question; and if you tell me the answer, then I also will tell you by what ἐξουσία I do these things. The baptism of John, whence was it?" (21:24-25a)	He answered them. "I will ask you a question; now tell me. Was the baptism of John from heaven or from men?" (20:3-4)	Jesus said to them. "I will ask you the question; answer me, and I will tell you by what ἐξουσία I do these things. Was the baptism of John from heaven or from men? Answer me?" (11:29-30)
And they argued with one another, "If we say 'From heaven,' he will say to us, 'Why then did you not believe him?' (21:25b	And they discussed it with one another, "If we say 'From heaven,' he will say, 'Why then did you not believe him?' (20:5)	And they argued with one another, "If we say, 'From heaven,' he will say, 'Why did you not believe him?' (11:31)
But if we say 'From men', we are afraid of the multitude; for all hold that John was a prophet." (21:26)	But if we say 'From men,' all the poeple will stone us; for they are convinced that John was a prophet." (20:6)	But shall we say 'From men'?" –they were afraid of the people, for all held that John was a real prophet. (11:32)
So they answered Jesus, "We do not know." And he said to them, "Neither will I tell you by what ἐξουσία I do these things." (21:27)	So they answered they did not know whence it was. And Jesus said to them, "Neithet will I tell you by what ἐξουσία I do these things." (20:7-8)	So they answered Jesus, "We do not know." And Jesus said to them, "Neither will I tell you by what ἐξουσία I do these things." (11:33)

(b) The Markan Text: 11:27-33

The cause of the conflict that occurs between the Jewish authorities and Jesus is brought to the reader's attention with the question the officials put to him:

> And they said to him, "Tell us by what ἐξουσία you do these things, or who is it that gave you this ἐξουσία?" (Mk 11:28)

> καὶ ἔλεγον αὐτῷ, Ἐν ποίᾳ ἐξουσίᾳ ταῦτα ποιεῖς; ἢ τίς σοι ἔδωκεν τὴν ἐξουσίαν ταύτην ἵνα ταῦτα ποιῇς;

Obviously the "things" to which they refer are Jesus' words and actions which are levelled against the temple and which appear to the authorities to be undermining their position as the guardians and power-brokers of the temple. Hence their question concerning his right to act in this way. In his defence, Jesus does not explain, but asks them a question: "Was the baptism of John from heaven or from men"? The phrase "from heaven" (ἐξ οὐρανοῦ) is reflective of the world view in antiquity which, as Schoenborn (1991, 544) explains, "combines elements of cosmology with the idea of God." He also adds that for people in antiquity this meant that "God himself is determinative of what is predicated to heaven." Obviously, then the phrase "from men" (ἐξ ἀνθρώπων) in this context denotes the alternative, that is, not of God.

In the story the author shows that the scribes in this instance do not resort to the usual method of appealing to Scripture or legal precedent as they would normally do in reply to questions of theology or morality. Clearly they recognise that the question put to them is politically charged, as was their initial question to Jesus. Consequently they refuse to answer, because either way their answer would convict them. If they said that John was from God they risked an uprising as the people looked forward to the Messiah or a precursor in the form of a prophet who would deliver them from the oppressive power of the Romans and restore Israel to its former promise. As already noted, this was a constant theme in the Jewish apocalyptic literature of the time. The "authorities" knew that the people would condemn them because they had not acted to prevent Herod from executing John as a man of God. They also feared the political consequences if they said he was not from God. Their relationship with the Romans was such that part of the deal in allowing the rulers of Judaea to hold office was that they would maintain law and order by keeping the people in check. If the people rose in rebellion then the Roman forces would move in to take control.[1] Jesus' reply to these men was not that he was keeping them guessing. Rather he was also using their tactics. He had already been accused by some of the scribes as being in league with Beelzebul (Mk 3:22). The acclaim that he received as he entered Jerusalem, and which is

---

[1] See Goodman (1987) 29-50, for discussion of the ruling classes and their relationship with Rome

recounted in the narrative just prior to this episode, was testimony that the people believed he was "from God," and that Jesus had a ground swell of supporters. He was leaving them to draw their own conclusions. In fact he was freely choosing not to reply to their question.

Jesus' Polemic against the Temple

(a) Entry into Jerusalem: Mk 11:1-10

As Mark records the event of Jesus' entrance into Jerusalem, it was the demonstration of support for him by the people (Mk 11:1-10) that seems to be one of the "things" that concerned the "authorities." Whether there were elements in this story of Jesus' journey into Jerusalem that were actually factual or whether the story was constructed to highlight the fact that Jesus had gained the following of the crowds, is difficult to know. However this episode, along with the other episodes (Mk 11:11-25) that occur in the text prior to the story of Jesus' confrontation with the "authorities" serve to provide the Markan audience with the reason for the concerted attack on Jesus.

All three synoptic versions contain this story. A reconstruction of the original story would probably be as follows:

> Jesus procured a colt and rode into Jerusalem amid the acclamation of the crowds who spread their garments and leafy palms on the road to welcome him. They greeted him loudly with the words: "Blessed is he who comes in the name of the Lord!"

The version of this story in Matthew's Gospel includes the response of the crowd referring to Jesus as the "Son of David" (Mt 21:9b). In the Lukan version of the story, Jesus is hailed as "king" (Lk 19:38). However in the Markan version there is no reference to Jesus as either Son of David or king. Rather he is praised as one who comes "in the name of the Lord" (Mk 11:9). Jesus is greeted with acclamation because it is "the kingdom of our father David that is coming" (Mk 11:10). Many interpretations of this episode in Mark's Gospel discuss this event as if it refers to the "kingship" of Jesus, when, in fact, there is no reference to Jesus as king. This is significant because in Mark's Gospel Jesus is accused by Pilate in the trial scene, of claiming to be king.

Duff (1992, 55) draws attention to the variety of interpretations regarding this episode in Mark's Gospel where Jesus enters Jerusalem to the acclaim of the crowds. Broadly speaking some scholars have interpreted the Markan account as a sign that "the messianic king has come to claim his city," while others have suggested that the context is intentionally ironic in order to "provoke the reader to reconsider his/her pre-suppositions about such topics as messiahship, discipleship, and the role of the kingdom of God."[2] Duff's view is that the readers' attention is drawn to "their knowledge and/or experience of typical Greco-Roman entrance processions in order to highlight the allusions to the divine warrior" (1992, 56). He provides a number of examples from the Greco-Roman world indicative of the variety of processions that were held for political, military and religious occasions when the conqueror or leader entered the city. Duff (1992, 64) explains that these entrance processions typically followed "a pattern whereby a ruler/general symbolically appropriates a city by way of ritual, whether that city be foreign or his own. The appropriation of the city is echoed both in the elements of the procession but, more important, by a ritual ceremony at the end." Duff then turns his attention to the Markan narrative, where he claims that the author has used allusions to the divine warrior in Zerachiah 14 "to shape his account of Jesus' entry into Jerusalem" (1992, 70). He explains that the pattern of entering into the city in fact does not follow the typical pattern, but that there is enough allusion in the narrative to draw the reader to make a comparison between the procession of a divine conqueror and the way Jesus comes into the city, and that Mark in fact "subverts those triumphal allusions" in order to challenge the expectations of those who believed that Jesus would inaugurate a kingdom like that of the warrior-king (1992, 70-71).

A fairly typical interpretation of this episode is that Mark is here confirming the kingship of Jesus, or as Tolbert (1989, 115) states, the episode illustrates "the kingly function of Jesus and the first enthusiastic recognition of it." Stock (1989, 291-2) draws attention to the Hebrew scripture references in relation to the expected messiah that are evident in the text:

> In view of the intent of the passage to describe Jesus' approach to Jerusalem as a messianic king, we may see in the phrase, "a colt *tied*," an evocation of Gen 49:8-12 ("Binding his foal to the vine and his ass's colt to the choice vine," 49:11) which proclaims the advent of a king from Judah. "On which no one has ever sat" is a common requirement in a beast used for religious purposes. Jesus comes as the Son of David messiah, but he does not come as a temporal ruler or with worldly pomp. He comes as a religious figure, a prince of peace, "humble and riding on a donkey" (Zech 9:9).

Duff (1992, 55) explains that other interpretations have emphasised the irony that the author of the Markan gospel is employing here. He cites Myers' comment that the triumphal entry is misnamed, since the procession was not meant to be triumphal as such. Myers (1988, 294) claims that the actual procession "resembling carefully choreographed street theatre, is designed to give intentionally conflicting messianic signals." Myers agrees with Horsley's observation that there are striking parallels between Menahem's procession into Jerusalem to liberate the city in 66 ACE and the

---

[2] In particular, Duff (1992) 55 discusses the views of Kelber (1974), Taylor (1966), and also Myers (1988).

Markan account of Jesus' march on Jerusalem (1988, 295). However, he argues that while there is military symbolism in the text, "it is expressly antimilitary in its tone. Jesus does not intend to fight for the temple state, and the Mount of Olives will in fact be used for the purpose of judgement (13:3)." He draws the conclusion that the procession "is filled with conflicting signals, as if it intends to be a satire on military liberators" (1988, 295).

Again how much factual material there is in this episode is difficult to tell. It may be that the author is drawing attention to Jesus' popularity with the crowd and his construction of the scene is to highlight the fact that the popularity of Jesus was on the same scale as other popular figures of the time. Another possibility could be that the author is drawing the reader's attention to the crowd's proclamation of Jesus as the Messiah at this point, and later in the narrative, will record the crowd's *volte-face* as they reject him before Pilate. Theologically, the allusions to the divine warrior and to other references to the Hebrew scriptures underscore that Jesus was the promised Messiah for whom the Jews were waiting.

However, as the story is told by the narrator, this does not explain why Jesus requisitioned a colt so that he could ride into Jerusalem in the first place. It was Jesus himself who organised his entry into the city (Mk 11:1-8). Claiming to be king would be inconsistent with the actions of Jesus that are recorded so far in the narrative. Nor does it seem that the author is using satire here to make his point. Rather in this episode and indeed throughout the second part of the Markan narrative emphasis is placed on the freedom with which Jesus acted in confronting those issues in the system of government which contravened the fundamental tenet of Judaism, namely the commandment of love of God and love of neighbour. Jesus' entry into Jerusalem was the first of these acts of confrontation with the establishment.

One possible explanation as to why Jesus chose to ride into Jerusalem is that he was deliberately challenging a monolithic system in which the requisition of transport was the prerogative of the wealthy and influential but was not accessible to the poor. An inscription found in recent times in the town of Burdur in southern Turkey provides evidence that the requisitioning of transport was a practice throughout the Roman empire.[3] The inscription written in both Latin and Greek was issued by Sextus Sotidius Strabo Libuscidianus, who, it seems, held the position of governor in the province of Galatia during the reign of Tiberius. The inscription is contemporaneous with the period in which Jesus lived and worked. There is evidence from other ancient literary sources in the form of edicts and letters giving directions regarding requisitioning of transport and which bears witness to the fact that the matter was problematic during the

---

[3] Work on deciphering this inscription was undertaken by David French and Stephen Mitchell in 1975-76. Mitchell's article (1976) provides a translation of the inscription with a commentary. Reference was made to this inscription in chapter two.

reign of Augustus and throughout the first and second centuries CE. Because laws and edicts were promulgated on this matter, it is apparent that people were being exploited by unscrupulous imperial officials, the military and powerful landowners regarding transportation. The edict that Sotidius decreed was ordered to be prominently displayed so that all might know the rules and regulations as to who was eligible to requisition transport, what were their entitlements and what payments were to be made to the suppliers of the transport. However the concluding paragraph is worth noting:

> I want nothing to be provided for those who transport grain or anything else of that sort either for their own use or to sell, and (nothing should be provided) for anyone for their own personal baggage animals or for their freedmen's or for their slaves' animals. Shelter and hospitality should be provided without payment for all members of my own staff, for persons on military service from other provinces and for freedmen and slaves of the best of princes and for the animals of these persons, in such a way that these do not exact other services without payment from people who are unwilling.

Mitchell (1976, 113) states that from evidence within the text of this inscription "there is no doubt that the *mandata* in question had come from Augustus himself. Since Sotidius also explicitly states that he had received these instructions in person, we must conclude that he had been appointed by Augustus and continued his term of office under Tiberius, when the edict was issued." It also seems that regulations regarding transport had been drawn up by Augustus, since Sotidius states that because of the widespread abuses that had crept into the system, he was "tightening up" the edict on transport that had previously been decreed by Augustus (1976, 107; 109). According to Mitchell (1976, 115) it was the interpretation of the regulations by subordinate authorities particularly in the provinces that caused resentment and drew complaint from the people. He states that "[t]he definition and enforcement of detailed regulations in line with the general guidelines in any particular locality was the responsibility of the governor, and the new edict clearly exemplifies this process."

What is significant here is that the governor was endeavouring to do the right thing by the people in setting down guidelines that would address the abuses that were occurring. The administration at the highest level tried to address transport issues resulting from a widespread increase in mobility and communication throughout the empire. The nature of the problems that ensued were many and complex. However on analysis the whole system was seriously flawed. Ultimate control of the movement of people throughout the empire was undertaken by the leader of Rome who initially drew up the regulations regarding transportation. It was he who gave the *mandata* to the governors in the provinces to ensure these regulations were followed, and who in turn interpreted these rules as they saw fit, often with a view to their own advantage. On the other side of the issue was the situation where, if people wanted to travel to or through another province, they were required to produce a *diploma*, or permit, from the officials in their home province. However these could easily be forged or bought from unscrupulous minor officials (1976, 125). While transport owners were supposed to provide only for those categories of people that the regulations defined, they too often succumbed to either harassment or bribery. Abuse within the system at whatever level was ever present. The poor and the outcasts had neither status or the money to access the system. In fact the whole system of transport further created a gulf between the wealthy and influential and the poor and the outcast of society. This state of affairs was not just a local problem particular to Sotidius' jurisdiction. Edicts which responded to the complaints of people regarding transport matters have been found to have come from Egypt, Syria, Asia Minor (Mitchell 1976; Llewelyn 1994, 58-92). Nor was the problem confined to the period in which Jesus lived. Evidence suggests that although Augustus, Tiberius and other Roman rulers of the first century concerned themselves with the regulation of transport and the abuses which these regulations spawned, the problems continued for the next four centuries (Mitchell 1976, 115; 131; Llewelyn 1994, 59-92).

As Mark presents the story, Jesus' entry into Jerusalem was not to petition about transport *per se*. The very abuses which directly and indirectly were the result of these regulations impacted on the whole of the social system creating situations of social tension, exploitation and an increasing gulf between the wealthy and the poor. Jesus' arrival in Jerusalem on "requisitioned" transport was a symbolic act to expose a system which denied people the possibility of exercising a fundamental human right, the freedom of movement.

The acclaim from the crowds affirmed their public support of Jesus and their belief in him as a "warrior-king," a messiah who had come to restore freedom to Israel. The episode is described in vivid messianic apocalyptic language to draw the reader's attention to the theological dimension of the person of Jesus as the "Anointed One" who was intent, as were the apocalyptic figures depicted in the Hebrew scriptures, on confronting the forces of oppression within the society. However, Jesus' action was not directed towards that of gaining acknowledgment as a warrior-king or as a military insurrectionist who would bring liberty to the people. Rather, this symbolic action was meant to confront both the authorities who perpetuated an unjust and exploitative system, and also to challenge the crowd whose recourse of action in oppressive situations was generally to complain to the authorities in the hope that someone "in authority" might act on their behalf. Jesus' action demonstrated that he regarded himself as a free person who was entitled to live and act freely.

(b) Entry into the Temple: Mk 11:11-25

Following the account of Jesus' arrival in Jerusalem is the section Mk 11:11-25 which forms a minor rhetorical unit comprising a mixture of literary forms of narrative, parable and pronouncement story. The segments can be divided as follows:

Introduction:	Jesus goes into the temple, looks around and then leaves. (Mk 11:11)
Reference to fig tree	Parable of the barren fig tree and the curse laid on it. (Mk 11:12-14)
Action of Jesus	Driving out the buyers and sellers from the temple. (Mk 11:15-17)
Reaction of authorities	Chief priests and scribes look for a way to have Jesus killed (Mk 11:18-19)
Reference to fig tree	Disciples notice that the fig tree has withered. (Mk 11:20-21)
Conclusion	Teaching of Jesus explaining his action. (Mk 11:22-25)

The genius of the author as a composer is evident here. These segments in fact are interrelated one with the other through the intercalation technique that the author adopts. In this case there is what might be called a double intercalation by which an image of spatial time and spatial place is conveyed.

As Myers (1988, 297) notes, many commentators have regarded the inclusion of the narrator's comment that Jesus entered Jerusalem, went into the temple and then left for Bethany, as something of an anti-climax to the previous story of Jesus' entry into Jerusalem. Consequently, questions arise as to its purpose in the text other than a mere comment by the narrator. Myers (1988, 297) agrees that it is an anti-climax, but states that it is part of the author's design of making the point that the expectation that Jesus would enter the city as a popular king is, in fact, not Jesus' intention:

> Mark has drawn the reader into traditional messianic symbolics, only to suddenly abort them. This prepares us for the shock when Jesus *does* "intervene" in the temple—not to restore, but to disrupt, its operations.

Myers and other interpreters have tended to bracket this episode (Mk 11:11) with the story of Jesus' entry into Jerusalem (11:1-10), and have not considered its importance in the rhetorical unit Mk 11:11-25, and in particular to the parable of the fig tree in Mk 11:12-14. It is also dramatically effective as an introduction to the events that unfold.

However, Myers (1988, 299) is correct when he states that the purpose of this initial visit to the temple is to assess the situation.

The narrator relates that in going into the temple, Jesus looks around at everything there (καὶ περιβλεψάμενος πάντα). Obviously Jesus is taking note of what is happening here. He does not react immediately to the situation but instead leaves the temple precincts. The reader is therefore left with the impression that whatever course of action is to follow, it is carried out with due deliberation and intention, not as ill-considered and reactionary. In the following verses (Mk 11:12-14) the narrator notes both the time and place. It is the following day and Jesus and his disciples make their way towards the temple. The narrator then introduces a story in which Jesus places a curse on the fig tree and which in fact is intended as a parable relating to the function of the temple. Unlike the parable of the sower or the mustard seed where Jesus tells the story, the parable in this case is told by the narrator. With reference to the parable of the fig tree, Fowler's explanation of a parable (1991, 146) is significant:

> A parable is … a narrative that stands over against something else and beckons us to dare to "carry over" (*metaphero* in Greek) an insight from one thing to another. Parables are thus metaphorical' they induce us to "carry over" insight. In the case of Mark's intercalations, a parabolic relationship is set up between two narratives by embedding one within the other. To the extent that the narratives exercise a referential function, they each refer to the other.

This parable of the fig tree in Mk 11:12-14 is the first segment of the dialogue between Jesus and the disciples which frames the story of Jesus' action in the temple and "stands over against" the action in the temple. The narrator relates that Jesus sees the fig tree from afar, and because it was in leaf presumed that it was bearing fruit.

As Oakman observes, the discussion of this parable has often centered on the question regarding the time or season for the tree to be bearing fruit, and while this is an important consideration, there is another important question, namely, not *"When* did Jesus not find fruit?, but *Why* did Jesus not find fruit?" (1993, 258). Oakman refers to the Augustan Age and the Principate which was promulgated as a time of peace and prosperity, but which in reality was a time when "many citizens of the Empire did not share in this prosperity and commerce" (1993, 258). With reference to the testimony of Josephus (*AJ* xvi. 154, xv. 291, 295; ii. 84ff), Oakman claims that the time of the Herodian regime in Palestine, bears testimony to this. He explains that "Herod the Great, by any standard, was a brutal dictator who established a police state, bled his subjects nearly to death through taxation, and established monuments to a prosperity shared only by the wealthy and the powerful" (1993, 258). In the time of Jesus there was "the consolidation of judicial power in the hands of the landlord-commercial class and their religious legitimation through alignment with (or identity as) those who controlled the Jerusalem temple, the use of debt to enlarge landed estates, and the shift to cash cropping and tenancy agriculture" (1993, 259).

The important clue to the meaning of this parable are the words "seeing the tree from afar." The tree looked as if it should be bearing fruit. However on closer inspection, it was not bearing any fruit at all because it was not the "season" (καιρός) for producing figs. Here, the narrator's explanation is what Camery-Hoggatt (1992, 68) calls a "common frame" by which he means that within the milieu of the author and his reader, there is a common body of knowledge that is taken for granted.[4] Tolbert (1989, 192-193) takes the view that the parabolic association here is "illustrative of the unfruitfulness, hard-heartedness, and opposition now poised to engulf Jesus ... It is a symbolic cursing of unfruitfulness." The interpretation that Heil (1992, 229) proposes is that the temple, like the fig tree, was doomed to destruction.

However, there is another meaning which is also important here. The temple, as does the fig tree, "from a distance" looks as if it is productive, that is it appears to be functioning as a place of worship of the God of Israel. But when one is able to really look around the temple completely, it becomes obvious that its lavishness masks its unproductiveness. Josephus (*JB* V.222-3) in perhaps somewhat exaggerated terms, describes how people generally perceived the impressiveness of the temple building:

> The exterior of the building wanted nothing that could astound either mind or eye. For, being covered on all sides with massive plates of gold, the sun was no sooner up than it radiated so fiery a flash that persons straining to look at it were compelled to avert their eyes, as from the solar rays. To approaching strangers it appeared *from a distance* [emphasis mine] like a snow-clad mountain; for all that was not overlaid with gold was of purest white ...

In focussing only on Jesus' action of cursing the fig tree, interpreters have missed the symbolism between the *apparent* productivity that masks the barrenness of the fig tree and the *apparent* productivity that masks the hypocrisy of those who as chief priests substituted the true worship of the God of Israel for the trappings of power and greed. Ostensibly the temple was built for the worship of God, but in reality it was built to impress the Romans and leaders of other nations in order that Herod and his officers might be regarded with due honour amongst the more powerful in the Roman world. At the same time, the intention was also to impress and appease the people. The combination of the ostentatious grandeur of the temple, as well as its functioning as the seat of Jewish government and commerce, gave the impression of political stability and economic progress. Yet Jesus compares it with the fig tree whose fulfilled time was

---

[4] Camery-Hoggatt (1992) draws on the work of Umberto Eco (1979).

only apparent. In contrast, the message Jesus had come to proclaim was that the time was now fulfilled for the arrival of a new social reality (Mk 1:15).

(c) Jesus Enters the Temple: Mk 11:15-17

The events in the temple would undoubtedly refer to yet another of the "things" for which Jesus was attacked by the authorities as it struck "at the very foundation of their position, privilege and power" (Kingsbury 1989, 78). The narrator states that Jesus entered the temple and drove out those who were buying and selling in the temple, upsetting the tables of the money-changers and the seats of the pigeon dealers as well as not allowing goods to be carried through the temple court.

Hamilton (1964, 371) makes the point that Jesus' actions could not be construed as that of an insurrectionist:

> He did not take anything. He did not burn or destroy records of indebtedness. He did not lead any force which could be interpreted as a revolutionary army. He simply suspended the economic function of the temple without taking any advantage of the act.

Myers (1988, 299) claims that the debate as to whether Jesus' actions were that of a Zealot, is futile. He states that from an ideological perspective this episode is "the centerpiece in Mark's unrelenting criticism of the political economy of the temple. Jesus attacks the temple institutions because of the way they exploit the poor." Generally scholars assume that it was the actual commercial operations taking place in the temple that was the focus of Jesus' wrath.[5] However, as Myers (1989, 300) points out, the temple in Jerusalem was fundamentally an economic institution with commercial activities as a normal part of its operation. In the Markan text it is the temple complex (ἱερόν) itself to which Jesus directs his criticism. The main sanctuary (ναός) is only used in reference to the passion and death of Jesus (Heil 1992, 6).

There is therefore another reason why the authorities took exception to Jesus' actions in the temple (ἱερόν). Hamilton (1964, 366-7) provides evidence that as well as being places of worship, the temples throughout the ancient world also functioned as banks. There is evidence of this throughout Greece, Egypt, Babylonia and Asia Minor (1964, 366). Even when the less influential temples no longer functioned as banks, the temple in Jerusalem continued to do so. Waetjen (1989, 183) points out that in fact the temple "served as the central bank of worldwide Judaism, and all of its assets and disbursements were controlled and administered by the priestly aristocracy." The mammoth size of the temple meant that many people were needed for its construction

---

[5] For example, Stock (1989) 296-297; Kingsbury (1989) 78.

which was completed just prior to the procuratorship of Florus (64-6 ACE). Neusner (1975, 23) states that "the population directly or indirectly was engaged in some way with the work of the temple." According to Josephus, 18,000 men were put out of work at the temple's completion. Whether the figures Josephus states are accurate or not, is probably not all that important. What it does convey is that the temple provided employment for many people. Besides the construction workers, there were also those who were employed in a variety of ways in the maintenance and general running of the temple (Neusner 1975, 23). As well as functioning as a banking facility, it also functioned as a centre for other businesses. The temple thus accrued a vast amount of wealth mostly gained through its system of taxation, its commercial enterprises and its funding of loans (Jeremias 1969, 3-57). The significance of Jesus' action of driving out the buyers and sellers from the temple becomes obvious in the light of those who held a proprietary interest in the temple economy. Hamilton (1964, 369) identifies these interest groups:

> Under the Roman procurators the sanhedrin replaced the Idumean kings as the effective governing instrument. From the point of view of Judaism it was the proper proprietor and director of the temple funds. From the point of view of Rome, the sanhedrin, like Herod and Archelaus before it, was merely a vassal. The Roman procurator of Judea had ultimate control of the financial resources of his district. Administration of finance was, along with command of troops and judicial authority, one of his main functions as procurator (governor). In fact, the title "procurator" was the term used for imperial finance officers generally. The procurator's financial responsibility was especially manifest in light of the fact that tribute from imperial provinces like Judea went directly into the *fiscus* of the emperor as his personal income.

Hamilton (1964, 370) adds that the precedent for the procurator's interference in the temple economy was set by the kings before them and that Jesus' action in suspending the temple economy in this way would have been taken by the officials of the temple as Jesus' claim to be king. While Hamilton provides sound evidence regarding the temple and the economic system his conclusion as to Jesus' reason for acting as he did is somewhat lame in that he concludes that Jesus' action was "Jesus' way of preparing for or witnessing to the conditions of "that day" with respect to the temple. He was probably acting in fulfilment of the obligation laid upon him by Zechariah" (1964, 372). The real fact of the matter was that Jesus' attack on the temple was a threat to all of those who felt they had a proprietary interest in the temple and its revenue.

Myers (1988, 302-303) and Borg (1994, 115-116) claim that the words that the narrator ascribes to Jesus are key to understanding the significance of Jesus' action:

> Is it not written "My house shall be called a house of prayer for all the nations"? [Isa. 56;7] But you have made it a "den of robbers" [Jer. 7:11] (Mk 11:17).

Most commentators have interpreted Mark's construction of Jesus' action as a prophetic fulfilment of the Hebrew Scriptures. However the allusion to the scripture texts in fact serves as an explanation of the meaning of this symbolic action of Jesus. The reference to Isaiah as Borg (1994, 115) explains "comes from one of the most inclusive visions of temple community in the Hebrew Bible. The temple was to include marginalised groups and outsiders: eunuchs, foreigners and outcasts." Both Myers and Borg point out that the reference to the temple as a "den of robbers" is not a criticism of those who were carrying out legitimate business in the temple precincts as such, but a criticism levelled at the elite in Jerusalem, in the same way as Jeremiah's sermon in the temple was levelled at the elite of Jerusalem in his time. According to Borg (1994, 115):

> It was they [the elite] who had acted unjustly, oppressing the helpless (aliens, orphans, and widows), even as they also affirmed, in Jeremiah's mocking threefold acclamation, "This is the temple of the LORD, the temple of the LORD, the temple of the LORD."

Jeremiah's sermon in the temple was followed by his prediction that destruction would follow in the wake of the exploitative practices of the Jerusalem elite (Jer. 7:32-34). The reference to the withered fig tree that was noticed by the disciples as they left the temple (Mk 11:20-21), was intended as a metaphor in that Jesus' reference to the fig tree in foliage is "carried over" to the allusion to Jeremiah's prediction of the destruction that awaited Jerusalem (Jer 7:32-34). This in turn is "carried over" by inference to the fate of Jerusalem in the first century CE. Jesus' action of placing a curse on the tree and its subsequent withering was therefore, a symbolic statement that the temple would suffer the same fate as that predicted in the "woe" that Jeremiah levelled at the temple of his day.

The actual events narrated in Mk 11:15-17 may or may not contain factual elements. However the words attributed to Jesus could be construed as a factual statement, given that Jesus' indictment of those whom he exposed as violators of the temple institution was well known both in the time of Jesus and in the subsequent Jesus tradition.

It would seem that Jesus' polemic against the temple would have had some bearing on the crowd's switch of allegiance from Jesus to their preference for Barabbas which is related in Mk 15:6-13. The description of their enthusiastic support of him as he entered Jerusalem (Mk 11:7-10) indicates that the people thought that a popular show of strength and confidence in Jesus as their leader would produce better economic conditions for them. However when he went so far as to attack the institution which they were led to believe would provide for their economic well-being they began to see the consequences of his action in another light. They could only cope with "creeping" changes to the system and were more than eager to support that. But Jesus' vision was one that demanded radical change both of attitude and action. They were afraid to risk their so-called security for a new freedom.

Confrontation with the Political Authorities

Following the account of Jesus' confrontation with the political authorities over his right to act against the functioning of the temple, the author factors into the narrative a series of episodes which both illustrate the growing hostility towards Jesus, as well as emphasising the contrast in the principles out of which both the authorities and Jesus are operating. Although the episodes are entities in themselves, they are linked to one another so that contrasts and comparisons are obvious.

(a) Parable of the Tenants: Mk 12:1-12

The placement of the parable of the wicked tenants immediately after the confrontation with the authorities serves to reiterate the message that Jesus was conveying through his action in the temple, namely the corrupt nature of those involved in the Temple's administration. Here, Jesus is addressing the chief priests, scribes and elders. The usual interpretation of this parable is that God is identified as the owner of the vineyard, Jesus is identified as the son of the owner and the wicked tenants are identified as the authorities whom Jesus is addressing (cf. Kingsbury 1989, 47; Tolbert 1989, 236-9). One of the clues to the meaning of this episode is that the Sanhedrin know that the parable is aimed at them (Mk 12:12b). Throughout Mark's Gospel, the images in the parables that Jesus employs in his teaching are those with which the audience can readily identify. Thus images of sowing seed would have been readily understood by listeners from rural areas. They would have also related to the notion of vineyards, tenant farmers and absentee landlords in a somewhat negative way as their experience of absentee landlords and tenant farmers was often one of oppression. The metaphor of the vineyard and God as the owner of the vineyard, was a vivid image often employed in the Hebrew scriptures as an image of God's loving and caring relationship with the people of Israel. Jesus takes up this metaphor and develops a parable that incorporates images from his audience's contemporary world in order to convey to this audience, namely the authorities, just how distorted was *their* image of God's relationship with the people of Israel. The parable suggests that the authorities regard themselves as the tenant farmers and God as the absentee landlord. As tenant farmers they are in charge. However they refuse to give to this absentee landlord what he regards as his due as owner of the property. They resort to killing the owner's messengers and eventually also kill his son. Thus they stop at nothing in the belief that when the time for the absentee owner's right to the land expires, they would inherit it. But as the parable states, the absentee landowner acts to prevent this from happening by destroying them and sending in new tenants. Many commentators have identified the messengers as the prophets and the son as Jesus. However, in the first place, Jesus' own image of God is not that of an absentee landlord. That, in fact, would have presented a negative image of God in the minds of the hearers, because of the association of ideas with their experience of absentee landlords. Throughout Mark's Gospel, Jesus presents an image of God that is relational. (Mk 1:35, 6:46, 11:25, 14:35). Therefore, it would follow that Jesus is not comparing himself to the "son" of the "absentee landlord" in the parable. Rather the main point of the parable is the mayhem that the "wicked tenants" perpetrate because of their wanton greed for power. Jesus directs his criticism at the authorities whose actions perpetrate the destructive forces occurring within Judaism. The narrator states that the authorities knew the parable was spoken against them and wanted to arrest Jesus but were afraid of the crowd's reaction (Mk 12:12).

(b) Questioning by the Pharisees and the Herodians: Mk 12:13-17

In the context of the narrative, the encounter with the Sanhedrin is followed by a report of a series of meetings with the various groups who are aligned in their attack on Jesus. This is a rhetorical device to recapitulate specific issues that Jesus is calling into question, and at the same time it serves to re emphasise the sectors of the establishment who formed the opposition.

The first meeting is with the Pharisees and the Herodians who come "to entrap him in his talk" (Mk 12:13). Immediately the reader is aware that the stage is set for further confrontation. The introduction to their topic confirms to the reader that even the opponents concede that Jesus acts with great freedom, even though their question is barbed: "Teacher, ... we know that you do not differentiate between people" (οὐ γὰρ βλέπεις εἰς πρόσωπον ἀνθρώπων).[6] Their very greeting, addressing him as "Teacher," alerts the reader to the hypocrisy that is evident in their questioning, for nowhere have they acknowledged him as a teacher. In fact they have repudiated his teachings. Jesus is asked whether or not taxes should be paid to Caesar. Instead of answering he asks for a denarius and directs the question to them: "Whose image and superscription is this?" As Myers (1988, 311) states Jesus asks his opponents to consider the "discourse of the coin." The image and the superscription represented

---

[6] Waetjen (1989) 188; Stock (1989) 306.

authority.[7] Oster (1982, 203) explains that coins were able to symbolically represent the power which "impinged upon every compartment of life and thought for the inhabitants of the Roman Empire."[8] The Gospel narrative does not indicate just what image and superscription is depicted. According to Kreitzer (1990, 213) one of the features that was common on the coins of Augustus was the comet or star "as a way of emphasising his relationship to the Divine Caesar." Liberty and victory also featured on coins, and the title "son of the Divine Caesar" was a common feature, which Augustus appropriated to himself and which successive emperors also adopted as their title (Ramage, 1987, 60-61). Oster explains that the symbolism of the globe became a political symbol on coins that were minted during the reign of Augustus and was "indicative of the use of cosmic Power language on coins contemporary with the life of Jesus and the early Church" (1982, 204). He outlines the pervasiveness of this power depicted on the coins (1982, 206):

> With Augustus' rapid and inexorable ascendancy to Power, the prevailing ethos of the world Power was magnified. Illustrative of this intensified sense of Power was the increasingly frequent use of the globe in imperial numismatic art. In his surpassed study of this topic, A. Schlachter categorized the numismatic evidence into six basic types. These are: (1) a small globe resting at the base of the bust of the Emperor ... (2) the Emperor sitting upon a stool which, in turn, rested upon the earth, (3) the Emperor stands with one foot on the world, (4) the Emperor holds the globe in the palm of his hand, (5) the Emperor was pictured sitting on the globe, and (6) cognate types with pedestal, etc, supporting the earth.
> As an example of Power language, it depicted the limitlessness of the power which the Emperor exercised, a power initiated and maintained by divine right and protection.

The question that the Pharisees were asking Jesus, was not related to the economy as such. It was really a test of whether Jesus would acknowledge the power of Rome or whether he would repudiate it. Either response would have convicted him one way or the other as either a traitor to the cause of Rome or as a traitor to the Jewish people who objected to paying tribute to Rome. As Myers (1988, 313) explains, the subject of taxation was a central issue and a major cause of rebellion from time to time.

Jesus responds to their reply in the form of a "pronouncement": "The things of Caesar render to Caesar, and the things of God to God" (Mk 12:17). The issue inherent in Jesus' response was not a simple matter of suggesting that they pay taxes to Caesar and pay their dues to God, or that they obey lawful authority as Alexander Sand (1990, 128) suggests. Neither was it a matter of suggesting that they do not pay taxes nor of not obeying foreign authority. Instead, the issue that Jesus raises becomes a question

---

[7] See photographic evidence of Augustan coins in Vierneisel & Zanker (1979) 26-33.
[8] See also Grant 1969; Sutherland 1976 and Sutherland 1987.

not of *his* allegiance but of *their* allegiance. It was a question of whose "power" they were going to recognise particularly as the Pharisees' disposition was generally that of accommodating to Rome on the one hand, and at the same time tending to be meticulous about the application of the Judaic law. The Herodians, for their part wanted to maintain their own sphere of power amongst the Jewish people, and at the same time maintain their connections with Rome. The onus of response is put back to them with Jesus' words: "Render (ἀπόδοτε) to Caesar what belongs to Caesar and to God what belongs to God." The Greek word ἀπόδοτε, is often translated in English as "repay," "give" or "give back."[9] However according to the Macquarie English Dictionary, the word "render" in legal terms means "to return; to make a payment in money, kind, or service, as by a tenant to his [sic] superior." As this incident follows the parable of the wicked tenants, the meaning of ἀπόδοτε as "render" seems more appropriate in this case. Implicit in Jesus' words is the challenge that whoever either the Pharisees and Herodians regard as their superior, be it Caesar or God, then they should render accordingly. They are free to judge and to act.

(c) Questioning of the Saducees: Mk 12:18-27

The second group to approach Jesus is the Sadducee delegation. According to Stock (1989, 308) there is no evidence that this group endured after the destruction of the temple, which would suggest that the Sadducees were closely allied with the Temple. As already mentioned, the Sadducees were from the wealthy aristocratic class and they jealously guarded their lineage. In the episode narrated in Mark's Gospel, the Sadducees appear to be asking questions of Jesus concerning the doctrine of resurrection from the dead. They provide a somewhat extreme example of divorce by which to test him. Myers (1988, 315) claims that "moral chaos is not the issue," but that "maintenance of socio-economic status through the posterity of seven sons is." Following Schüssler Fiorenza, Myers (1988, 315) explains that Jesus is here demonstrating "yet another way in which the kingdom subverts the dominant social order, in this case the patriarchal objectification of women." Here, Jesus is demonstrating his freedom in voicing his vision of another way of constructing the social order where the function of women, and men for that matter, are not that of serving the elite male-dominating class. However from a rhetorical perspective another interpretation also presents itself. As mentioned earlier, the episodes in this section of the narrative, while entities in themselves, are also interconnected. By using an extreme

---

[9] For example, The Revised English Bible; NRSV; Waetjen (1989) 51.

example to test Jesus' knowledge of the law, the author is caricaturing the Sadducees' emphasis on the law and their conservative interpretations of the law. At the same time the author is also making reference to their preoccupation with the matter of lineage. Jeremias (1962, 93) states that polygamy was allowed among the Jews at the time, but because of the cost in providing for a large household, polygamy was normally found only among the rich. In addition levirate marriage among the wealthy classes in Jerusalem which is attested in b. Yeb. 15b was also a practice (1962, 93). Obviously problems arose from such unions when the head of the household died leaving a number of wives. The response that Jesus gives deals not with the conundrum put to him, rather it exposes the Scribes' preoccupation with their place in the social system.

(d) Question of the Scribe: Mk 12:28-34

The incident described in Mk 12:28-34 has often been interpreted as either another testing of Jesus to ascertain if indeed he adheres to the law of Moses or that it is a shift in focus in that a scribe comes freely to Jesus to ask him what law he regarded as the most important. However the episode is rhetorically significant in that through the dialogue between Jesus and the scribe, the principle on which Jesus acts is clearly stated and the principle on which the scribes act becomes evident both in Jesus' reply to the scribe and his subsequent remark in 12:38-40.

As the narrator describes the event, a scribe approaches Jesus and asks him which is the greatest of the commandments. Freyne (1988, 47) claims that the approach from the scribes "is a covert attack on the temple and its cult." He points out that in praising the wisdom of Jesus, the scribe obviously "had to distance himself from his fellows in recognising that God's presence is no longer just linked to Jerusalem and its temple" (1988, 47). Freyne also points out that the reason that the scribes came down to Galilee from Jerusalem was to discredit Jesus because the Jerusalem authorities felt that Jesus was beginning to influence the scribes and should he do so, the political position of the aristocracy would be seriously threatened. Jesus' reply to the scribe is that the greatest commandment is to love God and to love neighbour as oneself. Implicitly the principle out of which Jesus acts is based on the commandment of love of God and love of neighbour. The first part of the commandment, love of God, takes up the issue of the supremacy of God, an issue with which Jesus confronted the Pharisees and the Herodians (Mk 12:13-17). The second part emphasises the love of neighbour. This was the issue that the question of the Sadducees in their focus on the trivia of the law fail to recognise as important (Mk 12:18-27). The scribe repeats what Jesus has uttered, and so the reader is left in no doubt that the scribe also knows the fundamental law of love of God and love of neighbour. Jesus' pronouncement that the scribe "was not far

from the Kingdom of God" (Mk 12:34) underscores the point that the scribes knew that
the disposition of love of God and love of neighbour was a prerequisite for inclusion in
the βασιλεία. Yet as the following incident demonstrates, the scribes actions betrayed
their evil disposition.

(e) Return to the Temple Precincts: Mk 12:35-44

The narrative continues with Jesus' return to the temple. He is no longer questioned by
the authorities. Instead, Jesus poses a question in the form of *haggadah,* a teaching
device where apparent contradictions are put forward in order to draw out a distinction
(Stock 1989, 315). It concerns the apparent contradiction of the scribes' teaching that
the Anointed One is the son of David, when in fact the psalmist states that David had
referred to the Anointed One as "Lord." It therefore, would seem to prove that the
Anointed One cannot be David's son. As Tolbert (1989, 255) observes, "Jesus'
enthymeme seems to challenge any literal attempt to trace Davidic lineage as a test of
messiahship." However, the point that the author is emphasising here, as Myers (1988,
319) points out, is not "genealogy, but ideology." Contrary to the view of some
scholars that Mark's Gospel is here asserting the identity of Jesus as the Davidic
Messiah (cf. Senior 1984, 94), it would seem that Myers is correct when he states that
in the interpretation of this scripture text that Jesus is presenting, the point is made clear
that the Messiah "is *not* David's son (12;37), rejecting both of the earlier messianic
acclamations, 10:47f. and 11:9f. He will not rehabilitate the old imperial vision: indeed
the Davidic tradition must submit to the authority of Messiah" (1988, 319). The
narrator reports that the crowd listened to Jesus "with delight." This was not just
because they were impressed by Jesus' cleverness in his teaching, but rather because
his teaching brought hope and no doubt, relief, that the Messiah they had been taught to
expect would in fact not be of the same ilk as the orthodox royal line. Rather, the
Anointed One would be someone who would inaugurate a new social order. Jesus then
instructs his audience to be wary of the scribes because of the inconsistency in their
behaviour. They obviously know the fundamental Jewish law of love of God and love
of neighbour, yet they act in such a way as to draw honour to themselves, to place
themselves first. Although they appear as righteous men because of their lengthy
prayers, in fact they use their power and status to oppress others, particularly the
marginalised in the society.

Jesus then draws attention to the widow who comes to the temple to place her
offering. The insights of Addison Wright regarding this story is an important
consideration here. Wright (1982, 262) claims that commentators have not seen the

point of this story and have overlaid it with interpretations that generally provide either
a pious contrast with the actions of the Scribes about which Jesus has commented in the
preceding verses, or that Jesus is commending her for her contribution no matter how
insignificant it may be.[10] However, as Wright (1982, 263) points out, this information
is not contained in the text. Nor is it consistent with the logic of the narrative. Again the
theme of the deceptiveness of appearances as in the parable of the fig tree and the
temple in Mk 11:12-21, is also taken up again here. The story follows from Jesus'
condemnation of the behaviour of the scribes who jealously guard their status and
power within the social system. They appear to place God first, yet they oppress the
poor and the marginalised by "devouring the property of widows." The widow who
places her temple offering is conditioned by their teaching of the law. The poor are
made to feel virtuous because they act unquestioningly out of a sense of "duty" to
provide for the temple as doing the will of God. In all probability they would have been
quite unaware that many of the ruling class acquired their wealth from the proceeds of
what was offered in tribute. The poor were forced to "render to Caesar" while being led
to believe that they were "rendering to God."

This scenario is followed by the disciple's comment on the magnificence of the
temple building. Again, the reader is reminded of the episode of the curse of the fig tree
where what seems apparent is really a facade. The dialogue between the disciple and
Jesus serves first of all to recapitulate all of the statements regarding the apparent
magnificence of the temple building and the corruption that it houses. Secondly it
serves as an introduction to Jesus' prediction of the temple's ultimate destruction.

The ἐξουσία of the Disciples

The theme of the ἐξουσία with reference to the disciples is taken up again in Mk
13:34. Here in parable form, the ἐξουσία of the disciples is affirmed as being like that
of servants in a household who have ἐξουσία, that is freedom to choose or to act. The
master is away and so the responsibility of ensuring that the household functions is left
to those servants. However the servants (δοῦλοι) are exhorted to watch so that they
are not taken unawares when the master of the household returns. Many commentaries
seem to disregard these verses or pass over them rather cursorily, yet as Myers rightly
points out, these verses are significant in the context of Mark's Gospel. He states that
this last parable is "an unassuming little folktale" which is at "the heart of Mark's

---

[10] See for example Dewey (1980) 154; Senior (1984) 46; Beavis (1988) 6; Stock (1989) 319;
Tolbert (1989) 226.

ideological discourse" (1988, 347). He explains that in it there are "proleptic echoes of the passion narrative and analeptic echoes of the story's two central political parables" (1988, 347). The analeptic echoes are evident in the introduction which "unmistakably alludes to the 'vineyard tenants': the unknown 'moment' (*kairos* = 12:2) is like a 'man' (=12:1) who went 'away' (*apodemos* = *apedemesin*, 12:1)" (1988, 347). The proleptic reference is to be found in the parable's warning to be awake and watchful. This, Myers (1988, 347) suggests, is the "very theme around which Mark will build the story of Jesus' final 'hour': Gethsemane." Both Myers (1988, 347) and Collins (1992, 87) state that the parable is directed not to the political opponents but to the discipleship of Mark's community.

The function of the parable in this context therefore, is to act as a link between the ending of the apocalyptic discourse (Mk 13:31) and the beginning of the passion narrative (Mk 14:1). In other words, it functions as a closure to the apocalyptic discourse of Mk 13 and at the same time acts as a preface to the next section which consists of the Passion and Resurrection narratives (Mk 14:1-16:8). The parable (Mk 13: 34-36) is embedded in the injunction to be alert (Mk 13:33; 37):

> Take heed, watch [literally: be wakeful] (ἀγρυπνεῖτε); for you do not know when the time will come (Mk 13:33).

> It is like a man going on a journey, when he leaves home and puts his servants in charge, each with his work, and commands the doorkeeper to be on the **watch** (ἵνα γρηγορῇ) (Mk 13:34).

> **Watch** (γρηγορεῖτε) therefore - for you do not know when the master of the house will come, in the evening, or at midnight, or at cock-crowing or in the morning (Mk 13:35).

> lest he come suddenly and find you asleep (Mk 13:36).

> And what I say to you I say, to all: **Watch** (γρηγορεῖτε) (Mk 13:37).

Here the use of the "hook" word γρηγορέω is suggestive of the tone and emphasis of urgency. In Mark's narrative, this injunction "to watch" will again be emphasised in the scene at Gethsemane immediately before Jesus is handed over to the authorities for trial.

Discipleship

The relationship between Jesus and the disciples has been the subject of much scholarly discussion. The behaviour or attitude of the disciples has generally been interpreted as that of misunderstanding the message of Jesus (Tyson, 1961, 263), and "failing" in their call as disciples. In more recent times, the view that seems to prevail, particularly from a narrative reading of the Gospel, is that the disciples are in conflict with Jesus and even become his opponents. For example, Kingsbury (1989, 112) summarizes the disciples' response in the following way:

> The end result of the disciples' incomprehension is apostasy, or defection: ... With the betrayal, abandonment, and denial of Jesus, the disciples have severed their bonds of loyalty to him. Incomprehension has subverted commitment.

Kelber (1976, 57) also refers to the conflict between Jesus and the disciples. The source of this conflict, it is claimed, is the disciples' rejection of the notion of a suffering Messiah. Consequently this conflict, as Kelber suggests, "is most sharply dramatized in the Passion Narrative." Matera (1993, 15-26) likewise emphasises the theme of conflict that he claims is evident throughout the Markan narrative.

However it would seem that neither the notion of misunderstanding nor that of conflict is precisely the case. Throughout the Gospel narrative there is the insistence that Jesus explained everything to his disciples or that he spoke plainly to them (Mk 4:34; 7:17-23; 9:28-29; 10:32-34) which seems to rule out the idea that there was a misunderstanding of the message of Jesus. The fact that the narrative states that the disciples were drawn to the discussions with Jesus after the temple incident and remained with him, also indicates that they were not opposed in principle to Jesus' criticism of the temple. However, it would seem that the disciples in the end were afraid to commit themselves to action because of what this would possibly entail, that is, the prospect of "losing one's life." The narrator draws attention to the disciples' fear in Mk 9:32. Not knowing what Jesus meant when he told them that the Son of man would be delivered into the hands of men and killed, and after three days would rise, they were afraid to ask him. Later in the Gospel narrative (Mk 10:32) it is reported that as Jesus set out with his disciples and followers for Jerusalem, the disciples reacted to Jesus with amazement while the followers were afraid:

> And they were on the road, going up to Jerusalem, and Jesus was walking ahead of them; and they [i.e. the disciples] were amazed, and those who followed were afraid.

Myers (1988, 351) suggests that discipleship for the Markan community presented a number of political options which would have been confusing and that it was difficult to envision a world in which there was no temple. This observation is based on Myers' supposition that the Markan audience in fact resided in or near northern Palestine, that the audience was largely of Jewish origin and that the events mentioned in the text occurred before the destruction of the temple. This means that for those of Jewish origin, the temple defined their identity in that it represented at least the vestige of the symbolic centre point of Jewish independence, in spite of the inherent corrupt operations within the temple system. The zealots, for example, wanted to purify the temple operations both from Jewish administration which had become subservient to Rome and from Roman influence as well. The way to achieve this was for them to take control of the social order. Jesus, in contrast, envisioned "an alternative social order beyond the temple-centered universe" (Myers 1988, 351). However, if one takes the view from evidence in the Gospel text that the Markan audience was comprised of people from a wide geographical area and not necessarily all of Jewish origin, then political options for discipleship would have taken on another dimension and would have hinged very much on their status as an illegal religious sect in the Roman dominated Mediterranean world. It would seem that historically, the statement in Mk 10:32 is most likely a reference to the discipleship of Jesus' own time and it was these disciples who could not envision a world without the temple. For the Markan audience, it would have been the example of the disciples' response of taking the option to go with Jesus to Jerusalem, depicted in Mk 10:32, to which the audience would have related and then appropriated to the range of options with which they were now confronted.

In Mk 10:32 therefore, there is the sense that the disciples are taking the option of going with Jesus to Jerusalem. They are not the ones who are afraid (οἱ δὲ ἀκολουθοῦντες ἐφοβοῦντο), but rather the ones who are amazed (Ἦσαν δὲ ἐν τῇ ὁδῷ ἀναβαίνοντες εἰς Ἱεροσόλυμα ... καὶ ἐθαμβοῦντο). In Mk 10:24, Jesus' teaching causes the disciples to be amazed (οἱ δὲ μαθηταὶ ἐθαμβοῦντο ἐπὶ λόγοις αὐτοῦ) Then Peter emphasises that the disciples have left everything to follow Jesus (Mk 10:28). Jesus' resolve to go to Jerusalem (Mk 10:32) again arouses the emotion of amazement in the disciples, but the emotion of fear in the unnamed followers. It would seem then, that the events that unfolded in Jerusalem and particularly those involving the consequences of Jesus' criticism of the temple and its functions, were the major factors which eventually changed the disciples' amazement to one of fear.

Anointing at Bethany: Mk 14:3-9

The story of the woman anointing Jesus at Bethany introduces the Passion narrative. Dewey (1980, 154) claims that the parallelism of this story with that of the widow in Mk 12:41-44 is intentional. Dewey notes the contrast between the widow's offering which is quite small because she is poor, and the woman at Bethany who in fact has paid a substantial amount for the ointment. She points out that the stories are connected by the "hook" word "poor" (τοὺς πτωχοὺς) which occurs twice in each account of the story. Dewey's conclusion is that Jesus praises both women because they show "the way of service or self-giving." However as Wright (1982, 262-3) states there is no reference in the story of the widow, suggesting that Jesus praised her. Rather the widow's situation is an example that Jesus uses to illustrate what he means by the oppressive practices of the temple. On the other hand, the woman who anoints Jesus is in fact praised, and what is more Jesus says that she will be remembered for what she has done. It is the contrast rather than the comparison which seems to be the major factor here. The point of comparison is that both women were oppressed by the structures and male dominated values of the society. The contrast is that the widow complied with the laws and paid her taxes dutifully, even though she had little means at her disposal. The woman who anointed Jesus, however, refused to allow the social customs and social disapproval to dictate and control her actions particularly when she judged it appropriate to provide an act of loving service.

While it may have been the author's intention to juxtapose the stories of these women at this point in the narrative, it would seem that the story of the anointing is also framed by the two incidents of plans to kill Jesus (Mk 14:1-2; Mk 14:10-11), thereby emphasising the contrast between the woman who wants to "restore" life and those who want to kill. The parallelism between this incident (Mk 14:3-9) and the incident related in Mk 3:1-6 is evident in that both are framed by plans to kill Jesus. The action of Jesus in healing the man with the withered hand (Mk 3:1-6) is prefaced by the narrator's statement that "some of them [i.e. the Pharisees] were looking for a reason to accuse Jesus" (Mk 3:2). Jesus challenges them with the question as to whether it is lawful on the Sabbath to do good or to do evil, to save life or to kill. Following the healing, the Pharisees begin to plot with the Herodians as to how they might kill Jesus (Mk 3:6). The anointing at Bethany likewise is prefaced by the statement that the chief priests and the teachers of the law were looking for a way to arrest Jesus and kill him (Mk 14:1). Following the anointing and Jesus' discussion with those present, Judas went to the chief priests and promised to seize the opportunity of handing him over to them (Mk 14:10).

By including the story of the woman anointing Jesus, the author re-emphasises the alternative vision that Jesus has proclaimed. In a sense it serves as a summary statement regarding discipleship. The woman freely chooses to act and to offer this form of service. Another point is the irony of the situation. Jesus has been preaching against the opulence of the rich and the exploitation of the poor. Here, in this scene people begin to question why the money was not given to the poor. Jesus' answer in fact challenges their right to question the freedom of someone who chooses to provide a service to another when in fact their support of the structures has done nothing to alleviate the suffering of the poor as the story of the widow illustrates.

Although the story in the Gospel of Luke states that the woman who anointed Jesus was "living an immoral life in the town" (Lk. 7:36), this is not stated in the Markan text.[11] It would seem that the focus the author of Mark's Gospel wishes to emphasise, is the clarity of the woman's action in contrast to the hypocrisy on the part of those present. In fact whether she was an immoral woman or not does not seem to be the author's concern. The duplicity of Judas and the immorality of his action is even more accentuated in the light of the woman's action.

The fact that the narrator mentions that the ointment was very expensive, "worth more than a year's wages" (Mk 14:10), is significant here. The author is stating that although Jesus has been on the side of the poor, it is not the amount of money one has or does not have money that is the real issue in this case. What is at issue is the denial of access to equality and dignity. The woman's extravagance in this instance, is not a preoccupation with riches as was the case with the extravagance of Herod and the ruling authorities. The woman's action was a preoccupation with a gratuitous service, which the wealthy did not seem to provide.

An important point that Senior (1984, 47) makes here is that the woman's action is "good news" and that it was to have universal significance:

> In the final discourse Jesus had instructed the community to continue with its preaching of the Gospel "to all nations" (13:10). Here the global sense of the mission is put in even more striking terms — *eis holon ton kosmon* — "to the whole world" (14:9). Wherever the Gospel is preached her story will be told because this story *is* Gospel, the "Good News": of Jesus' liberating death and the call to respond to it.

The subtle rhetoric in the statement attributed to Jesus is also important. The statement is both an affirmation of the woman's action and at the same time it can be interpreted as a subversive statement of the rhetoric of praise given to the rulers in the empire for their extravagant deeds. The woman's act of so-called "extravagance" as "good news" can be compared with the propaganda surrounding the extravagances of Augustus for which he was hailed as "good news" for the whole world and for which he was praised as the one bringing liberty to the nations. The inference in Jesus' comment (Mk 14:9) is that what constitutes bringing liberty to the world is freedom of action in ministering to another with compassion. Liberty is not about the action of a few "providing" for the poor. The indictment that Jesus levels at those around the table who complain of the woman's actions, is that it is because of their attitude, actions and life-style that there will always be the poor who are caught in this cycle of dependence and so become the

---

[11] See Schüssler Fiorenza's discussion of the status of the woman in the Gospel texts (1989) 128.

object of the charity and favour of the "do-gooders." The woman who would normally be without independent means for her livelihood, in fact breaks out of the recipient model of others' charity and she herself takes the opportunity of caring extravagantly for another with compassion. By her action she is also affirming Jesus and his message of good news of liberation of the poor. The meaning of discipleship in this incident is concerned with subverting the dominant notion that power to act was the prerogative of the elite few.

The Passover Meal

(a) Preparation

Mark's account of Jesus' instructions to his disciples regarding preparations for the Passover meal is yet another indication, like that of his preparation for the journey into Jerusalem, where Jesus had planned his next move with deliberation. The format that the author adopts follows the same pattern as the account of Jesus' preparation for his journey into Jerusalem. Robbins (1976, 23) following the schema outlined by Taylor (1966, 536), states that there are three common elements in these two accounts: (a) the two disciples are given the promise that they will encounter a sign and so be able to carry out the instructions (b) Jesus gives them the correct words to say so that the one whom they are to meet will know from whom they come, (c) the disciples find everting just as Jesus had told them and they are able to follow instructions to the letter. Taylor (1966, 536) provides the following comparison:

xi. 1-6		xiv. 13-16	
1.	ἀποστέλλει δύο τῶν μαθητῶν αὐτοῦ	13.	ἀποστέλλει δύο τῶν μαθητῶν αὐτοῦ
2.	καὶ λέγει αὐτοῖς ὑπάγετε εἰς τὴν κώμην... καὶ ; εὑρήσετε...		καὶ λέγει αὐτοῖς ὑπάγετε εἰς τὴν πόλιν... καὶ ἀπαντήσει ὑμῖν...
3.	εἴπατε ὁ κύριος...		εἴπατε
		14.	ὁ διδάσκαλος ...
4.	καὶ ἀπῆλθον καὶ εὗρον ...	16.	καὶ ἐξῆλθον ... καὶ εὗρον
6.	καθὼς εἶπεν ὁ Ιησοῦς καὶ...		καθὼς εἶπεν αὐτοῖς καὶ...

Taylor (1966, 538) states that although these stories cannot be considered as doublets since the subject matter is quite different, he claims that the format indicates that these stories were written by the one author. However, it could also be argued that the way of telling a story was formulated along the lines of a conventional pattern of relaying a story, and that these particular stories may have circulated in the Christian community before they were incorporated into the Gospel text, and perhaps with little alteration. Both stories, however indicate that Jesus had friends or acquaintances in Jerusalem which suggests the possibility that Jesus had some prior knowledge or even prior experience of Jerusalem before the events which immediately led to his execution (Taylor 1966, 539).

(b) Passover Feast

The major feasts were times of political upheaval. Josephus lists the number of people who were trapped in Jerusalem in the siege during the Passover of 70 CE (*BJ* vi. 420, vii. 210ff) which would have totalled 1,200,000 (Jeremias (1969, 78). The numbers cited by Josephus are probably an exaggeration. However, according to Jeremias (1969, 84) who has revised some of his own previous calculations, the increase in the number of people in the city "amounted to several times the population in Jerusalem." Tension ran high at Passover time because of the increase in population and consequently the Roman military was reinforced with extra soldiers in case riots broke out. As Horsley & Hanson (1985, 34-37) explain, riots in the city at Passover time were not uncommon.[12] The narrator in Mark's Gospel states that the plan that the authorities had in mind was to delay arresting Jesus until after the festival season to avoid the possibility of rioting amongst the people. In what amounted to an undercover operation, the authorities sought "inside" help in locating Jesus. However, it seems that when Judas was prepared to lead them to Jesus' whereabouts, they decided to act there and then. This suggests that the authorities were intent on apprehending Jesus in spite of it being the festival season.

Myers (1988, 360) claims that Jesus and the disciples had to "resort to covert means" in order to avoid being arrested. The coded arrangements by which Jesus and the disciples secured a safe place in order to celebrate Passover suggests they were avoiding detection. It was Jesus, however, who knew there was an informer in the group (14:18).

The Passover feast was both a religious and a political festival, a celebration of "freedom." It was religious in that the Jews recalled and celebrated God's intervention

---

[12] See also Crossan (1994) 127-128.

in the deliverance of their ancestors from the slavery of Egypt. It was also a political festival in that it gathered the Jews in solidarity to focus their allegiance to Judaism and also to remind those under whose political power they dwelt that they were still a political force in the eastern part of the Mediterranean world.

Myers correctly points out that for Mark, the Passover meal that Jesus had arranged was not intended to be a celebration of Judaism's past. Jesus had repudiated the temple cult, and so this Passover meal was symbolically articulating another reality, one that pointed to a new exodus, a new liberation. It is, as Myers (1988, 363) states "Mark's final assault upon the Jewish symbolic field." The repudiation of the temple cult is obvious as Myers (1988, 363) points out:

> suddenly we realize that Jesus is *not* after all participating in the temple-
> centered feast of Passover (note that Mark never mentions the eating of
> the lamb). Instead he is expropriating its symbolic discourse (the ritual
> meal) in order to narrate his new myth, that of the Human One who gives
> his life for the people.

The Arrest

It is at the end of the supper that the narrator indicates that the ἐξουσία of the disciples is about to be ultimately challenged. Drawing on the symbolism of both Zechariah 13:7 and Ezechiel's parable (34;11-16:23) which states that the shepherd will be struck down and that all the sheep will be scattered, Jesus predicts the outcome of his arrest and the subsequent "scattering" of the disciples. However, in spite of the imminent arrest, Peter chooses to proclaim his loyalty and support even in the face of death.

The narrator then relates the events following the supper meal. The theme of watching and staying awake is taken up again in this episode. After the closing hymn of the ritual, Jesus goes out with his disciples to the Mount of Olives where he predicts that the disciples will eventually "fall away" from him. Immediately Peter protests his allegiance whatever the circumstances (Mk 14: 26-31). Going on a little further with the disciples, Peter James and John, Jesus entreats them to watch with him as he faces his ordeal (μείτατε ὧδε καὶ γρηγορεῖτε, Mk 14:34). But already they begin to grow weary. The commitment of the disciples to following Jesus at this point is stated in the words of Jesus when he finds the disciples asleep: "The spirit is willing (πρόθυμος), but the body is weak" (Mk 14:38b). Mann points out that the Greek word πρόθυμος, is used here in the sense of being "ready" or "eager" or "fully engaged" (1986, 592). The implication here is that Jesus acknowledges the disciples' willingness to be fully engaged at one level, but they were unable to face the reality of events which Jesus had predicted. Their own safety and needs were to take precedence.

Within the context of the narrative, the reality that Jesus' arrest was imminent perhaps had not been fully comprehended by the disciples. When Judas arrived with the cohort of soldiers under cover of darkness and apprehended Jesus, everyone deserted him and fled as Jesus had predicted. As Myers (1988, 368) states: "The sheep have scattered; the discipleship narrative has collapsed." It is obvious then, that the reaction of the disciples was not one of misunderstanding or one of opposition, but rather, one of fear at the prospect of their fate if they were to be seen in league with Jesus. The disciples were not prepared to submit themselves to the fate of martyrdom alongside their leader, Jesus. They no doubt would have been well aware of two well known occurrences where people were executed for insurrection. The news of the fate of those who attempted to assassinate Herod in their zeal for the law, would have circulated amongst the population. These "zealots" as Hengel (1989, 258) points out, were betrayed before they could carry out their act and they were brought before Herod. According to Josephus (*AJ* XV, 289) they refused to show any sign of repentance for what they had planned to do and confessed openly of their intention. Consequently they were led away and after enduring "every kind of torture" they were put to death. On another occasion, as Josephus (*BJ* I, 648-655) recalls, two teachers destroyed the symbol of the eagle that had been placed in the Temple. They were arrested and brought before Herod who asked them if it was their intention to pull the eagle down. When they confessed that they had done so and that they were unafraid of the consequences of their action, Herod had them burnt alive and the others that were with these two, were beheaded. These events would have occurred within the life time of the disciples. If Jesus was brought before the authorities and condemned as an insurrectionist, then their fate would also be sealed if they were regarded as being part of his company. In fact Peter is eventually singled out and accused of being a follower of Jesus, a charge that he emphatically denies.

Waetjen is of the opinion that the statement "they all fled" refers to the community of his followers, not just the eleven. He explains:

> When "all" insist that they will remain loyal to him, more than eleven appear to be involved. This is substantiated by the narrator's return to the inclusive designation of "disciples" in 14:32 and the note of 15:41 that "many ... women" accompanied him up to Jerusalem. Therefore it is not only the eleven who take flight. All of the disciples, both men and women, desert him, and Jesus is left alone with his captors.

While it is true that Mark often uses the term δώδεκα (the Twelve) the word μαθντής (disciple) as Nepper-Christensen (1991, 373) points out, is seldom used in the synoptic Gospels to designate the "wider circle" of his followers or listeners. He explains that although the word μαθηταί (disciples) is used in Mk 6:35, the word δώδεκα occurs in the parallel episode in Lk 9:12. While it seems certain that all the followers of Jesus deserted him, the author of the Gospel in this instance seems to be specifically referring to the response of the Twelve.

The Trial Scenes

After Jesus is apprehended, he is then submitted to two interrogation episodes. The first is when he is brought before the Sanhedrin, that is, the Jewish authorities, and the second is when he is brought before Pontius Pilate who represents Roman authority. Scholars have noted a certain similarity in the two trial scenes and which, they argue, seems to suggest that these accounts were constructed along the same pattern (Beavis 1987, 586). The outline of the pattern which largely follows that proposed by Beavis (1987, 584-588) is depicted below:

Trial before the Sanhedrin

14:53	Setting: Jesus led before the Sanhedrin
14:55-59	False witnesses called to give testimony
14:60	First Question: "Have you no answer to make?"
14:61a	Silence
14:61b	Second Question: "Are you the Christ?"
14:62	Answer: "I am and you will see the Son of Man seated at the right hand of the Power and coming with the clouds of heaven."
14:63-65	Condemnation.

Trial before Pilate

15:1	Setting: Jesus led to Pilate
15.2	First Question: "Are you the King of the Jews?"
15:3	Answer: "You have said so." [Chief priests accuse Jesus of many things]
15:4	Second Question: "Have you no answer to make?"
15:5	Silence
15:6-13	[Barabbas released]
15:14-15	Condemnation

In the chiastic patterning of the Gospel of Mark, it has been earlier demonstrated that Mk 8:27-33 forms the centre point or climax of the Gospel narrative. The themes contained in this section are brought to fulfilment in the trial scenes. The question as to the identity of Jesus stated in Mk 8:27-29 is the concern of Jesus' inquisitors in the trial scenes. The prediction that Jesus would be brought to trial before the elders, chief priests and scribes in Mk 8:31-32 is the situation in the trial scene before the Sanhedrin. As Beavis (1987, 594-596) states, the patterning was intentionally designed to help the reader to relate to the deeper christological meaning in the Gospel text. The relationship to the trials scenes in the Passion narrative is evident as the following schema indicates:

Caesarea Philippi

8:27(a)	Setting: Jesus and disciples at Caesarea Philippi
8:27(b)	First Question: Who do men say I am?
8:28	Answer: John the Baptist ... Elijah ... one of the prophets
8:29(a)	Second Question: Who do you say I am?
8:29(b)	Answer: You are the Christ
8:30	Response: Jesus charged them to tell no one
8:31-32(a)	Statement: Prediction of the Passion
8:32(b)	Response: Peter rebukes Jesus
8:33	Response: Jesus rebukes Peter

Collins (1993, 19) claims that the Pre-Markan Passion narrative does not contain the trial scene of Jesus' arraignment before the Sanhedrin and that the account of this trial in the Markan text is "a Markan composition which is based on older traditions"(1993, 19). Collins' reconstruction of the trial scene is as follows:

> And they led Jesus away to the high priest. In the morning, the chief priests took counsel, bound Jesus, led him away and handed him over to Pilate. And Pilate asked him, "Are you the king of the Jews?" He answered and said to him, "You say [so]." And the chief priests accused him of many things. Pilate asked him again, saying, "Do you not answer anything? Look how many things they accuse you of." But Jesus answered no further, so that Pilate marvelled. He had Jesus whipped and handed him over to be crucified.

The function of the trial scene in the text is to emphasise Jesus' claim to be the Messiah (Collins 1993, 19). Jesus is charged with blasphemy because he asserts, in response to the high priest's question, that he is the Messiah. However, the admission hardly warrants the charge of blasphemy (Donahue 1973, 96). According to Donahue (1973, 97) the charge of blasphemy was "to clarify the content of his [i.e. the author's] Christological statement." Such an explanation provides historical credibility to the narrative for as Collins (1993, 21-22) points out, a claim such as this would relate "to the council's responsibility to keep order and its commitment to support Roman rule." Historically, if there was such a trial, then Jesus' appearance before the Sanhedrin would have been a preliminary hearing before he was sent to Pilate for trial and sentence.

In the trial scenes that are constructed, Jesus elects not to answer the questions put to him, and he neither confirms nor denies the charges against him. This action is in contrast to that of the Zealots who, when on trial would mostly acknowledge their political intention in order to prove their commitment to their cause even if this meant being executed. In a sense, they would convict themselves and die a martyr's death. Jesus' silence suggests that his cause was not that of the Zealots, and that he did not choose a martyr's death. He chose to teach and to act the way he did during his life, and it was the authorities who chose to execute him.

Donahue (1973, 97) claims that the condemnation of Jesus "serves a double purpose, one in the structure of the trial and the other in the context of the gospel." He explains that in the trial narrative its purpose is its reference to the Sanhedrin's need to find witnesses so that Jesus can be killed. With reference to its connection to the gospel as a whole, Donahue states that "the mortal opposition to Jesus, begun in 3:6 and which appears at crucial places in the gospel, reaches its apex here. From now on the Passion narrative is simply the playing out of what takes place in this scene."

There has been much debate as to who were responsible for executing Jesus.[13] Some have suggested that it was the Sanhedrin who sentenced Jesus to death and that Pilate ratified their decision. Some commentators see Mark's depiction of Pilate as being somewhat sympathetic, but unable to appease the crowd. Others have claimed that the Romans saw Jesus as a real threat to the stability of the area and to their position and that after allowing a preliminary hearing as a concession to the chief priests, Pilate acted on behalf of the Romans to put an end to possible trouble from Jesus. However, the inclusion of these two trial scenes which follow much the same format within the Gospel narrative, would seem to suggest that the author is stating that the Jewish authorities and the Romans were both responsible for the death of Jesus.

Peter's Denial

The author of Mark's Gospel, it would seem, intentionally places the account of Peter's "trial" between the two trial scenes in which Jesus is interrogated in order to emphasise the challenge to the ἐξουσία of both Jesus and Peter. The account of Peter's trial is divided into three segments which is recognised as a Markan technique (Dewey 1976, 97).

14:66-67a	Introduction
14:67b-68	First accusation and denial
14:60-70a	Second accusation and denial
14:70b-71	Third accusation and denial
14:72	Conclusion

Both the intercalation and the progression of three stages in the story of Peter's denial suggests that the episode is a Markan construction. The narrator indicates to the reader that even though all the others have fled, Peter demonstrates his loyalty up to a point by following Jesus at a distance. However when he is recognised by one of the servant girls as being with Jesus, he emphatically denies knowing Jesus. Peter's Galilean dialect also arouses suspicion as Galilee was the seed-bed for insurrection in the first

---

[13] See discussion by Sanders (1985), 294-318. Also Myers (1988), 269-374.

century CE. His inquisitors are not the chief priests, but a servant girl and some bystanders who would have had no power to convict him and who probably would not have gained a hearing from the authorities in any case. However, in spite of this Peter is afraid of the consequences should someone inform on him. Therefore, he continues to deny knowing Jesus. The story comes to a climax when the cock crows. In the context of the story the incident of the cock crowing, performs two functions. The first draws the reader back to the connection as Dewey (1976, 102) states, with Jesus' warning to the disciples to be alert because the Son of Man might unexpectedly return "in the evening, or at midnight, or when the cock crows or at dawn" (Mk 13:35). The cock begins to crow at the end of the third night watch. The incident also functions to heighten the dramatic impact of the story as it provides the signal to Peter that Jesus' prediction had come to pass. Peter had denied Jesus three times. This had happened in spite of Peter's strong protest earlier, that he would never deny Jesus (Mk14:29-31).

Stock (1989, 376) draws attention to the contrast between the trial that Jesus is undergoing and the "trial" to which Peter is being subjected:

> Uppermost in Mark's narrative plan is the contrast between Peter's conduct in the courtyard below and Jesus' conduct in the court-room above. Jesus makes a solemn, free confession before the highest authorities of the land that will cost him his life, while Peter, among the serving men and women, cannot so much as acknowledge that he had walked in the footsteps of the man of Nazareth.

Collins (1993) does not include this incident in her reconstruction of the Pre-Markan narrative. Historically, of course, this incident could have occurred as Peter would have been able to provide first-hand information as to what had taken place. This is unlike the trial scenes of Jesus in which there would not have been any witnesses (Sanders 1985, 299). That the disciples fled in fear seems to have been the case. However, it would seem that the author's purpose in structuring this episode into the Gospel narrative "serves as a crucial reflection on discipleship" (Senior 1984, 102). According to Dewey (1976, 108-9) the author's main concern is not so much that Peter denies knowing Jesus, but rather it is what Peter denies and the way in which he disclaims Jesus that the author wishes to emphasise:

> Peter separates himself from Jesus in a progression from a noncommital "I don't understand" to a public cursing. Within this context are Mk's thematic concerns: (1) Peter curses Jesus—and at the same time that Jesus is condemned to death; (2) in doing so Peter fulfils Jesus' prediction and becomes subject to the general curse that the Son of Man will be ashamed of those who were ashamed of Jesus (8:38); (3) Peter denies Jesus as a Nazarene; (4) Peter denies his own Galilean identity (an identity he shares with Jesus).

In the context of the ἐξουσία of the disciples it would appear that historically, fear dictated Peter's denial of Jesus. Modern commentators of this episode are quick to judge Peter's denial as failure or as apostasy, for example Dewey (1976, 113), Waetjen (1989, 226). This is probably not taking the situation into account sufficiently. As already pointed out, any associates of those leading an insurrection would also have been executed along with their leader. Fear at the prospect of this kind of death is understandable. In such a political climate, it would have required radical commitment of heroic proportions. Ultimately, of course Peter was faced with the reality of crucifixion. The radical nature of Jesus' death is de-emphasised by commentators who glibly state that Peter was weak or cowardly for denying his association with Jesus. The reality for the Markan community in the Mediterranean world would have been such that Christians were faced with decisions of radical proportions in situations which called for risk and which challenged their freedom to act.

The Execution of Jesus: Mk 15:15-41

(a) The Charges against Jesus

At the end of the second trial scene, the narrator states that Pilate was prevailed upon by the crowd to release Barrabas, an insurrectionist. Pilate puts the question to them as to whom they would prefer to be released, and their answer is Barrabas. Again it is difficult to know just what is historical fact here. In the structure of the narrative, the scene is also a reflection on discipleship. Peter had denied Jesus, but the crowd, who once had listened to the teachings of Jesus "with delight" (Mk 12:37b), now actively seek his execution (Mk 15:13-14). The narrator states that the crowd was stirred up and manipulated by the Jewish authorities, and so the blame is apportioned to them for Jesus' execution. Nevertheless the crowd is also implicated in the decision. The author of Mark's Gospel intimates that Pilate and the chief priests were not united in their reasons for executing Jesus. It would seem that in one sense, Pilate tests the crowd's reaction, as he ultimately had the power of ordering the execution. Some commentators have suggested that each of the Gospel authors present Pilate in a somewhat sympathetic light (McGing 1991, 417-418), while the secular authors such as Philo and Josephus depict him as a cruel and calculating person who used his power of office accordingly (McGing 1991, 424-438). Hengel (1989, 104-105) provides an example from Josephus' account of Pilate's action of taunting the people by having a unit of soldiers bring the effigies of the emperor on standards and placed in Jerusalem as a sign of Roman power. Apparently, this had been tried before by other Roman authorities, but Pilate went against previous practice by having this done at night. This incident occurred at the beginning of Pilate's term of office. Later he set up consecrated shields in front of the official residence, with the name of the emperor inscribed on them. Hengel (1989, 105) states that presumably offence was caused by the inscription, although the nature of it was not handed down. However, in both cases Pilate had to face the enraged people. Pilate resorted to calling in the Roman troops to quell the rioting of the crowd, which resulted in a large loss of life.

If there is historical fact in Pilate's question to the crowd on the occasion of Jesus' arrest, it could well have been that Pilate's intentions may have not been all that benign. Even if this was a total reconstruction on the part of the Markan author, the depiction of Pilate is not actually one of sympathy for Pilate's predicament that he had no real choice but to hand Jesus over to be crucified. While the Markan author does not spell it out explicitly, the Markan audience would have been aware of the power of the Roman procurators and governors, and were no doubt aware of the stories that had circulated regarding Pilate's ruthlessness. The statement that Pilate wanted to appease the crowd, indicates his concern to not let matters get out of control. This would have reflected badly on his ability to govern effectively, if news of rioting in Jerusalem reached Rome. Sanders (1985, 302-303) draws attention to the fact that Josephus testifies that Herod executed John because his preaching was drawing enthusiasm amongst the people. He also cites Josephus' account of the Egyptian rebels who were overthrown in a pitched battle and that Pilate called in the cavalry and the *hoplites* against the Samaritans. Pilate certainly had the means at his disposal to quell an out of control crowd quickly and effectively. Sanders explains that Jesus was not a solitary figure preaching against the evils of his day. Although Jesus did not have the number of followers that would constitute an army, he did have sufficient numbers that could pose a threat to social order. According to Sanders (1985, 303-304) "He [Jesus] like John the Baptist, falls in between the solitary woe-sayer and the Egyptians. The leader is executed but not the followers. There were enough followers to make it expedient to kill Jesus, rather than simply flog him as a nuisance and release him." It would seem that the conduct of the crowd in calling for Jesus' execution, was not because they despised him, but because they were afraid of the consequences if they chose to act or speak out on behalf of Jesus.

Within the context of the Gospel narrative, the whole scene is constructed by the Markan author for rhetorical effect regarding the nature of discipleship. The Markan audience knows where the Jewish authorities stand in relation to Jesus, and also knows where the Roman authorities stand in relation to Jesus. In this scene the audience is alerted to the crowd's position. Although the Twelve had fled when Jesus was arrested, they are not implicated in the actual decision of Jesus' execution.

It would seem that Mark is emphasising that the Jewish authorities and the Romans regarded Jesus not just as an ordinary criminal, but as a pretender who with the following that he had, might indeed claim kingship. Jesus was a threat to the public order because he had a following (Borg 1987, 180). He was sentenced to be executed because he presumed to challenge the authority of Rome (Myers 1988, 386).

While Roman officialdom tolerated the title of "client king" with regard to Herod, because it was expedient to do so, it did not tolerate it elsewhere. It was Rome who appointed Herod as "king" in the first place. Jesus' preaching of the "reign of God" was interpreted by Roman officials as a claim by Jesus of assuming kingship. Therefore, contrary to some scholars who argue that Pilate did not take the Jewish authorities' concerns regarding Jesus with too much seriousness, it would seem that the reason Pilate sentenced Jesus to death was because he feared Jesus' power and feared what this would mean for his position as governor of the region if higher authorities from Rome had to intervene.

Sanders (1985, 305-308) explores the suggestions regarding the charges that were laid against Jesus and which resulted in Jesus' execution. He claims that the so-called charge of blasphemy would not have constituted sufficient grounds for execution, either from the Jewish establishment or from the Roman authorities. Other people had claimed to be speaking on behalf of God but had not been executed for doing so. The suggestion by Pilate that Jesus had been accused of claiming to be the Messiah would also not have constituted sufficient grounds for execution. Again, others individuals had claimed that role also, and had not been taken all that seriously. Sanders therefore concludes that it was because of Jesus' action against the temple and the threat of its inevitable destruction, as well as his noticeable following among the people that "could have led the Romans to think that Jesus was a threat to public order" (1985, 302). The Jewish authorities would have opposed Jesus on these grounds as well, since the temple was the centre of Jewish religious, political and economic life. Sanders draws attention to the story in Jer 26 where Jeremiah is threatened with death because he predicted the destruction of the temple.

(b) The Way to Calvary

Jesus is handed over to be crucified, and it is the Roman soldiers who lead him away. Another important consideration here is the role of the Roman soldiers in the whole affair of Jesus' execution. In the normal course of events, they are the ones who have to take orders. Here, however the soldiers are given free reign over Jesus and they exert what little power they have at their disposal to viciously attack him. The Markan author seems to be emphasising that the exercise of power over another, no matter from what level of social status this power comes, is destructive of another person's dignity. Prisoners of conscience down through the course of history have been subjected to such atrocities perpetrated by soldiers and guards who choose to exercise the little power they have over prisoners who are in their custodial care. In the Markan account, the soldiers lead Jesus away to the place of execution. They force (ἀγγαρεύω) a passer-by from the country, Simon of Cyrene, to carry Jesus' cross. Somewhat pious interpretations of this scene have made out that Simon's action was generous or at least helpful. This has missed the author's point. In fact Simon was forced into service, a practice which subject nations hated and tried to avoid (Llewelyn 1994, 86-87). Normally it was only the higher officials who could legally enforce such service. However, minor officials, in whatever capacity, also took it upon themselves to exercise their power in this way when the opportunity presented itself. In forcing Simon to carry Jesus' cross, the Roman soldiers exercise what little "official" power they had, to force another person to their demands.

Schmidt (1995,1-18) who interprets the crucifixion narrative against the background of Roman triumphal processions, postulates that Mark writes for a Roman audience. Drawing on elements that were constitutive of these processions, Schmidt (1995, 16) claims that Mark is presenting "an *anti*-triumph in reaction to the contemporary offensive self-divinization efforts of Gaius and especially Nero. In other words, he [i.e. the Gospel author] intends to portray Jesus parabolically to a Roman gentile audience as the true epiphanic triumphator." The parallels that Schmidt draws between the Roman triumphator and Jesus are convincing. However Myers (1988, 384) also admits that there are allusions to Roman processions but points out that in his case the parallel is to that of "defeated military foes on parade." As an example, he cites Josephus' description of Simon bar Giora's execution. This man was "the general and self-proclaimed king of the rebel resistance at the time of the fall of Jerusalem" (1988, 384). He was taken to Rome and taken in triumphal procession with other political prisoners to the temple of Jupiter Capitolinus. Here, a noose was put around his neck and he was dragged to the forum to be tortured by those who led him, and eventually slain. There were celebrations when his death was announced. Myers (1988, 385) explains that in the provinces with lesser "kings," a local public march to the executioner's stake sufficed for the same lesson in imperial omnipotence."

(c) Calvary: The Place of Execution

Schmidt (1995, 10) draws attention to the name "Golgotha," that the Markan author attributes to the place where Jesus is taken for execution, and notes particularly that Mark, somewhat untypically with reference to proper names, translates it as "the place of the skull" (Mk 15:22). Schmidt explains that the Hebrew word "Golgotha" denotes more generally the word "head" rather than "skull." He notes the coincidence that the name of the place of triumph is the Temple of Jupiter Capitolinus "which was the terminus of every Roman triumph" (1995, 11). It was so named because of the legend that during the laying of the foundation for a temple on a Roman hill, a human head was discovered. This symbol was appropriated by the Romans that the place of the temple was to be "the head" of all Italy and was known thereafter as the Capitoline Hill (1995, 10-11). Schmidt concedes that it "may be a coincidence," but claims that "to an audience prepared by the context to look for double meanings, it would be a glaring and meaningful coincidence" (Schmidt 1995, 11).

(d) The Inscription

The narrator in Mark's Gospel states that it was the third hour when Jesus was crucified. The inscription indicating to the passers-by the crime for which Jesus was being executed read simply "King of the Jews." The Markan author is stating here that the wording on the inscription was indicative as to how those who were responsible for Jesus' execution, described his "crime." However in spite of many interpretations to the contrary, (cf. Danker, 1961, 49; Waetjen 1989, 223; Stock 1989, 403), the Markan author does not have Jesus refer to himself as "king." This would be politically inconsistent with Jesus' views in the light of his experience of kingship in the Mediterranean world of the first century CE. It would also be inconsistent in the context of Mark's theme of freedom in the narrative. The Markan narrative has consistently demonstrated that the ἐξουσία of Jesus was not "a power to act over others" as "kings" in the Mediterranean world were want to do, but in fact "a power to act with and for others." The message of Jesus is concerned with the reign of God (βασιλεία), not with kingship as such. In drawing attention to the inscription fixed on to the cross, the Markan author is emphasising the irony of the situation. It is the "authorities" of this world, Herod, the Chief Priests and their Scribes, the Roman government and even the Roman soldiers who are threatened by Jesus' announcement of the inauguration of the βασιλεία where the concept of freedom is to take on a new meaning. In its simple statement, and unlike the monumental inscriptions to the "kings and rulers" of this world, such as the *Res Gestae* of Augustus, the inscription on the cross symbolically and provocatively conveys a message which challenges the claim to the kind of power that the "rulers" of this world claim for themselves and which Jesus had called into question:

> You know that those who are supposed to rule over the gentiles lord it over (κατακυριεύουσιν) them, and their great men exercise authority over (κατεξουσιάζουσιν) them. But it shall not be so among you; but whoever would be great among you must be your servant, and whoever would be first among you must be slave of all. For the Son of man also came not to be served but to serve, and to give his life as a ransom for many (Mk 10:42-45).

The inscription placed on the cross is given public prominence, not just during the time that Jesus was on the cross, but through the media of those Christian writings which bear testimony to the event of Jesus' death.

The genius of Mark's construction of the Passion narrative, is that not only are there allusions to Roman practices, there are also allusions to Jewish expectations of the apocalyptic advent of the Messiah. Myers (1988, 391) states that the author's depiction of Jesus' death on the cross is the culmination of the other "apocalyptic moments," the baptism and transfiguration of Jesus. He explains:

> Mark, however, has given us narrative clues that identify all the apocalyptic moments with the one event of the cross. We recall that three times Jesus has predicted that his audience would "see" the advent of the Human One: once to his disciples (9:1), once referring to the powers themselves (13:25), and once addressing the Sanhedrin (14:62). We now realise that the narrative of Jesus' execution does indeed fulfil his word: at the cross "some of" the disciples (represented by the women "watching" in 15:40) and the whole political spectrum of powers (including members of the Sanhedrin) are all present. They are "seeing" the advent of the Human One on the cross. That this is the moment spoken of in 8:29f and 13:24f is further confirmed by the two representative "apocalyptic portents." The sun darkens (the cosmic symbol), and the sanctuary curtain is rent in two (the political symbol). The world order has been overthrown, the powers have fallen (13:24f).

The Challenge to Freedom

In Markan scholarship, the exclamation by the Roman centurion who stands guarding the cross (Mk 15: 39), has generally been regarded as a profession of faith. Bornkamm interprets the exclamation as "a miracle and a sign" and makes the observation that "when Israel lets her Messiah die at the hands of the Romans, the first confession of faith in him comes from the lips of a pagan" (1973: 168). This notion of "conversion" on the part of the centurion is also the view of such scholars as Matera (1982, 136); Jackson, (1987, 16-37); and Stock (1989, 414). To regard the centurion's statement as a "miracle" (Bornkamm 1973, 168) or a "conversion" Harrington (1990, 628) is, as Myers correctly states, to have missed "one of the most salient lessons of the whole story, which is that those in power indeed "know who Jesus is" and are out to destroy him, whereas those who follow him are often unsure who he is, but struggle to trust him nevertheless" (1988, 394). While Myers acknowledges that the Markan text does contain radical reversals, and on that score, the traditional view of the centurion's "conversion" would not be out of the question, he argues that there are clues in the narrative which suggest otherwise.

Firstly, Myers draws attention to the words in the text that the centurion was standing over against Jesus on the cross. He explains that "such spatial attention usually in Mark connotes opposition, not solidarity" (1988, 393). The Greek word ἐναντίος, meaning "contrary" or "hostile," occurs in Mk 6:48, in the scene where the disciples are having difficulty on the lake because the wind was against (ἐναντίος) them. Secondly, Myers (1988, 393) points out that the centurion does not defect from his role in reporting to Pilate, as was his "duty," that Jesus had died. This action, according to Myers, would rule out any notion of discipleship on the part of the centurion. Perhaps the most significant clue to which Myers draws attention, is the centurion's statement (Mk 15:39): "This man was a son of God." Apart from two instances which could be regarded as apocalyptic moments where the heavenly voices proclaim Jesus as the "beloved Son" (1:11; 9: 7), and the opening statement by the narrator who announces the "Good news" of Jesus Christ [son of God] (1:1), all the other instances where Jesus is named as "son of God," namely, 3:11; 5: 7; 6: 3; 14: 61, are all uttered by opponents of Jesus. Myers poses the question as to why then should the centurion's statement be considered "trustworthy," that is, should it be regarded as a statement of conversion, given that the clues in the narrative suggest that the centurion has not defected from his allegiance to Pilate.

Throughout the trial scenes in the Passion narrative, the Gospel author has graphically depicted Pilate as standing in opposition to Jesus. Myers is surely correct then, when he claims that the words of the centurion do not constitute a confession of faith at all, but rather reflect "the hostile response of those struggling to gain power over Jesus by "naming him." This, Myers (1988, 394) explains, is the more appropriate political discourse at this point in the Markan narrative, and he adds that "[t]he only difference between the exclamation of the centurion and that of the demon or high priest is that Jesus cannot silence or repudiate it, for he is dead. It is therefore up to the reader to discern."

Indeed, in naming Jesus as "Son of God," the centurion confirms the fact that at this point in the narrative, the power of Rome has prevailed. Having subjected Jesus to an ignominious death, Roman officialdom has effectively put an end to Jesus' "power to act." In the context of the Gospel narrative as a whole, the words of the centurion stand in tension with the opening words of the Gospel, "The beginning of the gospel of Jesus Christ, the Son of God." In recounting the circumstances of Jesus' death, the author of Mark's Gospel places before his audience an array of responses to the passion and death of Jesus, from that of faithful "watching" on the part of some women disciples to defection by Peter and the other disciples, and from remorse and despair on the part of Judas to open hostility on the part of the crowd and the Jewish and Roman authorities.

The Burial of Jesus

The account of the burial of Jesus in Mark's Gospel highlights a number of issues regarding the concept of ἐξουσία in reference to discipleship. Firstly there is the involvement of Joseph of Arimathea in the burial of Jesus. Unlike the other Gospel accounts of the burial of Jesus which imply that Joseph, although a member of the Sanhedrin was not implicated in the death of Jesus, the Markan account makes no such allowances. For Mark, Joseph was "a respected member of the Council"(14:43), the implication being that his view would have held sway in the Council's deliberations in sentencing Jesus to death.

Interpretations that have viewed the Markan Joseph sympathetically, for example Bornkamm (1973, 168) have probably been influenced by the Matthean version "Joseph was a disciple of Jesus" (Mt 27: 57) or the Lucan account "He was ... a good and righteous man, who had not consented to their purpose and deed" (Lk 23:50), or the Johannine account "Joseph of Arimathea who was a disciple of Jesus, but secretly for fear of the Jews" (Jn 19:38). Brown claims that the Matthean account is probably "reading Joseph's postresurrectional career in to the account by describing Joseph as a disciple" (1988: 245). This no doubt can be said of the Lucan and Johannine accounts as well. Mark has a different agenda. In Mk 15:43 the author makes the claim that Joseph was a respected member of the Council and it was the whole council that had sought testimony against Jesus (Mk 14: 55) to put him to death and that "they all condemned him" (Mk 14:64b).[14] In Mark's interpretation of the events connected with the execution of Jesus, it is the Jewish Establishment as a whole that was responsible for having Jesus put to death. It was out of their office of authority that the members of the Sanhedrin took action. It was also in acting out of the authority of his office that Joseph approached Pilate to ask for the body of Jesus for burial.

According to Myers (1988: 395), a political reading suggests that Joseph's action was one of expediency. His action of petitioning Pilate to release the body of Jesus for burial was an expedient measure to avoid what he and probably the whole council perceived may have turned into a protest by the general public who would have

---

[14] Brown (1988) 238 n. 20, explains that the term εὐσχήμων means "prominent, honourable, outstanding." Therefore it seems likely that amongst the Sanhedrin, Joseph could be regarded as prominent, honourable, outstanding and respected.

objected that the dead were left unburied on the Sabbath. Brown (1988: 236) provides an example of the directive in the Deuteronomic Law with regard to the disposal of the body of an executed criminal :

> And you shall hang him on a tree. His body should not remain all night on the tree; but you shall bury him the same day, for a hanged man is accursed by God. You shall not defile your land, which the Lord your God gives you for an inheritance" (Deut: 21:22-23).

Brown also points out that in the *Temple Scroll* 64:10-13 and also in Philo this text from Deuteronomy is cited with reference to crucifixion. Likewise, he cites Josephus' comment with regard to the Jewish practice of burying the dead:

> The Jews are so careful about funeral rites that even those who are crucified because they were found guilty are taken down and buried before sunset.[15]

Therefore it would seem that, from the Markan author's point of view, the motive behind Joseph of Arimathea's action in approaching Pilate was not because he wanted to secure an honourable burial for Jesus, but rather, because of his status as a member of the Council he had to uphold the observance of the Law. Nevertheless, although Joseph held a considerable degree of status because he was a member of the Sanhedrin and thereby held authority with regard to Jewish law, he would have been well aware that Roman governance was the political rule of law and in that respect he needed to act with caution. According to Brown (1988, 241) Joseph's reason for caution may have been his fear of coming under suspicion as a sympathiser of Jesus and his cause. After all, as Brown points out, "Jesus had been found condemned as one who did not deny that he was King of the Jews and accordingly was guilty of *maiestas* in Roman eyes" (1988, 241). It possibly would have been out of fear of being regarded as a disciple of Jesus and being implicated in the treason for which Jesus had been accused, that Joseph had to summon up courage before approaching Pilate (τολμήσας εἰσῆλθεν πρὸς τὸν Πιλᾶτον).[16] Myers (1988, 395) draws attention to the fact that Joseph had to make bold his petition before Pilate, which is indeed indicative of the power and control that Rome wielded in the provinces. A socio-political reading of this story therefore, points to a closer historical reality than do the other Gospel accounts of the same story. Although Mark describes Joseph as someone who "was looking for the kingdom of God" (Mk 15:43), this does not

---

[15] Brown (1988) 236 n. 12, cites *J.W.* 4.5.2.
[16] BAGD, 822

necessarily indicate that he was a disciple. The scribe who approached Jesus regarding the commandments (Mk 12: 28-34) was told that he was "not far from the kingdom of God," yet this did not constitute him as a disciple of Jesus. That Joseph was not a disciple of Jesus is probably the reality as Brown claims (1988, 241):

> In relation to one crucified for *maiestas*, a prefect would not have been likely to give the body to a disciple of Jesus (Matthew) or to one who had argued for not punishing him (Luke). A desire to make a hero out of the King of the Jews would scarcely have been encouraged.

The second dimension of ἐξουσία in connection with discipleship that is emphasised in the story is in reference to the burial of Jesus which was carried out in haste without the proper burial rites that Jews were normally given. This is brought out in the narrative with the mention that the women went to the tomb after the Sabbath in order to carry out the burial rites appropriately. There is no mention in Mark's Gospel that the tomb was Joseph's tomb, as is the case in Matthew's Gospel (Mt 27:60). Brown (1988, 242) explains that "[a]n honourable burial would scarcely have been given by a Sanhedrist who voted for Jesus to be condemned to death on the grounds of blasphemy." In the Markan account it is the women, Mary Magdalene and Mary the mother of Joses who observe where Jesus was buried (Mk 15:47), and Mary Magdalene, Mary the mother of James, and Salome who sought to provide Jesus with an honourable burial. The fact that the women take note of where the body had been buried and take action to provide an honourable burial by bringing spices with which to anoint the body, serves to emphasise their lack of fear in being associated with Jesus.

Myers (1988, 395) also draws attention to the tragic pathos in the story. It is Joseph who puts Jesus in the tomb, an action which calls to mind the action of John's disciples who, on hearing of the Baptist's execution, take his body away for burial. Myers states that Jesus' disciples "cannot even be as faithful in death as John's disciples were" (1988, 395-396). It is at this point in the story that, as Myers states, "[t]he discipleship community has disappeared. Except for the women."

However, the women's role at this point in the narrative is also generally interpreted conventionally, as being "true" disciples, the implication being that the women were more faithful disciples than the men. In fact, this interpretation is perhaps somewhat exclusive in relation to the concept of discipleship that Mark's Gospel portrays. It is in the final scene where the women are commissioned by the young man at the tomb to announce to the disciples and to Peter that Jesus would meet with them in Galilee, that they are confronted with the challenge to take action. Already in the Passion Narrative, the narrator had indicated that the women expressed their allegiance to Jesus in "watching" at the foot of the cross, and it is the women who also go to the tomb in order to carry out the proper burial rites. They acted with courage, in spite of the fact that the Roman authorities could interpret their actions as allegiance to someone who was convicted of *maiestas*, and also in spite of the fact that the Jewish authorities could interpret their actions as allegiance to a blasphemer. However, it is in the dialogue with the young man at the tomb that their commitment to discipleship is also challenged. They are given the task of reporting to Peter and the other disciples that the mission of Jesus was to begin again in Galilee and that he would be there to meet them. In spite of the defection by Peter and the disciples, it is in Galilee to where they are being invited to enter again into discipleship with Jesus. The narrator states that the women are afraid. The Markan narrative is left open-ended. The reader can only speculate that the author of this Gospel through the voice of the narrator is setting the challenge of ἐξουσία before his audience. The women as well as the men are called into the circle of discipleship. The challenge to all as disciples, is to act with ἐξουσία in continuing to proclaim the "good news" of Jesus, the Anointed One.

Conclusion

Jesus challenged the so-called "conventional wisdom" of the time (Borg 1987, 182). In teaching and acting with ἐξουσία, Jesus was regarded by the established classes as a threat to their status and power as "keepers" of this conventional wisdom. Borg (1987, 182) states that

> "[t]o a large extent, it was the conventional wisdom of the time—the 'dominant consciousness' of the day—that was responsible for the death of Jesus. The high priest and his circle were both the servants and guardians of the dominant consciousness. Shaped by it and in a sense subservient to it, they were also concerned to preserve it.

The other so-called "conventional wisdom," or "dominant consciousness" which Jesus challenged was that of the power of Rome. Ultimately, it was the dominant ethos of power over the lives and destiny of others which the Romans forced on subject nations and promulgated as freedom, and to which even the "conventional wisdom" of Judaism bowed, that was exposed with Jesus' proclamation of a new freedom within the reign of God.

Contrary to the thinking of some modern day Christian piety, Jesus was not simply someone who was a victim of political forces. Rather, as Borg (1987, 183-184) claims, Jesus "provocatively challenged the ethos of his day. He was killed because he sought, in the name and power of the Spirit, the transformation of his own culture. He issued a call for a relationship with God that would lead to a new ethos and thus a new politics." The subsequent followers of the "Way" of Jesus undertook the proclamation of the "good news."

Fitzmyer (1991a, 331) states that the early Christians acknowledged Jesus' victory over a humiliating death by proclaiming Jesus as Lord (κύριος) over and against the "widespread belief in Roman emperors as κύριοι (e.g. Augustus [ÄgU 1197, I, 15])." This Christian response is attested in the writings of Paul, for example 1 Cor 8:6: "For there is one Lord, Jesus Christ, through whom are all things and through whom we exist."

Therefore, over and against the widespread propaganda that Augustus had inaugurated a golden age of liberty under the Roman empire, the author of Mark's Gospel provides a testimony that it was Jesus of Nazareth who had inaugurated a new age of freedom within the βασιλεία.

CHAPTER SEVEN

Epilogue: The World before the Text

The approach to an interpretation of a biblical text will be determined by the questions one brings to the text. As Sandra Schneiders (1991, 154) explains

> to start with the question is to root one's research in the open search for truth. Method remains necessary, but it will be developed in function of the question, not the other way round.

It has already been stated in the introduction to this study, that the concern that prompted my exploration of the concept of freedom in the Gospel of Mark is the question regarding the significance from a Christian perspective, of the meaning of freedom in and for the contemporary world. Sandra Schneiders names this apect of the interpretative process of a biblical text as the interest in "the world *before* the text", or the interest in the transformative potential of the text.

While there have been a number of studies on the various segments of Mark's Gospel which contain the term ἐξουσία, only one other study to date, that which has been undertaken by Karl Scholtisseck (1992), has explored the actual term ἐξουσία in Mark's Gospel from a thematic perspective. In his study of the ἐξουσία motif, Scholtissek begins with a consideration of the question that is posed within the text itself "What is this? A new teaching! With ἐξουσία he commands even the unclean spirits, and they obey him." (Mk 1: 27). Scholtissek points out that this verse contains both the question and the answer, and he proceeds by way of a thorough exegetical analysis to demonstrate how the ἐξουσία motif is central to an understanding of Mark's christology. He has interpreted the ἐξουσία theme in terms of identifying the christological dimension of *Vollmacht* inherent in the ἐξουσία pericopes, and the consequent implications of this interpretation for Christian faith.

While acknowledging Scholtissek's important contribution to an understanding of Mark's christology from the perspective of the ἐξουσία motif, the question that prompted my particular interest in the study of the ἐξουσία motif in Mark's gospel began at a different point. My starting point was not the text, but rather the question regarding Christian praxis in the face of dominant power that oppresses and enslaves other human beings in so many arenas of human social living in the postmodern world. This question which pertains to "the world *before* the text" necessitated a consideration of the "world *behind* the text" that is "the ancient world of the author(s) and her or his historical, theological, and ideological agenda as well as the community to which the text was originally addressed and the ancient world in which that community lived" (Schneiders 1991, 113). It also necessitated a consideration of the "world *of* the text", that is the linguistic system contained in the text and which generates its meaning (Schneiders 1991, 113).

In order to identify Christian *praxis* with reference to freedom, it was important to return to the foundational texts of the Christian tradition. The Gospel of Mark was the obvious starting point, as this Gospel is generally considered to be the earliest gospel narrative of the teaching and actions of Jesus, and would have been composed within the life time of people who possibly would have known Jesus, or would have experienced something of the socio-political climate that Jesus experienced.

What has emerged from a consideration of "the world *behind* the text" of Mark's Gospel is the emphasis on the ideology of power that prevailed throughout the Roman occupied world of the early Christian era. The system of government, the expansion policies and practices of the Roman Republic as well as the economic, cultural and social dimensions that directed, governed and shaped the living conditions of the populace were all influenced directly and indirectly by the ideology of power that was promulgated by Augustus during his life time. It also influenced the subsequent legacy of power that shaped policy and practice in the Mediterranean world long after the death of Augustus. The literature of the Augustan period and the early Roman empire provides evidence of an atmosphere of unrest among the ordinary people as they struggled against this ideology of domination and its effect on their lives. The modern reader is thus able to gain an insight into what it meant for people of the first century to experience being powerless within such a climate of dominant power.

This study of the "world *behind* the text" of Mark's Gospel necessitated a study of the "world *of* the text" of other "texts" such as literature, art, architecture and inscriptions, that have come down to us from that period. An exploration of the "world *of* these texts" identified the linguistic codes and symbols which pointed to the message or meaning of these other texts. In particular the linguistic codes and symbols evident in the text of the *Res Gestae* inscription pointed to the perspective regarding the ideology of power that prevailed during the reign of Augustus. The subsequent promulgation of this ideology of power through the medium of the *Res Gestae* text inscribed on monuments throughout the Roman occupied world, was a legacy that Augustus bequeathed to future generations. This was a legacy of an ideology of power to which subsequent emperors of the Roman empire subscribed. It was within the climate of this socio-political world that the message of Jesus was also proclaimed.

The next phase in the interpretive process of the "world *of* the text," as Schneiders also explains:

consists of the testimony of the participants in the originating events that has been incorporated in the linguistic text. Because the testimony is incorporated into a text, it becomes a work, an artistic entity constructed according to a particular genre, for example, narrative, poetry, proclamation, or discourse. This is the basis of its capacity to "project a world" (1991:167).

My exploration of the "the world *of* the text" of Mark's Gospel, and in particular with respect to that of the linguistic aspects pertaining to the ἐξουσία motif in this text, has identified the nature of the freedom with which Jesus taught and acted, and which ran counter to the climate of domination in the socio-political Mediterranean world of the first century. The "world *of* the text" of Mark's gospel emphasises how the challenge to the prevailing ideology of power extended not only to the structures of government and those exercising power through these structures, but also to those who claimed allegiance to Jesus as his disciples. For the followers of Jesus, claiming discipleship meant being called to a radical understanding of the meaning of ἐξουσία and also a radical way of living out of this new understanding. This is the world projected by the text.

A socio-political reading of Mark's Gospel with particular attention to the ἐξουσία motif contained in "the world *of* the text" and "the world behind the text," provides a way for taking the tradition of Mark's message of freedom "into a possible alternative reality" (Schneiders 1991, 167) with respect to identifying dominanting and oppressive structures and practices that currently operate in postmodern society. It also offers a challenge for a contemporary Christian response to dominant power that denies people their freedom. This "alternative reality" constitutes what Schneiders (1991, 167) has named as the "world *before* the text." The engagement with the "world *behind* the text" and the "world *of* the text" with reference to the ἐξουσία theme in Mark's Gospel, has thus generated new insights and understandings which have the potential to expand our consciousness of the meaning and appropriation of Mark's concept of freedom as that of truly liberating power.

APPENDIX

Abbreviations

AHR	*The American Historical Review*
AJP	*American Journal of Philology*
ANRW	*Aufstieg und Niedergang der Römischen Welt*
BA	*Biblical Archaeologist*
BAGD	W. Bauer, W.F. Arndt, F.W. Gingrich and F.W. Danker. 1979. *A Greek-English Lexicon of the New Testament and Other Early Christian Literature.* 2nd ed. Chicago/London: University of Chicago Press.
BTB	*Biblical Theology Bulletin*
CBQ	*Catholic Biblical Quarterly*
CRINT	Compendia rerum iudaicarum ad Novum Testamentum
CP	*Classical Philology*
DBI	R. J. Coggins and J.L. Houlden. 1990. *A Dictionary of Biblical Interpretation.* London: SCM Press; Philadelphia, Trinity Press International.
DCM	*The Dictionary of Classical Mythology.*
DELL	*Dictionnaire étymologique de la langue latine*
EDNT	*Exegetical Dictionary of the New Testament*
EJ	V. Ehrenberg and A.H.M. Jones, *Documents Illustrating the Reigns of Augustus and Tiberius.*
FS	Festschrift
GEL	*Greek-English Lexicon of the New Testament*
HSCP	Harvard Studies in Classical Philology
JAW	*Jahresbericht für Altertumswissenschaft*
JRS	*Journal of Roman Studies*
JBL	*Journal of Biblical Literature*
JSNT	*Journal for the Study of the New Testament*

JSOT	*Journal for the Study of the Old Testament*
JTS	*Journal of Theological Studies*
KeT	*Kleine Texte für theologische und philologische Vorlesungen und Übungen*
LCL	Loeb Classical Library
LS	C.T.Lewis and C. Short., *A Latin Dictionary*
NF	Neue Folge
NJBC	*The New Jerome Biblical Commentary.* Ed. Raymond E. Brown, Joseph A. Fitzmyer, Roland E. Murphy. London: Geoffrey Chapman, 1994.
NovT	*Novum Testamentum*
NTS	*New Testament Studies*
OCCL	*The Oxford Companion to Classical Literature*
OLD	*Oxford Latin Dictionary*
PGL	*A Patristic Greek Lexicon*
RB	*Revue Biblique*
RG	*Res Gestae*
SBLDS	Society of Biblical Literature Dissertation Series
StTh	*Studia theologica*
TDNT	*Theological Dictionary of the New Testament.* 10 vols. Grand Rapids: Eerdmans, 1964-76.
TLL	*Thesaurus Linguae Latinae*
WSt	*Wiener Studien: Zeitschrift für Klassische Philologie und Patristik*
ZNW	*Zeitschrift für die neutestamentliche Wissenschaft*

Ancient Sources

Aristotle
Ar. Rhetorica
    1.2.3
    1.9.33

Augustus
Res Gestae

Cassius Dio
History
    51.2
    54.1
    56.33

M. Tullius Cicero
Philippics
    3.2.1-5
    4.2.4
    5.16.42-5

Demetrius
On Style
    221.222

Isocrates
Evagoras

Josephus
Antiquitates Judaicae
    12.414-9
    14.136-7
    14.188-91
    14185-264
    14.265-7
    14.325
    14.381.3
    14.384
    1.388
    15.195
    15.199
    15.200
    15.267
    15.268-73
    15.275-6
    15.332
    15.380-425

De bello Judaico
    1.99
    1.283
    1.284
    1.285
    1.387-92
    1.401-14
    1.422
    11.4-7
    2.14-92
    2.94-7
    11117
    2.167
    2.168

Livy
    1.60.4
    2.1.1
    2.1.2
    2.1.7
    2.2.5
    1.15.3
    4.20.7

Rhetorica ad Herennium
    4.42.54

Strabo
Geography
    5.3.9

Suetonius
Augustus
    2.22.1
    2.43.1
    2.86.1
    2.101.1
    2.101.2
    2.101.4

Xenophon
Agesilaus

Bibliography

ACHTEMEIER, Paul J. 1975. *Mark*. Proclamation Commentaries. Philadelphia, Pennsylvania: Fortress Press.

ANDERSON, Hugh. 1989. "Jesus: Aspects of the Question of His Authority." In *The Social World of Formative Christianity and Judaism: Essays in Tribute to Howard Clark Kee*. Edited by Jacob Neusner, Peder Borgen, Ernest Frerichs, Richard Horsley. Philadelphia: Fortress, 290-310.

APPLEBAUM, Shimon. 1976. "The Social Economic Status of the Jews of the Diaspora." CRINT 2, 701-727.

APPLEBAUM, Shimon. 1977. "Judaea as a Roman Province: the Countryside as a Political and Economic Factor." *ANRW* II. 8, 355-396.

AUNE, David, E. 1989. *The New Testament in Its Literary Environment*. Philadelphia: Westminster Press.

BALDWIN, Charles S. 1928. *Medieval Rhetoric and Poetic (to 1400): Interpreted from Representative Works*. New York: Macmillan.

BALZ, Horst. 1990. ἐγκαίνια, ίων, τά. *EDNT* 1, 376.

BARDON, Henry. 1968 [1940]. *Les Empereurs et les lettres latines d'Auguste à Hadrien*. Paris: Société d'Edition "Les Belles Lettres."

BARINI, Concepta. 1937. *Res Gestae Divi Augusti ex Monumentis Ancyrano, Antiocheno, Apolloniensi*. Scriptores graeci et latini, iussu Beniti Mussolini consilio R. Academiae Lynceorvm editi. Romae: Typis Regiae Officinae Polygraphicae.

BARTLETT, John R. 1985. *Jews in the Hellenistic World: Josephus, Aristeas, the Sibylline Oracles, Eupolemus*. Cambridge et al.: Cambridge University Press.

BARTON, I.M. (ed). 1989. *Roman Public Buildings*. Exeter: University of Exeter.

BAUMBACH, Günther. 1990. γραμματεύς, έως, ό. *EDNT* 1, 259.

BEAVIS, Mary Anne. 1987. "The Trial before the Sanhedrin (Mark 14:53-65): Reader Response and Greco-Roman Readers." *CBQ* 49, 581-596.

BEAVIS, Mary Anne. 1988. "Women as Models of Faith in Mark." *BTB* 18, 3-9.

BERGER, Klaus. 1984. "Hellenistische Gattungen im Neuen Testament." *ANRW* II. 25.2, 1031-1432.

BEST, Ernest. 1981. *Following Jesus: Discipleship in the Gospel of Mark*. JSNT Supplement Series 4. Sheffield: JSOT Press.

BEYER, Hermann. W. 1964. διακονέω, διακονία, διάκονος. *TDNT* 2, 81-93.

BILEZIKIAN, Gilbert G. 1977. *The Liberated Gospel: A Comparison of the Gospel of Mark and Greek Tragedy*. Grand Rapids, Michigan: Baker Book House.

230   Bibliography

BITZER, Lloyd. 1968. "The Rhetorical Situation." *Philosophy and Rhetoric* 1, 1-14.

BLOUT, Brian K. 1993. "A Socio-Rhetorical Analysis of Simon of Cyrene: Mark 15:21 and Its Parallels." *Semeia* 64, 171-198.

BÖCKLE, Franz. 1980. *Fundamental Moral Theology*. Translated by N.D. Smith. Dublin: Gill & Macmillan.

BORG, Marcus J. 1984. *Conflict, Holiness & Politics in the Teachings of Jesus*. Studies in the Bible and Early Christianity, vol. 5. New York: Edwin Mellen Press.

BORG, Marcus J. 1987. *Jesus: A New Vision*. San Francisco: Harper & Row.

BORG, Marcus J. 1994. *Jesus in Contemporary Scholarship*. Valley Forge, Pennsylvania: Trinity Press International.

BORING, M. Eugene. 1991. "Mark 1:1-15 and the Beginning of the Gospel." *Semeia* 52: 43-81.

BOTHA, Pieter J.J. 1993. "The Historical Setting of Mark's Gospel: Problems and Possibilities." *JSNT* 51. 27-55.

BROUGHTON, T.R.S. 1975. "Roman Asia." In *An Economic Survey of Ancient Rome*. Edited by Tenney Frank. vol. IV. New York: Octagon Books.

BROWN, John Pairman. 1983. "Techniques of Imperial Control: The Background of the Gospel Event." In *The Bible and Liberation: Political and Social Hermeneutics*. Edited by Norman Gottwald. (Revised Edition of A Radical Religion Reader). Maryknoll: Orbis, 367-377.

BRUNT, P.A. 1988. *The Fall of the Roman Republic and Related Essays*. Oxford: Clarendon Press.

BRUNT, P.A. & J.M. MOORE. 1967. *Res Gestae Divi Augusti: The Achievements of the Divine Augustus*. London: Oxford University Press.

BRYAN, Christopher. 1993. *A Preface to Mark: Notes on the Gospel and Its Literary and Cultural Settings*. New York/Oxford: Oxford University Press.

BUDESHEIM, Thomas L. 1971. "Jesus and the Disciples in Conflict with Judaism." *ZNW* 62, 190-209.

BULTMANN, Rudolf. 1952. [1948]. *Theology of the New Testament*. vol 1.Translated by Kendrick Grobel. London: SCM Press.

BURRIDGE, Richard A. 1992. *What Are the Gospels? A Comparison with Graeco-Roman Biography*. Cambridge: Cambridge University Press.

CAIRNS, Francis. 1984. "Propertius and the Battle of Actium (4.6)." In *Poetry and Politics in the Age of Augustus*. Edited by Tony Woodman & David West. Cambridge: Cambridge University Press, 129-168.

CAMERY-HOGGATT, Jerry. 1992. *Irony in Mark's Gospel*. Cambridge: Cambridge University Press.

CAPLAN, Harry. 1968. [1954]. *Cicero: [Cicero] Ad.C. Herennium: de Ratione Dicendi (Rhetorica ad Herennium)*. vol. 1 of 28. LCL. London: William Heinemann.

CARNEY, T.F. 1975. *The Shape of the Past: Models and Antiquity*. Lawrence, Kansas: Coronado Press.

CARTER, John. 1989. "Civic and Other Buildings." In *Roman Public Buildings*. Edited by I.M. Barton. Exeter: University of Exeter, 31-65.

CASSON, Lionel. 1974. *Travel in the Ancient World*. London: George Allen & Unwin.

CASTELOT, John J. and Aelred CODY. 1990. "Religious Institutions of Israel." *NJBC* 252-1283.

CHAMPLIN, Edward. 1989. "The Testament of Augustus." In *Rheinisches Museum für Philologie*. Edited by Carl Werner Müller. NF 132. Frankfurt am Main: J.D. Sauerländer.

CHARLESWORTH, M.P. 1924. *Trade Routes and Commerce in the Roman Empire*. Cambridge: Cambridge University Press.

COLLINS, Adela Yarbro. 1988. "Narrative, History and Gospel." *Semeia* 43, 145-153.

COLLINS, Adela Yarbro. 1992. *The Beginning of the Gospel*. Minneapolis: Fortress Press.

COLLINS, Adela Yarbro. 1993. "The Genre of the Passion Narrative." *StTh* 47, 3-28.

CROSSAN, John Dominic. 1973. "Mark and the Relatives of Jesus." *NovT* 15, 81-113.

CROSSAN, John Dominic. 1993 [1991]. *The Historical Jesus: The Life of a Mediterranean Peasant*. North Blackburn, Victoria : Collins Dove.

CROSSAN, John Dominic. 1994. *Jesus: A Revolutionary Biography*. San Francisco: Harper.

CUSS, Dominique. 1974. *Imperial Cult and Honorary Terms in the New Testament*. Fribourg, Switzerland: The University Press.

D'ANGELO, Mary Rose. 1992. "Abba and 'Father': Imperial Theology and the Jesus Traditions." *JBL* 111/4, 611-630.

DANKER, Frederick W. 1970. "The Demonic Secret in Mark: A Reexamination of the Cry of Dereliction (15 34)." *ZNW* 61, 48-69.

DANKER, Frederick W. 1982. *Benefactor: Epigraphic Study of a Graeco-Roman and New Testament Semantic Field*. St Louis, Missouri: Clayton Publishing House.

DEWEY, Kim E. 1976. "Peter's Curse and Cursed Peter." In *The Passion of Mark: Studies on Mark 14-16*. Edited by Werner H. Kelber. Philadelphia: Fortress Press, 96-113.

DEWEY, Joanna. 1980. *Markan Public Debate: Literary Technique, Concentric Structure and Theology in Mark 2:1-3:6.* SBL Dissertation Series 48. Missoula: Scholars Press.

DEWEY, Joanna. 1991. "Mark as Interwoven Tapestry." *CBQ* 51, 221-36.

DEWEY, Joanna. 1994. "Textuality in an Oral Culture: A Survey of the Pauline Traditions." *Semeia* 65, 37-65.

DIEHL, Ernst. (ed) 1910 [1908]. *Res Gestae Divi Augusti.* Kleine Texte für theologische und philologische Vorlesungen und Übungen, 29/30. Bonn: A. Marcus und E. Weber.

DI LELLA, Andrew A. 1990. "Daniel." *NJBC* 406-420.

DONAHUE, John R. 1971. "Tax Collectors and Sinners: An Attempt at Identification." *CBQ* 33, 39-61.

DONAHUE, John R. 1973. *Are You the Christ? The Trial Narrative in the Gospel of Mark.* SBLDS 10. Missoula, Montana: Society of Biblical Literature for the Seminar on Mark.

DONAHUE, John R. 1976. "Introduction: From Passion Traditions to Passion Narrative." In *The Passion of Mark: Studies on Mark 14-16.* Edited by Werner H. Kelber. Philadelphia: Fortress Press, 1-20.

DONAHUE, John R. 1992. "The Quest for the Community of Mark." In *The Four Gospels: 1992.* FS Franz Neirynck. Edited by F. Van Segbroeck et al. vol II. Bibliotheca Ephemeridum Theologicarum Lovaniensium. Leuven: Leuven University Press, 817-838.

DORMEYER, Detlev. 1989. *Evangelium als literarische und theologische Gattung.* Erträge der Forschung, Band 263. Darmstadt: Wissenschaftliche Buchgesellschaft.

DORMEYER, Detlev and Hubert FRANKEMÖLLE. 1984. "Evangelium als literarische Gattung und als theologischer Begriff. Tendenzen und Aufgaben der Evangelienforschung im 20. Jahrhundert, mit einer Untersuchung des Markusevangeliums in seinem Verhältnis zur antiken Biographie." *ANRW* II. 25.2: 1543-1704.

DUCKWORTH, George, E. 1959. "Vergil's Georgics and the Laudes Galli." *AJP* 80: 225-37.

DUCKWORTH, George, E. 1962. *Structural Patterns and Proportions in Vergil's Aeneid: A Study in Mathematical Composition.* Ann Arbor: The University of Michigan Press.

DUFF, Paul Brooks. 1992. "The March of the Divine Warrior and the Advent of the Greco-Roman King: Mark's Account of Jesus' Entry into Jerusalem." *JBL* 11, 55-71.

ECO, Umberto. 1979. *The Role of the Reader: Explorations in the Semiotics of Texts.* Bloomington, IN: Indiana University Press.

EHRENBERG,V. & A.H.M. JONES. 1976. *Documents illustrating the Reigns of Augustus and Tiberius.* 2nd edn. Oxford: Clarendon Press.

ELLIOTT, J.K. 1971. "The Conclusion of the Pericope of the Healing of the Leper and Mark i.45." *JTS* 22, 153-157.

ELLIS, E. Earle. 1992. "The Date and Provenance of Mark's Gospel." In *The Four Gospels: 1992*. FS Franz Neirynck. Edited by F. Van Segbroeck et al. vol II. Bibliotheca Ephemeridum Theologicarum Lovaniensium. Leuven: Leuven University Press, 801-815.

ELSNER, John. 1991. "Cult and Sculpture: Sacrifice in the Ara Pacis Augustae." *JRS* 81, 50-61.

ERNOUT, A.& A. MEILLET. 1959. Dictionnaire étymologique de la langue latine: Histoire des mots. 4th ed. Paris: Librairie C. Klincksieck.

EVANS, Craig, A. 1989. "Jesus' Action in the Temple: Cleansing or Portent of Destruction." *CBQ* 51, 237-270.

FARR, James. 1989. "Understanding Conceptual Change Politically." In *Political Innovations and Conceptual Change*. Edited by Terence Ball, James Farr, Russell L. Hanson. Cambridge: Cambridge University Press.

FEARS, J. Rufus. 1980. "Rome: the Ideology of Imperial Power." *Thought* 55: 98-109.

FEARS, J. Rufus. 1981. "The Cult of Virtues and Roman Imperial Ideology." *ANRW* II. 17.2, 827-948.

FELDMAN, Louis II. (trans.). [1965] 1981. *Josephus: Jewish Antiquities, Books XVIII-XIX*. vol 9 of 10. LCL. Cambridge MA.: Harvard University Press; London: William Heinemann.

FIEDLER, Peter. 1990. ἁμαρτία, ας, ἡ ἁμαρτάων ἁμάρτημα, ατος, τό. *EDNT* 1, 65-67.

FITZMYER, Joseph, A. 1991. "The Languages of Palestine in the First Century AD." In *The Language of the New Testament: Classical Essays*. Edited by Stanley E. Porter. JSNT Supplement Series 60, 126-162.

FITZMYER, Joseph, A. 1991a. κύριος, ου ὁ κυριαχός. EDNT 2, 328-331.

FRANKEMÖLLE, Hubert. 1993. συναγωγή, ης, ἡ επισυναγωγή, ης, ἡ. *EDNT* 3, 293-296.

FRIEDERICH, Gerhard. 1964. εὐαγγελίζομαι, εὐαγγέλιον, προευαγγελίζομαι, εὐηαγγελιστής. *TDNT* II, 707-737.

FOERSTER, Werner. 1964. ἔξεστιν, ἐξουσία, ἐξουσιάζω, κατεξουσιάζω. In *TDNT* II, 560-575.

FOSTER, B.O.(trans.). 1967 [1919]. *Livy, Books I-II*. vol. 1 of 14. LCL. London: William Heinemann/ Cambridge, MA: Harvard University Press.

FOWLER, Robert, M. 1991. *Let the Reader Understand: Reader-Response Criticism and the Gospel of Mark*. Minneapolis: Fortress.

FREESE, John Henry (trans.). [1926] 1982. *Aristotle: The "Art" of Rhetoric*. vol. 22 of 23. LCL. Cambridge, MA: Harvard University Press.

FREYNE, Sean. 1980. *The World of the New Testament* . New Testament Message, vol. 2. Dublin: Veritas.

FREYNE, Sean. 1982. "The Disciples in Mark and the *Maskilim* in Daniel. A Comparison." *JSNT* 16, 7-23.

FREYNE, Sean. 1988. *Galilee, Jesus and the Gospels: Literary Approaches and Historical Investigations.* Philadelphia: Fortress Press.

GAGÉ, Jean. 1977. [1935] *Res Gestae Divi Augusti ex monumentis Ancyrano et Antiocheno latinis Ancyrano et Apolloniensi Graecis.* Paris: Société d'Edition "Les Belles Lettres."

GARDTHAUSEN, Viktor. 1904. *Augustus und seine Zeit.* (3 Tiele in 6 Bänden). Teil 1, Band 3. Mit Karte. Leipzig: Teubner. (Reprint Aalen: Scientia, 1964).

GARNSEY, Peter & Greg WOOLF. 1990 [1989]. "Patronage of the Rural Poor in the Roman World." In *Patronage in Ancient Society.* Edited by Andrew Wallace-Hadrill: London; New York: Routledge, 153-167.

GIESEN, Heinz. 1991. ἐπιτιμάω. *EDNT* 2, 42-43.

GILL David W.J. & Bruce W. WINTER. 1992. "Acts and Roman Religion." In *The Book of Acts in its First Century Setting.* vol 2, *The Book of Acts in its Graeco-Roman Setting.* Edited by W.J. Gill & Conrad Gempf. Grand Rapids, Michigan: William B. Eerdmans; Carlisle: Paternoster Press, 79-103.

GLARE, P.G.W. (ed.). 1977. *Oxford Latin Dictionary.* Fascicle VI. Oxford, Clarendon Press.

GOODMAN, Martin. 1987. *The Ruling Class of Judaea: The Origins of the Jewish Revolt against Rome A.D. 66-70.* Cambridge: Cambridge University Press.

GOTTWALD, Norman K. 1993. "Social Class as an Analytic and Hermeneutical Category in Biblical Studies." *JBL* 112/1, 3-22.

GRAMS, Rollin. 1991. "The Temple Conflict Scene: A Rhetorical Analysis of Matthew 21-23." In *Persuasive Artistry: Studies in New Testament Rhetoric in Honor of George A. Kennedy.* Edited by Duane F. Watson. JSNT.S 50. Sheffield: JSOT Press, 41-65.

GRANT, Michael. 1969. *From Imperium to Auctoritas: A Historical Study of AES Coinage in the Roman Empire 49 B.C.- A.D. 14.* Cambridge MA: Cambridge University Press.

GRIMAL, Pierre. 1951 [tr.1988]. *The Dictionary of Classical Mythology.* Paris: Presses Universitaires de France. Translated by A.R. Maxwell-Hyslop. Oxford: Basil Blackwell.

HAMILTON, Neil, Q. 1964. "Temple Cleansing and Temple Bank." *JBL* 83, 365-372.

HAMMOND, Mason. 1963/64. "*Res Olim Dissociabiles: Principatus Ac Libertas:* Liberty under the Early Roman Empire." *HSCP* 67/68, 93-113.

HANHART, Karel. 1992. "Son, Your Sins are Forgiven (Mk 2.5)." In *The Four Gospels: 1992*. FS Franz Neirynck. Edited by F. Van Segbroeck et al. vol II. Bibliotheca Ephemeridum Theologicarum Lovaniensium. Leuven: Leuven University Press, 997-1016.

HARDY, E.G. (ed). 1923. *The Monumentum Ancyranum*. Oxford: Clarendon.

HARRINGTON, Daniel J. 1990. "The Gospel according to Mark." In *NJBC*. 596-629.

HEIL, John Paul. 1992. *The Gospel of Mark as a Model for Action: A Reader-Response Commentary*. New York; Mahwah, N.J.: Paulist Press.

HENDRIX, Holland. 1992. "Benefactor/Patron Networks in the Urban Environment: Evidence from Thessalonica." *Semeia* 56, 41-58.

HENGEL, Martin. 1981. *The Charismatic Leader and His Followers*. Translated by J. Greig. New York: Crossroad.

HENGEL, Martin. 1985. *Studies in the Gospel of Mark*. Translated by John Bowden from the German. Philadelphia: Fortress Press.

HENGEL, Martin. 1989. *The Zealots: Investigations into the Jewish Freedom Movement in the Period from Herod 1 until 70 A.D.* Translated by David Smith. Edinburgh: T. & T. Clark.

HESTER, James D. 1991. "Placing the Blame: The Presence of Epideictic in Galatians 1 and 2." In *Persuasive Artistry: Studies in New Testament Rhetoric*. FS George A. Kennedy. Edited by Duane F. Watson. JSNT.S 50. Sheffield: JSOT Press, 281-307.

HEUSS, Alfred. 1975. "Zeitgeschichte als Ideologie: Bemerkungen zu Komposition und Gedankenführung der Res Gestae Divi Augusti." In *Monumentum Chiloniense. Studien zur augusteischen Zeit*, FS Erich Burck. Edited by E. Lefèvre. Amsterdam: Adolf M. Hakkert, 55-95.

HOOK VAN, Larue (trans.). 1945. *Isocrates*. vol.3 of 3. LCL. London: William Heinemann, Cambridge, MA: Harvard University Press..

HORSLEY, G.H.R. 1981. *New Documents Illustrating Early Christianity. A Review of the Greek Inscriptions and Papyri published in 1976*. Vol 1. North Ryde, Australia: The Ancient History Documentary Research Centre of Macquarie University.

HORSLEY, Richard A. & John S. HANSON. 1985. *Bandits, Prophets, and Messiahs: Popular Movements at the Time of Jesus*. San Francisco: Harper & Row.

HORSLEY, Richard.A. 1993. *Jesus and the Spiral of Violence: Popular Jewish Resistance in Roman Palestine*. Minneapolis: Fortress Press.

HOWATSON, M.C. (ed). 1989. *The Oxford Companion to Classical Literature*. 2nd edn., Oxford: Oxford University Press.

HÜBNER, Hans. 1991. λεγιών, ῶνος, ἡ. *EDNT* 2, 345-347.

JACKSON, Howard M. 1987. "The Death of Jesus in Mark and the Miracle from the Cross." *NTS* 33, 16-37.

JACOBSON, David, M. 1988. "King Herod's 'Heroic' Public Image." *RB* 95, 386-403.

JEREMIAS, Joachim. 1958. "Chiasmus in den Paulusbriefen." *ZNW* 49: 145-56.

JEREMIAS, Joachim. 1969. *Jerusalem in the Time of Jesus: An Investigation into Economic and Social Conditions during the New Testament Period*. Philadelphia: Fortress Press.

JUDGE, Edwin. 1985. *On Judging the Merits of Augustus*. Protocol of the Forty-Ninth Colloquy (29 April 1984). Berkeley CA: Center for Hermeneutical Studies in Hellenistic and Modern Culture, Graduate Theological Union and University of California (Berkeley).

JUDGE, Edwin. (ed.). 1985a.[1983]. "Augustus in the Res Gestae." In *Augustus and Roman History: Documents and Papers for Student Use*. North Ryde, Australia: Macquarie University, 131-171.

JUDGE, Edwin. (ed.). 1985b.[1983]. "Res Publica Restituta: A Modern Illusion." In *Augustus and Roman History: Documents and Papers for Student Use*. North Ryde, Australia: Macquarie University, 172-203.

KAIMIO, Jorma. 1979. *The Romans and the Greek Language*. Commentationes Humanarum Litterarum, 64. Helsinki: Societas Scientiarum Fennica.

KAMIERSKI, Carl R. 1992. "Evangelist and Leper: A Socio-Cultural Study of Mark 1:40-45." *NTS* 38, 37-50.

KÄSEMANN, Ernst. 1968. *Jesus Means Freedom*. Translated by Frank Clarke from the German *Der Ruf der Freiheit*. 3rd rev. edn. Philadelphia: Fortress Press.

KEE, Howard Clark. 1977. *Community of the New Age: Studies in Mark's Gospel*. Philadelphia: Westminster Press.

KELBER, Werner. 1974. *The Kingdom in Mark: A New Place and a New Time*. Philadelphia: Fortress Press.

KELBER, Werner K. 1976. "The Hour of the Son of Man and the Temptation of the Disciples." In *The Passion of Mark: Studies on Mark 14-16*. Edited by Werner H. Kelber. Philadelphia: Fortress Press, 41-57.

KELBER, Werner. 1987. "Narrative as Interpretation and Interpretation of Narrative: Hermeneutical Reflections on the Gospels." *Semeia* 39, 107-134.

KENNEDY, George. 1983. *Greek Rhetoric under Christian Emperors*. Princeton: University Press.

KENNEDY, George. 1984. *New Testament Interpretation through Rhetorical Criticism*. Chapel Hill and London: University of North Carolina Press.

KERR, Walter C.A. (trans.). [1926] 1969. *Cicero: Philippics*. vol 15 of 28. LCL London: William Heinemann, Cambridge, MA: Harvard University Press.

KINGSBURY, Jack Dean. 1989. *Conflict in Mark: Jesus, Authorities, Disciples*. Minneapolis: Fortress Press.

KINGSBURY, Jack Dean. 1990. "The Religious Authorities in the Gospel of Mark." *NTS* 36, 42-65.

KINGSBURY, Jack Dean. 1993. "The Significance of the Cross within Mark's Story." *Interpretation* 47, 370-379.

KREITZER, Larry. 1990. "Apotheosis of the Roman Emperor." *BA* 53, 210-217.

LACEY, W.K. and B.W.J.G. WILSON. (eds. and trans.). 1970. *Res Publica: Roman Politics and Society according to Cicero*. London: Oxford University Press.

LAFARGUE, Michael. 1989. "Sociohistorical research and the Contextualization of Biblical Theology." In *The Social World of Formative Christianity and Judaism: Essays in Tribute to Howard Clark Kee*. Edited by Jacob Neusner, Peder Borgen, Ernest S. Frerichs and Richard Horsley. Philadelphia: Fortress Press, 3-16.

LAMPE, G.W.H. (ed.). 1961. *A Patristic Greek Lexicon*. Oxford: Clarendon.

LARSEN, J.A.O. 1973. "Demokratia." *CP* 68: 45-46.

LATTKE, Michael. 1990. *Hymnus: Materialien zu einer Geschichte der antiken Hymnologie*. Novum Testamentum et Orbis Antiquus 19. Freiburg, Schweiz: Universitätsverlag / Göttingen: Vandenhoeck & Ruprecht.

LATTKE, Michael. 1993. "Ten Theses on Christian Freedom or Are you Afraid of Christian Freedom?" *Colloquium* 25, 37-38.

LAUTON, Annemarie. 1946. Die Sprache des Augustus im Monumentum Ancyranum. *Inaugural -Dissertation zur Erlangung der Doktorwürde an der philosophischen* Fakultät der Leopold-Franzens-Universität zu Innsbruck. Innsbruck.

LAUTON, Annemarie. 1949. "Zur Sprache des Augustus im Monumentum Ancyranum." *WSt* 64, 107-23.

LEMCIO, Eugene, E. 1986. "The Intention of the Evangelist Mark." *NTS* 32, 187-206.

LENSKI, Gerhard E. 1966. *Power and Privilege : A Theory of Social Stratification*. New York: McGraw-Hill.

LEWIS, Charlton T. & Charles SHORT. 1951. [1879]. *A Latin Dictionary*. Founded on Andrew's Edition of Freund's Latin Dictionary. Oxford: Clarendon Press.

LLEWLYN, S.R. 1994. *New Documents Illustrating Early Christianity. Vol 7. A Review of the Greek Inscriptions and Papyri published in 1982-83*. North Ryde, Australia: The Ancient History Documentary Research Centre of Macquarie University.

LOHSE, Eduard. 1971. σάββατον, σαββατισμός, παρασκευή. *TDNT* 7. Grand Rapids: Ecrdmans, 1-35.

LOHSE, Eduard. 1976. *The New Testament Environment*. Translated by John E. Steely from the German *Umwelt des Neuen Testaments*. rev.ed. (Göttingen: Vandenhoeck & Ruprecht, 1974). 4th impression. London: SCM Press.

LUTER, A. Boyd & Michelle V. LEE. 1995. "Philippians as Chiasmus: Key to the Structure, Unity and Theme Questions." *NTS* 41: 89-101.

LÜHRMANN, Dieter. 1987. *Das Markusevangelium*. Handbuch zum Neuen Testament, 3. Tübingen: J.C.B. Mohr (Paul Siebeck).

LUZ, Ulrich. 1990. βασιλεία, ας, ἡ. *EDNT* 1, 201-205.

MACK, Burton L. 1988. *A Myth of Innocence: Mark and Christian Origins*. Philadelphia: Fortress Press.

MACK, Burton L. 1990. *Rhetoric and the New Testament*. Minneapolis: Fortress Press.

MACMULLEN, Ramsay. 1986. "Personal Power in the Roman Empire." *AJP* 107, 512-524.

MACRO, Anthony D. 1972. "The Cities of Asia Minor under the Roman Imperium." *ANRW* II 7.2, 658-697.

MAGIE, David. 1950. *Roman Rule in Asia Minor To the end of the Third Century after Christ.*. Vols. 1 (Text) & 2 (Notes). Princeton, New Jersey: Princeton University Press.

MALBON, Elizabeth Struthers. 1989. "The Jewish Leaders in the Gospel of Mark: A Literary Study of Marcan Characterization." *JBL* 108, 259-281.

MALBON, Elizabeth Struthers. 1993. "Text and Contexts: Interpreting the Disciples in Mark." *Semeia*. 62, 81-102.

MANDELL, Sara R. 1991. "Did the Maccabees Believe That They Had a Valid Treaty with Rome?" *CBQ* 53, 202-220.

MANN, C.S. 1986. Mark: *A New Translation with Introduction and Commentary*. Garden City, N.Y: Doubleday.

MARCHANT, E.C. (trans.) 1946 [1925]. *Xenophon: Scripta Minora*. LCL. Cambridge, MA: Harvard University Press; London: William Heinemann.

MARCUS, Ralph. 1976. (trans.) 1976 [1927]. *Josephus: Jewish Antiquities, Books XII-XIV*. vol. 7 of 9. LCL. Cambridge, MA: Harvard University Press; London: William Heinemann.

MARCUS, Ralph. 1976. (trans.) 1980 [1927]. *Josephus: Jewish Antiquities, Books XV-XVII*. vol. 7 of 10. LCL. Cambridge, MA: Harvard University Press; London: William Heinemann.

MARXSEN, Willi. 1968. *Introduction to the New Testament: An Approach to Its Problems*. Translated by G. Buswell. Philadelphia: Fortress Press.

MASON, Hugh, J. 1974. *Greek Terms for Roman Institutions: A Lexicon and Analysis*. American Studies in Papyrology, vol 13. Toronto: Hakkert.

MATERA, Frank J. 1982. *The Kingship of Jesus*. SBLDS 66, Chico, CA: Scholars Press.

MATERA, Frank J. 1993. "He Saved Others; He Cannot Save Himself: A Literary-Critical Perspective on the Markan Miracles." *Interpretation*. 47, 15-26.

MATTINGLY, Harold & Edward A. SYDENHAM. 1923. *Roman Imperial Coinage*. London: Spink & Son.

MCGING, Brian C. 1991. "Pontius Pilate and the Sources." *CBQ* 53, 416-438.

MELLOR, Ronald. 1981. "The Goddess Roma." *ANRW* II.17.2: 950-1030.

MINETTE DE TILLESSE, Caetano. 1992. "Structure théologique de Marc." In *The Four Gospels*. FS Franz Neirynck. Edited by F. Van Segbroeck et al. vol II. Bibliotheca Ephemeridum Theologicarum Lovaniensium. Leuven: Leuven University Press, 905-933.

MITCHELL, Stephen. 1976. "Requisitioned Transport in the Roman Empire: A New Inscription from Pisidia." *JRS* 66, 106-131.

MOMMSEN, Th[eodor]. (ed). 1883. *Res Gestae Divi Augusti: Ex Monumentis Ancyrano et Apolloniensi*. Berlin: Weidmann.

MOSKALEW, W. 1982. *Formular Language and Poetic Design in the Aeneid*. Leiden: E.J. Brill.

MOULTON, James Hope & George MILLIGAN. 1930. *The Vocabulary of the Greek Testament: Illustrated from the Papyri and Other Non Literary Sources*. Grand Rapids: Eerdmanns.

MOXNES, Halvor. 1988. *The Economy of the Kingdom: Social Conflict and Economic Relations in Luke's Gospel*. Philadelphia: Fortress Press.

MURPHY-O'CONNOR, Jerome. 1990. "John the Baptist and Jesus: History and Hypotheses." *NTS* 36, 359-374.

MYERS, Ched. 1988. *Binding the Strong Man: A Political Reading of Mark's Story of Jesus*. Maryknoll, New York: Orbis.

NEIRYNCK, Frans. 1990. "Synoptic Problem." *NJBC* 587-595.

NEPPER-CHRISTENSEN, Poul. 1991. μαθητής, ου, ὁ. *EDNT* 2. 372-374.

NESTLE, Dieter. 1967. *Eleutheria: Studien zum Wesen der Freiheit bei den Griechen und im Neuen Testament*. Tübingen: J.C.B.Mohr (Paul Siebeck).

NEUSNER, Jacob. 1982. *First-Century Judaism In Crisis: Yohanan ben Zakkai and the Renaissance of Torah*. Augmented Edition. New York; Ktav Publishing House.

NEWSOME, James D. 1992. *Greeks, Romans, Jews: Currents of Culture and Belief in the New Testament World*. Philadelphia: Trinity Press International.

NEYREY, Jerome H. 1986. "The Idea of Purity in Mark's Gospel." *Semeia* 35, 91-128.

NIEDERWIMMER, Kurt. 1966. *Der Begriff der Freiheit im Neuen Testament*. TBT 11. Berlin: Alfred Töpelman.

NIEDERWIMMER, Kurt. 1990. ἐλεύθερος, ἐλευθερόω, ἐλευθερία, ας ἡ, ἀπελεύθερος, ου, ὁ. *EDNT* 1, 432-434.

OAKMAN, Douglas E. 1994. "Cursing Fig Trees and Robbers' Dens; Pronouncement Stories Within Social-Systemic Perspective, Mark 11:12-25 and Parallels." *Semeia* 64, 253-272.

ONG, Walter. 1987. "Text as Interpretation: Mark and After." *Semeia* 39, 7-26.

OSTER , Richard. 1982. "Numismatic Windows into the Social World of Early Christianity: A Methodological Inquiry." *JBL* 101, 195-223.

PANIMOLLE, Salvatore A. 1988. *La libertà cristiana: La libertà dalla legge nel Nuovo Testamento e nei primi Padri della Chiesa*. Città del Vaticano: Libreria Editrice Vaticana.

PERRIN, Norman. 1976. "The High Priest's Question and Jesus' Answer." In *The Passion of Mark: Studies on Mark 14-16*. Edited by Werner H. Kelber. Philadelphia: Fortress Press, 80-91.

PESCH, Rudolf. 1968. *Naherwartungen: Tradition und Redaktion in Mk 13*. Düsseldorf: Patmos-Verlag.

PÖHLMANN, Wolfgang. 1991. εὐθύς, εὐθέως *EDNT* 2. 77-78.

POWELL, Mark Allen. 1993. "Towards a Narrative Understanding of Mark." *Interpretation* 47, 341-345.

PREMERSTEIN, A. von. 1964. [1932]. "Gliederung und Aufstellung der Res gestae divi Augusti in Rom und im pisidischen Antiochien." *Klio* 25 = NF 7, 197-225.

PRICE, S.R.F. 1984. *Rituals and Power: The Roman Imperial Cult in Asia Minor*. Cambridge: Cambridge University Press.

RÄISÄNEN, Heikki. 1990. *The 'Messianic Secret' in Mark*. Translated by Christopher Tuckett. Edinburgh: T & T Clark.

RAMAGE, Edwin S. 1987. *The Nature and Purpose of Augustus' "Res Gestae."* Stuttgart: Steiner.

RHOADS, David. 1976. *Israel in Revolution 6-74 C.E.* Philadelphia: Fortress Press.

RHOADS, David. 1993. "Losing Life for Others in the Face of Death." *Interpretation* 47, 358-368.

RHOADS, David & Donald MITCHIE. 1982. *Mark as Story: An Introduction to the Narrative of a Gospel*. Philadelphia: Fortress Press.

RICH, John. 1990. "Patronage and Interstate Relations in the Roman Republic." In *Patronage in Ancient Society*. Edited by Andrew Wallace-Hadrill. London/New York: Routledge, 117-135.

RICHARDSON, J.S. 1991. "*Imperium Romanum*: Empire and the Language of Power." *JRS* 81, 1-9.

ROBBINS, Vernon K. 1976. "Last Meal: Preparation, Betrayal, and Absence." In *The Passion of Mark: Studies on Mark 14-16.* Edited by Werner H. Kelber. Philadelphia: Fortress Press, 21-38.

ROBBINS, Vernon K. 1987. "The Woman Who Touched Jesus' Garment: Socio-Rhetorical Analysis of the Synoptic Accounts." *NTS* 33, 502-515.

ROBBINS, Vernon K. 1992. *Jesus the Teacher: A Socio-Rhetorical Interpretation of Mark.* With a new introduction. Minneapolis: Fortress Press.

ROBBINS, Vernon K. 1992a. "Using a Socio-Rhetorical Poetics to Develop a Unified Method: The Woman Who Anointed Jesus as a Test Case." SBL Sem. papers 1992. Atlanta: Scholars Press, 302-319.

ROBBINS, Vernon K. 1993. "Introduction: Using Rhetorical Discussion of the Chreia to Interpret Pronouncement Stories." *Semeia* 64, vii-xvii.

ROBBINS. Vernon K. 1994. "Socio-Rhetorical Criticism: Mary, Elizabeth and the Magnificat as a Test Case." In *The New Literary Criticism and the New Testament.* Edited by Edgar V. McKnight and Elizabeth Struthers Malbon. Valley Forge, Pennsylvania: Trinity Press International.

ROBERTS, W. Rhys (ed./trans.). 1902. *Demetrius on Style. The Greek text of Demetrius De elocutione.* Edited after the Paris Manuscript with introduction, translation, facsimiles. Cambridge: Cambridge University Press.

ROBINSON, Geoffrey. 1994. *A Change of Mind and Heart: The Good News according to Mark.* Revesby, N.S.W.: Parish Ministry Publications.

ROHDE, Joachim. 1993. πρεσβύτερο." *EDNT* 3, 148.

ROHRBAUGH, Richard. 1993. "The Social Location of the Markan Audience." *Interpretation* 47. 380-395.

ROLFE, J.C, (trans.). 1970. [1951] *Suetonius.* XL vol. 1 of 2. LCL. London: William Heinemann.

SALDARINI, Anthony. 1988. "Political and Social Roles of the Pharisees and Scribes in Galilee." *SBL* Sem. Papers 1988. Atlanta, Georgia: Scholars Press, 200-209.

SANDERS, E.P. 1985. *Jesus and Judaism.* London, SCM Press.

SANTIROCCO, Matthew S. 1988. *Unity and Design in Horace's Odes.* Chapel Hill: University of North Carolina Press.

SCHMIDT, T.E. 1995. "Mark 15: 16-32: The Crucifixion Narrative and the Roman Triumphal Procession." *NTS* 41, 1-18.

SCHNEIDERS, Sandra M. 1991. *The Revelatory Text.* San Francisco: Harper.

SCHNELLE, Udo. 1994. *Einleitung in das Neue Testament.* Göttingen: Vandenhoeck & Ruprecht.

SCHOENBORN, Ulrich. 1991. οὐρανός, οῦ, ὁ. *EDNT* 2, 544.

SCHOLTISSEK, Klaus. 1992. *Die Vollmacht Jesu. Traditions- und redaktionsgeschichtliche Analysen zu einem Leitmotiv markinischer Christologie.* Münster: Aschendorff.

SCHOLTISSEK, Klaus. 1993. *Vollmacht im Alten Testament und Judentum. Begriffs-und motivgeschichtliche Studien zu einem bibeltheologischen Thema.* Paderborn: Ferdinand Schöningh.

SCHRAGE, Wolfgang. 1971. συναγωγή ἐπισυναγωγή ἀρχισυνάγωγος ἀποσυνάγωγος *TDNT* 7, 798-852.

SCHÜSSLER FIORENZA, Elisabeth. 1985. "The Followers of the Lamb: Visionary Rhetoric and Social-Political Situation." In *Discipleship in the New Testament.* Edited by Fernando F. Segovia. Philadelphia: Fortress Press, 144-165.

SCHÜSSLER FIORENZA, Elisabeth. 1987. "Rhetorical Situation and Historical Reconstruction in 1 Corinthians." *NTS* 33, 386-403.

SCHÜSSLER FIORENZA, Elisabeth. 1989. *In Memory of Her: A Feminist Theological Reconstruction of Christian Origins.* New York: Crossroads.

SCOTT, M. Philip. 1985. "Chiastic Structure: A Key to the Interpretation of Mark's Gospel." *BTB* 15, 17-26.

SEGERT, Stanislav. 1984. "Semitic Poetic Structures in the New Testament." *ANRW.* II. 25.2, 1433-1462.

SELVIDGE, Maria J. 1984. "Mark 5:25-34 and Leviticus 15:19-20: A Reaction to Restrictive Purity Regulations." *JBL* 103, 619-623.

SENIOR, Donald. 1984. *The Passion of Jesus in the Gospel of Mark.* Wilmington, Delaware: Michael Glazier.

SHIPLEY, Frederick W. (trans.) 1979. [1924]. *Velleius Paterculus: Compendium of Roman History. Res Gestae Divi Augusti.* LCL. Cambridge MA: Harvard University Press.

SHULER, Philip L. 1982. *A Genre for the Gospels: The Biographical Character of Matthew.* Philadelphia: Fortress Press.

SCHÜRER, Emil. 1979 *The History of the Jewish People in the Age of Jesus Christ (175 B.C.—A.D. 135).* Vol. 2. Revised and edited by Geza Vermes, Fergus Millar and Matthew Black. Edinburgh: T. & T. Clark.

SKINNER, Quentin. 1989. "Language and Political Change." In *Political Innovations and Conceptual Change.* Edited by Terence Ball, James.Farr, Russell L. Hanson. Cambridge: Cambridge University Press.

SMALLWOOD, E. Mary. 1981. *The Jews under Roman Rule, from Pompey to Diocletion: A study in political relations.* Leiden: E.J. Brill.

SÖDING, Thomas. 1995. "Leben nach dem Evangelium: Konturen markinischer Ethik." In *Der Evangelist als Theologe: Studien zum Markusevangelium.* Edited by Thomas Söding. Stuttgarter Bibelstudien 163. Stuttgart: Verlag Katholisches Bibelwerk.

SPERBER, Daniel. 1977. "Aspects of Agrarian Life in Roman Palestine I. Agricultural Decline in Palestine during the Later Principate." *ANRW* II.8, 397-443.

STARR, Chester G. 1952. "The Perfect Democracy of the Roman Empire." *AHR* 58, 1-16.

STIBBE, Mark W.G. 1990. "Semiotics." *DBI*, 618-620.

STRANGE, James F. 1992. "Some Implications of Archeology for New Testament Studies." In *What Has Archeology To Do With Faith?* Edited by James H. Charlesworth and Walter P. Weaver. Faith and Scholarship Colloquies. Philadelphia: Trinity Press International.

STOCK, Augustine. 1989. *The Method and Message of Mark.* Wilmington, Delaware.

SULLIVAN, Richard D. 1977. "The Dynasty of Judaea in the First Century." *ANRW* II. 8, 296-354.

SUTHERLAND, C.H.V. 1976. *The Emperor and the Coinage: Julio-Claudian Studies.* London: Spink & Son.

SUTHERLAND, C.H.V. 1987. *Roman History and Coinage 44 BC—AD 69: Fifty Points of Relation from Julius Caesar to Vespasian.* Oxford: Clarendon Press.

TALBERT, Charles H. 1974. *Literary Patterns, Theological Themes, and the Genre of Luke-Acts.* Missoula, Montana: SBL & Scholars Press.

TANNEHILL, Robert. 1977. "The Disciples in Mark: The Function of a Narrative Role." *JR* 57, 386-405.

TANNEHILL, Robert, C. 1981. "Introduction: The Pronouncement Story and its Types." *Semeia* 20, 1-13.

TANNEHILL, Robert, C. 1981a. "Varieties of Synoptic Pronouncement Stories." *Semeia* 20, 101-119.

TANNEHILL, Robert C. 1984. "Types and Functions of Apophthegms in the Synoptic Gospels." *ANRW.* II. 25.2, 1792-1929.

TAYLOR, Lily Ross. 1931. *The Divinity of the Roman Emperor.* Middletown, Connecticut: American Philological Association.

TAYLOR, Vincent. 1966. *The Gospel According to St Mark: the Greek Text with Introduction, Notes and Indexes.* 2nd edition. London and Basingstoke: Macmillan.

THACKERAY, H. St. J. (trans.) [1927].1976. *Josephus: The Jewish War, Books I-III.* vol. 2 of 9. LCL. Cambridge, MA: Harvard University Press; London: William Heinemann.

THACKERAY, H. St. J. (trans.) [1933] 1979. *Josephus: The Jewish War, Books IV-VII* vol. 3 of 9. LCL. Cambridge, MA: Harvard University Press; London: William Heinemann.

THEISSEN, Gerd. 1977. *Sociology of Early Palestinian Christianity*. Translated by John Bowden. Philadelphia, Fortress Press.

THEISSEN, Gerd. 1991. *The Gospels in Context: Social and Political History in the Synoptic Tradition*. Translated by Linda M. Maloney. Minneapolis: Fortress Press.

THIBEAUX, Evelyn R. 1992. "Known to be a Sinner: The Narrative Rhetoric of Luke 7:36-50." *Unpublished paper presented to the Society of Biblical Literature, Rhetoric and the New Testament Section*. Georgetown University.

TIEDE, David L. 1984. "Religious Propaganda and Gospel Literature." *ANRW* II. 25.2, 1705-1729.

TOLBERT, Mary Anne. 1989. *Sowing the Gospel: Mark's World in Literary-Historical Perspective*. Minneapolis: Fortress.

TREBILCO, Paul. 1994. "Asia." In *The Book of Acts in its First Century Setting*. vol 2, *The Book of Acts in its Graeco-Roman Setting*. Edited by W.J. Gill & Conrad Gempf. Grand Rapids, Michigan: William B. Eerdmans; Carlisle: Paternoster Press, 291-362.

TYSON, Joseph B. 1961. "The Blindness of the Disciple in Mark." *JBL* 80, 261-268.

VAN IERSEL, B.M.F. 1995. "Concentric Structures in Mark 1:14-3:35 (4:1): With Some Observations on Method." *Biblical Interpretation* 3, 75-97.

VAN IERSEL, B.M.F. 1998. *Mark: A Reader-Response Commentary*. Translated by W. H. Bisscheroux. JSNT: Supplement Series 164. Sheffield: Sheffield Academic Press.

VIERNEISEL, Klaus and Paul ZANKER (eds). 1979. *Die Bildnisse des Augustus. Herrscherbild und Politik im kaiserlichen Rom*. München: Glyptothek München.

VINSON, Richard B. 1991. "A Comparative Study of the Use of Enthymemes in the Synoptic Gospels." In *Persuasive Artistry: Studies in New Testament Rhetoric in Homor of George A. Kennedy*, ed. Duane F. Watson, 41-65. *JSNT*. S 50, Sheffield: JSOT Press, 119-141.

VOELZ, James W. 1984. "The Language of the New Testament." *ANRW* II. 25.2, 893-977.

VOLKMANN, H. 1942. *Res Gestae Divi Augusti*. Teil I. Kritische Textausgabe. *JAW* 276 [Supplementband], 1-37.

VOLKMANN, H. 1942. "*Res Gestae divi Augusti*. Teil II. Besprechung des Schrifttums der Jahre 1914-41." *JAW* 279: 1-94.

VOLLENWEIDER, Samuel. 1989. *Freiheit als neue Scöpfung: Eine Untersuchung zur Eleutheria bei Paulus und in seiner Umwelt*. Göttingen: Vandenhoeck & Ruprecht.

WAETJEN, Herman C. 1989. *A Reordering of Power: A Socio-Political Reading of Mark's Gospel*. Minneapolis: Fortress Press.

WEBER, Ekkehard. 1970. *Augustus, Meine Taten - Res Gestae Divi Augusti Nach dem Monumentum Ancyranum, Apolloniense und Antiochenum.* (Lateinisch-Griechisch-Deutsch). München: Heimeran.

WEEDEN, Theodore J. 1976. "The Cross as Power in Weakness." In *The Passion of Mark: Studies on Mark 14-16.* Edited by Werner H. Kelber. Philadelphia: Fortress Press, 115-129.

WEINSTOCK, Stefan. 1960. "Pax and the 'Ara Pacis'." *JRS* 50, 44-58.

WELCH, John (ed). 1981. *Chiasmus in Antiquity: Structures, analysis, exegesis.* Hildesheim: Gerstenberg.

WENGST, Klaus. 1987. *Pax Romana and the Peace of Jesus Christ.* Translated by John Bowden. Philadelphia: Fortress Press.

WESTERMANN, W. L. 1911. "The Monument of Ancyra." *AHR* 17, 1-11.

WHITEHORNE, John. 1992. "Augustus as 'Theos' in Contemporary Papyri." *Proceedings 19th International Congress Papyrology, II.* Cairo: 421-34.

WHITMAN, Cedric H. 1958. *Homer and the Heroic Tradition.* Cambridge, MA: Harvard University Press.

WINK, Walter. 1991. "Jesus and the Domination System." *SBL* Sem. papers 1991. Atlanta: Scholars Press, 265-286.

WINK, Walter. 1991a. "Neither Passivity Nor Violence: Jesus' Third Way." *Foundations and Facets Forum 7*, 5-25.

WIRSZUBSKI, Chaim. 1950. *Libertas as a Political Idea at Rome During the Roman Republic and Early Principate.* Cambridge: Cambridge University Press.

WRIGHT, Addison G. 1982. "The Widow's Mites: Praise or Lament." *CBQ* 44, 256-265.

WUELLNER, Wilhelm. 1987. "Where is Rhetorical Criticism Taking Us?" *CBQ* 47, 448-463.

YAVETZ, Zvi. 1984. "The Res Gestae and Augustus' Public Image." In *Caesar Augustus: Seven Aspects.* Edited by Fergus Millar and Erich Segal. Oxford: Clarendon Press, 1-36.

ZANKER, Paul. 1988. *The Power of Images in the Age of Augustus.* Jerome Lectures; (16th ser.) Translated by Alan Shapiro. Ann Arbor: University of Michigan Press.

ZMIJEWSKI, Josef. 1991. νηστεία. *EDNT.* 2, 465.

Bd. 1   MAX KÜCHLER, Schweigen, Schmuck und Schleier. Drei neutestamentliche Vorschriften zur Verdrängung der Frauen auf dem Hintergrund einer frauenfeindlichen Exegese des Alten Testaments im antiken Judentum. XXII + 542 Seiten, 1 Abb. 1986. [vergriffen]

Bd. 2   MOSHE WEINFELD, The Organizational Pattern and the Penal Code of the Qumran Sect. A Comparison with Guilds and Religious Associations of the Hellenistic-Roman Period. 104 Seiten. 1986.

Bd. 3   ROBERT WENNING, Die Nabataer – Denkmäler und Geschichte. Eine Bestandesaufnahme des archäologischen Befundes. 364 Seiten, 50 Abb., 19 Karten. 1986. [vergriffen]

Bd. 4   RITA EGGER, Josephus Flavius und die Samaritaner. Eine terminologische Untersuchung zur Identitätsklärung der Samaritaner. 4 + 416 Seiten. 1986.

Bd. 5   EUGEN RUCKSTUHL, Die literarische Einheit des Johannesevangeliums. Der gegenwartige Stand der einschlägigen Forschungen. Mit einem Vorwort von Martin Hengel. XXX + 334 Seiten. 1987.

Bd. 6   MAX KÜCHLER/CHRISTOPH UEHLINGER (Hrsg.), Jerusalem. Texte – Bilder – Steine. Im Namen von Mitgliedern und Freunden des Biblischen Instituts der Universität Freiburg Schweiz herausgegeben... zum 100. Geburtstag von Hildi + Othmar Keel-Leu. 240 S., 62 Abb.; 4 Taf.; 2 Farbbilder. 1987.

Bd. 7   DIETER ZELLER (Hrsg.), Menschwerdung Gottes – Vergöttlichung von Menschen. 8 + 228 Seiten, 9 Abb., 1988.

Bd. 8   GERD THEISSEN, Lokalkolorit und Zeitgeschichte in den Evangelien. Ein Beitrag zur Geschichte der synoptischen Tradition. 10 + 338 Seiten. 1989.

Bd. 9   TAKASHI ONUKI, Gnosis und Stoa. Eine Untersuchung zum Apokryphon des Johannes. X + 198 Seiten. 1989.

Bd. 10   DAVID TROBISCH, Die Entstehung der Paulusbriefsammlung. Studien zu den Anfängen christlicher Publizistik. 10 + 166 Seiten. 1989.

Bd. 11   HELMUT SCHWIER, Tempel und Tempelzerstörung. Untersuchungen zu den theologischen und ideologischen Faktoren im ersten jüdisch-römischen Krieg (66–74 n. Chr.). XII + 432 Seiten. 1989.

Bd. 12   DANIEL KOSCH, Die eschatologische Tora des Menschensohnes. Untersuchungen zur Rezeption der Stellung Jesu zur Tora in Q. 514 Seiten. 1989.

Bd. 13   JEROME MURPHY-O'CONNOR, O.P., The Ecole Biblique and the New Testament: A Century of Scholarship (1890–1990). With a Contribution by Justin Taylor, S.M. VIII + 200 Seiten. 1990.

Bd. 14   PIETER W. VAN DER HORST, Essays on the Jewish World of Early Christianity. 260 Seiten. 1990.

Bd. 15   CATHERINE HEZSER, Lohnmetaphorik und Arbeitswelt in Mt 20,1–16. Das Gleichnis von den Arbeitern im Weinberg im Rahmen rabbinischer Lohngleichnisse. 346 Seiten. 1990.

Bd. 16   IRENE TAATZ, Frühjüdische Briefe. Die paulinischen Briefe im Rahmen der offiziellen religiösen Briefe des Frühjudentums. 132 Seiten. 1991.

Bd. 17   EUGEN RUCKSTUHL/PETER DSCHULNIGG, Stilkritik und Verfasserfrage im Johannesevangelium. Die johanneischen Sprachmerkmale auf dem Hintergrund des Neuen Testaments und des zeitgenössischen hellenistischen Schrifttums. 284 Seiten. 1991.

Bd. 18   PETRA VON GEMÜNDEN, Vegetationsmetaphorik im Neuen Testament und seiner Umwelt. Eine Bildfelduntersuchung. XII + 558 Seiten. 1991.

Bd. 19   MICHAEL LATTKE, Hymnus. Materialien zu einer Geschichte der antiken Hymnologie. XIV + 510 Seiten. 1991.

Bd. 20   MAJELLA FRANZMANN, The Odes of Solomon. An Analysis of the Poetical Structure and Form. XXVIII + 460 Seiten. 1991.

Bd. 21   LARRY P. HOGAN, Healing in the Second Temple Period. 356 Seiten. 1992.

Bd. 22   KUN-CHUN WONG, Interkulturelle Theologie und multikulturelle Gemeinde im Matthäusevangelium. Zum Verhältnis von Juden- und Heidenchristen im ersten Evangelium. 236 Seiten. 1992.

Bd. 23   JOHANNES THOMAS, Der jüdische Phokylides. Formgeschichtliche Zugänge zu Pseudo-Phokylides und Vergleich mit der neutestamentlichen Paränese XVIII + 538 Seiten. 1992.

Bd. 24   EBERHARD FAUST, Pax Christi et Pax Caesaris. Religionsgeschichtliche, traditionsgeschichtliche und sozialgeschichtliche Studien zum Epheserbrief. 536 Seiten. 1993.

Bd. 25   ANDREAS FELDTKELLER, Identitätssuche des syrischen Urchristentums. Mission, Inkulturation und Pluralität im ältesten Heidenchristentum. 284 Seiten. 1993.

Bd. 26   THEA VOGT, Angst und Identität im Markusevangelium. Ein textpsychologi-
          scher und sozialgeschichtlicher Beitrag. XIV + 274 Seiten. 1993.

Bd. 27   ANDREAS KESSLER/THOMAS RICKLIN/GREGOR WURST (Hrsg.), Peregrina
          Curiositas. Eine Reise durch den orbis antiquus. Zu Ehren von Dirk Van Damme.
          X + 322 Seiten. 1994.

Bd. 28   HELMUT MÖDRITZER, Stigma und Charisma im Neuen Testament und seiner
          Umwelt. Zur Soziologie des Urchristentums. 344 Seiten. 1994.

Bd. 29   HANS-JOSEF KLAUCK, Alte Welt und neuer Glaube. Beiträge zur Religionsge-
          schichte, Forschungsgeschichte und Theologie des Neuen Testaments. 320 Seiten.
          1994.

Bd. 30   JARL E. FOSSUM, The Image of the invisible God. Essays on the influence of
          Jewish Mysticism on Early Christology. X + 190 Seiten. 1995.

Bd. 31   DAVID TROBISCH, Die Endredaktion des Neuen Testamentes. Eine Untersu-
          chung zur Entstehung der christlichen Bibel. IV + 192 Seiten. 1996.

Bd. 32   FERDINAND ROHRHIRSCH, Wissenschaftstheorie und Qumran. Die Geltungs-
          begründungen von Aussagen in der Biblischen Archäologie am Beispiel von
          Chirbet Qumran und En Feschcha. XII + 416 Seiten. 1996.

Bd. 33   HUBERT MEISINGER, Liebesgebot und Altruismusforschung. Ein exegetischer
          Beitrag zum Dialog zwischen Theologie und Naturwissenschaft. XII + 328 Seiten.
          1996.

Bd. 34   GERD THEISSEN / DAGMAR WINTER, Die Kriterienfrage in der Jesusforschung.
          Vom Differenzkriterium zum Plausibilitätskriterium. XII + 356 Seiten. 1997.

Bd. 35   CAROLINE ARNOULD, Les arcs romains de Jérusalem. 368 pages, 36 Fig.,
          23 Planches. 1997.

Bd. 36   LEO MILDENBERG, Vestigia Leonis. Studien zur antiken Numismatik Israels, Palästinas
          und der östlichen Mittelmeerwelt. XXII + 266 Seiten, Tafelteil 144 Seiten. 1998.

Bd. 37   TAESEONG ROH, Die «familia dei» in den synoptischen Evangelien. Eine redaktions-
          und sozialgeschichtliche Untersuchung zu einem urchristlichen Bildfeld. ca. 272 Seiten.
          1998. (in Vorbereitung)

Bd. 38   SABINE BIEBERSTEIN, Verschwiegene Jüngerinnen – vergessene Zeuginnen. Gebro-
          chene Konzepte im Lukasevangelium. XII + 324 Seiten. 1998.

Bd. 39   GUDRUN GUTTENBERGER ORTWEIN, Status und Statusverzicht, im Neuen
          Testament und seiner Umwelt. VIII + 372 Seiten. 1999.

Bd. 40   MICHAEL BACHMANN, Antijudaismus im Galaterbrief? Beiträge zur Exegese eines polemischen Schreibens und zur Theologie des Apostels Paulus. X + 238 Seiten. 1999.

Bd. 41/1 MICHAEL LATTKE, Oden Salomos. Text, Übersetzung, Kommentar. Teil 1. Oden 1 und 3–14. XII + 312 Seiten. 1999.

Bd. 42   RALPH HOCHSCHILD, Sozialgeschichtliche Exegese. Entwicklung, Geschichte und Methodik einer neutestamentlichen Forschungsrichtung. VIII + 308 Seiten. 1999.

Bd. 43   PETER EGGER, Verdienste vor Gott? Der Begriff z^ekhut im rabbinischen Genesiskommentar Bereshit Rabba. VII + 440 Seiten. 2000.

Bd. 44   ANNE DAWSON, Freedom as Liberating Power. A socio-political reading of the ἐξουσία texts in the Gospel of Mark. XIV–258 Seiten. 2000.

UNIVERSITÄTSVERLAG FREIBURG SCHWEIZ
VANDENHOECK & RUPRECHT GÖTTINGEN

ORBIS BIBLICUS ET ORIENTALIS (eine Auswahl)

UNIVERSITÄTSVERLAG FREIBURG SCHWEIZ
VANDENHOECK & RUPRECHT GÖTTINGEN

INSTITUT BIBLIQUE DE L'UNIVERSITÉ DE FRIBOURG EN SUISSE

L'Institut biblique de l'Université de Fribourg en Suisse offre la possibilité d'acquérir un

certificat de spécialisation
CRITIQUE TEXTUELLE ET HISTOIRE DU TEXTE ET DE L'EXÉGÈSE DE L'ANCIEN TESTAMENT
(Spezialisierungszeugnis Textkritik und Geschichte des Textes und der Interpretation des Alten Testamentes)

en une année académique (octobre à juin). Toutes les personnes ayant obtenu une licence en théologie ou un grade académique équivalent peuvent en bénéficier.

Cette année d'études peut être organisée

☞ autour de la critique textuelle proprement dite (méthodes, histoire du texte, instruments de travail, édition critique de la Bible);

☞ autour des témoins principaux du texte biblique (texte massorétique et masore, textes bibliques de Qumran, Septante, traductions hexaplaires, Vulgate, Targoums) et leurs langues (hébreu, araméen, grec, latin, syriaque, copte), enseignées en collaboration avec les chaires de patrologie et d'histoire ancienne, ou

☞ autour de l'histoire de l'exégèse juive (en hébreu et en judéo-arabe) et chrétienne (en collaboration avec la patrologie et l'histoire de l'Église).

L'Institut biblique dispose d'une bibliothèque spécialisée dans ces domaines. Les deux chercheurs de l'Institut biblique consacrés à ces travaux sont Adrian Schenker et Yohanan Goldman.

Pour l'obtention du certificat, deux examens annuels, deux séminaires et un travail écrit équivalent à un article sont requis. Les personnes intéressées peuvent obtenir des informations supplémentaires auprès du Curateur de l'Institut biblique:

Prof. Dr. Adrian Schenker
Institut Biblique
Université, Miséricorde
CH-1700 Fribourg / Suisse
Fax +41 – (0)26 – 300 9754

Nachdem Sie das Diplom oder Lizentiat in Theologie, Bibelwissenschaft, Altertumskunde Palästinas/ Israels, Vorderasiatischer Archäologie oder einen gleichwertigen Leistungs- ausweis erworben haben, ermöglicht Ihnen ab Oktober 1997 ein Studienjahr (Oktober – Juni), am Biblischen Institut in Freiburg in der Schweiz ein

Spezialisierungszeugnis
BIBEL UND ARCHÄOLOGIE
(Elemente der Feldarchäologie, Ikonographie, Epigraphik,

Religionsgeschichte Palästinas/Israels)

zu erwerben.

Das Studienjahr wird in Verbindung mit der Universität Bern (25 Min. Fahrzeit) organisiert. Es bietet Ihnen die Möglichkeit,

☞ eine Auswahl einschlägiger Vorlesungen, Seminare und Übungen im Bereich "Bibel und Archäologie" bei Walter Dietrich, Othmar Keel, Ernst Axel Knauf, Max Küchler, Silvia Schroer und Christoph Uehlinger zu belegen;

☞ diese Veranstaltungen durch solche in Ägyptologie (Hermann A. Schlögl, Frei- burg), Vorderasiatischer Archäologie (Markus Wäfler, Bern) und altorientalischer Philologie (Pascal Attinger, Esther Flückiger, beide Bern) zu ergänzen;

☞ die einschlägigen Dokumentationen des Biblischen Instituts zur palästinisch-isra- elischen Miniaturkunst aus wissenschaftlichen Grabungen (Photos, Abdrücke, Kar- tei) und die zugehörigen Fachbibliotheken zu benutzen;

☞ mit den großen Sammlungen (über 10'000 Stück) von Originalen altorientalischer Miniaturkunst des Biblischen Instituts (Rollsiegel, Skarabäen und andere Stempel- siegel, Amulette, Terrakotten, palästinische Keramik, Münzen usw.) zu arbeiten und sich eine eigene Dokumentation (Abdrücke, Dias) anzulegen;

☞ während der Sommerferien an einer Ausgrabung in Palästina / Israel teilzunehmen, wobei die Möglichkeit besteht, mindestens das Flugticket vergütet zu bekommen.

Um das Spezialisierungszeugnis zu erhalten, müssen zwei benotete Jahresexamen abge- legt, zwei Seminarscheine erworben und eine schriftliche wissenschaftliche Arbeit im Umfange eines Zeitschriftenartikels verfaßt werden.

Interessenten und Interessentinnen wenden sich bitte an den Curator des Instituts:

PD Dr. Christoph Uehlinger
Biblisches Institut
Universität, Miséricorde
CH-1700 Freiburg / Schweiz
Fax +41 – (0)26 – 300 9754

The Book

The subject of this book is the concept of freedom from the perspective of the Christian context as it is articulated in the Gospel of Mark. In this gospel, the social and political environment of the first century Mediterranean world is reflected. The articulation of the concept of freedom in Mark's Gospel is discussed against the background of Roman political ideology of this period. The *Res Gestae* of Augustus, which according to the sources was completed not long before Augustus died in 14CE, reflects the Roman ideology of freedom *(libertas)* which was promulgated throughout the Mediterranean world in the first century CE.

The Gospel of Mark stands in the same socio-political environment as the *Res Gestae,* even though it was written some fifty to sixty years after the *Res Gestae* was composed. A socio-political reading of Mark's Gospel, with particular reference to the ἐξουσία motif contained in the text, identifies a world in which the domination of Rome, politically, economically and culturally, impacted on the eastern sector of the Roman empire, and more specifically, as it impacted on the lives of the Jewish people living in the region of Palestine. It is against this background of political domination that the message of freedom in the Gospel of Mark is articulated.